IDA LUPINO, DIRECTOR

IDA LUPINO, DIRECTOR

HER ART AND RESILIENCE IN TIMES OF TRANSITION

Therese Grisham and Julie Grossman

RUTGERS UNIVERSITY PRESS

NEW BRUNSWICK, CAMDEN, AND NEWARK, NEW JERSEY, AND LONDON

Library of Congress Cataloging-in-Publication Data
Names: Grisham, Therese, 1953– author. | Grossman, Julie, 1962– author.
Title: Ida Lupino, director : her art and resilience in times of transition / Therese Grisham and
Julie Grossman.
Description: New Brunswick, New Jersey : Rutgers University Press, 2017. | Includes
bibliographical references and index.
Identifiers: LCCN 2016032170| ISBN 9780813574912 (hardback) | ISBN 9780813574905 (pbk.) |
ISBN 9780813574929 (e-book (epub))
Subjects: LCSH: Lupino, Ida, 1918–1995—Criticism and interpretation. | BISAC: PERFORMING
ARTS / Film & Video / History & Criticism. | SOCIAL SCIENCE / Women's Studies. |
PERFORMING ARTS / Film & Video / Direction & Production.
Classification: LCC PN1998.3.L89 G75 2017 | DDC 791.43028092—dc23
LC record available at https://lccn.loc.gov/2016032170

A British Cataloging-in-Publication record for this book is available from the British Library.

∞ The paper used in this publication meets the requirements of the American National Standard for Information Sciences—Permanence of Paper for Printed Library Materials, ANSI
Z39.48–1992.

www.rutgersuniversitypress.org

Manufactured in the United States of America

CONTENTS

Preface vii

Note on Quotations xi

PART ONE

Introducing Ida Lupino, Director and Feminist Auteur 1

    A Rejection of Hollywood 3

    Lupino Directs 6

    Director Lupino and Colleagues 10

    The Filmakers' Films 12

    Lupino and the Censors 18

    Lupino as Feminist Auteur 28

    Postwar Hollywood, American Society and Culture 38

    Close-up on *Outrage* 42

    Empathy and a Cinema of Engagement 47

    Italian Neorealism or American Realisms? 49

    Looking Backward? *Outrage* and *M* 53

PART TWO

Lupino's Ingenious Genres: Early Films and *The Trouble with Angels* (1966) 61

    The Social Problem Film and Film Noir 63

    Home Noir 82

    Home Is Where the Noir Is 86

Doubled Dreams in *Hard, Fast and Beautiful* 89

Doubled Domesticity in *The Bigamist* 96

Doubled Trauma: *Outrage* 100

A Mighty Girl: Lupino and *The Trouble with Angels* 110

PART THREE

Lupino Moves to Television 119

Industrial Contexts: Film to Television 119

Directing for Television 123

"No. 5 Checked Out" 126

Ida Lupino, Television Director 133

On Close Readings of 1950s and 1960s Television 136

"The Return": Norma Desmond and Ida Lupino Haunt
the Small Screen 138

Mr. Adams and Eve 149

Directed Episodes, 1956–1968 161

Comedies 167

Action, Thrillers, Mysteries 174

Westerns 191

Acknowledgments 203

Notes 205

Works Cited 221

Index 233

PREFACE

In June 1945, an article titled "Her Thinking Bothers Ida Lupino" was published that provides one key to the life and work of a groundbreaking creative woman in modern America. In the article, Lupino described herself as a "jigger," by which she meant her restlessness, and "one who thinks jagged thoughts" (Holliday). Lupino's language discloses her nervous energy, as well as her aggressively unconventional way of looking at the world. Passionately critical of norms, Lupino had tremendous insight into modern social institutions, especially in terms of how they affect women. She wielded the weapon of "jagged thoughts"—her anticonformism—as offense and defense, from her position as an outsider working in film behind the scenes. She was an outsider throughout her career as filmmaker despite her considerable success as an actress.

Around the same time as this article appeared, Lupino played the part of torch-singer Petey Brown in Raoul Walsh's *The Man I Love*, which was not released until 1948. In it, her own non-singer's voice was dubbed in the song "The Man I Love" by the voice of Peg La Centra. In her next "musical film noir," *Road House* (Jean Negulesco, 1948), however, perhaps owing to her decision-making roles behind the scenes (see Biesen 69), Lupino had it her own "jagged" way. Her deep, smoky voice was not replaced by one more melodious or on-key. Playing Lily Stevens, a hardboiled blues and jazz singer (a young man in the audience tells his date, "She reminds me of the first woman that ever slapped my face"), Lupino is, hands down, the centerpiece of the film. Singing Harold Arlen and Johnny Mercer's "One for My Baby (and One More for the Road)," she gives a low-down, slow take on a song made famous by Fred Astaire in the musical film it was written for, *The Sky's the Limit* (Edward H. Griffith, 1943). Critics in 1948 were delighted with her phrasing: "Her gravel-toned voice lacks range but has the more essential quality of style, along the lines of a femme Hoagy Carmichael" (*Variety*, 9/22/48; qtd. in Biesen 73). Vince Keenan writes in *Noir City* that Lupino established "the chanteuse as a self-reliant figure leading life on her own terms" (qtd. in Hinkson).

The critics raved far less about *Road House* than they did about Lupino's role in it, "one of the best performances of her career" (qtd. in Hinkson). Lupino was, during this period just prior to becoming a director, a rising star, fast becoming one of Hollywood's most powerful women (Biesen 69). Perhaps her most celebrated performance was *The Hard Way* (1943), whose title can be seen as a description of the challenges Lupino faced, even as a powerful woman, in her lesser-known role as independent filmmaker from 1949 to 1953, during a time when no other women were directing films for Hollywood distribution.

Lupino always preferred writing to all the other work she did behind and in front of the camera: in 1965, she admitted that "writing is my first love" (Bart); ten years later, she repeated, "Writing is always what I wanted to do" (Loynd). Not surprisingly, she also loved and composed music. In the late 1930s, her piece *Aladdin Suite* was performed by the Los Angeles Philharmonic. In 1941, Lupino said, "When you write a piece of music, it's something you can play and listen to for years to come. When your film is carried away in cans to the storehouse, what do you have? A lot of cold press clippings" (Strauss). Despite the fact that one of Lupino's hallmarks as a media innovator was her leadership inside the industry, she was drawn to music and writing because they allowed her to express herself artistically at a distance from the suffocating demands of Hollywood.

In the 1970s, Lupino tried to make a film called "Will There Really Be a Morning," based on Frances Farmer's autobiography of the same name. The title is taken from a poem by another creative woman wanting "a room of her own"—Emily Dickinson. The endeavor fell through, but it is fascinating to wonder what Lupino would have done with this story about female trauma, modern social institutions, and the absurdities of celebrity, themes with which Lupino was occupied throughout her career.

This book focuses on Ida Lupino's directing work. In her bracing examinations of the socially prescribed limits on human freedom and desire, Lupino's art transgressed seemingly intractable boundaries around gender roles and social and media conventions. She called attention to the often destructive nature of those roles and conventions, while implying that there are always possibilities for asserting creative and meaningful agency.

Through odd pathways on the margins of our separate projects on film, the authors of this book found each other, discovering a mutual passion and predilection for "jagged thoughts" on Lupino's life, art, and historical context. We sincerely hope that *Ida Lupino, Director: Her Art and Resilience in Times of Transition* will help readers discover and value the fascinating films and television work of Ida Lupino.

NOTE ON QUOTATIONS

Quotes are taken verbatim from the films and television episodes themselves, unless otherwise noted, as in our consultation of several television scripts in Part Three.

IDA LUPINO, DIRECTOR

PART ONE

INTRODUCING IDA LUPINO, DIRECTOR AND FEMINIST AUTEUR

Ida Lupino's consistent thematic preoccupations with the oppressiveness of gender roles; her searing critique of American social institutions in the context of postwar society and American consumerism; and her courage, ingenuity, and powers of professional and artistic negotiation constitute an important story of feminist authorship that has not been fully articulated by scholars and critics. In our reading of Lupino's life, her acting, writing, producing, and her directing not only of films but also television, we hope to give Lupino a more prominent place in American (and European) film history, one she richly deserves. We begin *Ida Lupino, Director: Her Art and Resilience in Times of Transition* with a brief biography that discusses her writing, contemporary accounts of her work, and her legacy as a media trailblazer, one who deftly changed careers in mid-life and faced challenges related to her gender as a powerful woman in Hollywood. Throughout Part One, we contextualize this account of her thoughts about her career and the themes with which she was occupied as a woman and a filmmaker. We describe the postwar Hollywood film industry and the rise of independent production linked with a new American realism and "message pictures," of which The Filmakers, Lupino's independent production company, was a part. In the concluding section of Part One, we present a close-up on *Outrage*, a transitional film among Lupino's early works inflected by Italian neorealism and German Expressionism, a blend of film noir in its examination of the failure of the American Dream and the social problem film. In Part Two, we concentrate more fully on the influence of the social problem genre and film noir in Lupino's early films.

Given Ida Lupino's unusual life and versatile career in film and television from the 1930s through the 1970s, it is not surprising that she grew restless with her celebrated acting career and strove to undertake new artistic projects. In the late 1940s, Lupino began to concentrate on independent film production and became a director, writer, and producer. This book explores her groundbreaking work to establish The Filmakers, which she co-founded with writer Malvin Wald and producer Collier Young,[1] and her subsequent creative work behind the scenes in film and television.

Like many women before and after her, from Mary Pickford in the early years of film to Jodie Foster and Angelina Jolie, among others, today, Lupino turned to directing after having established herself as an

FIGURE 1 Malvin Wald, Ida Lupino, and Collier Young: The Filmakers (The Malvin Wald Collection, Brooklyn College of New York)

actress. Because of her success in acting and insider status in Hollywood, she was able to smooth the way for her production work, marshaling talent for The Filmakers; writing and directing the company's films on controversial topics (including unwed motherhood, rape, and bigamy); and disarming the Production Code Administration censors.

The cards were stacked against her, with only one woman before her, Dorothy Arzner, who made her final film in 1943, having directed sound films in Hollywood. Lupino then became the only woman to direct films in Hollywood in the immediate postwar era. While her acting career gave her some power and influence as a filmmaker, her gender certainly made her an outsider. In the next section, we discuss the strategies Lupino employed to succeed in Hollywood. Given the obstacles her outsiderdom posed, it is worth considering at the outset some of the reasons why Lupino took on such a challenge. What motivated her to decide to work behind the scenes?

A Rejection of Hollywood

Lupino had long felt ambivalent about being an actress. Her frustration with Hollywood can be seen early on in her career. In 1942, a Warner Bros. press release quotes Lupino saying that she was "tired of acting"— this, at the ripe age of twenty-four ("Ida Wants to Be Herself"). Fatigued by the pressures of performance that extended to her life off the screen, Lupino commented that actors are "expected to act all the time." "I don't want to smile all the time," she said. "I may want to sit glumly in a corner. After all, you can't act your life away" ("Ida Wants to Be Herself").

It wasn't just the limelight that bothered Lupino. It was her acute sense of the superficiality of life in front of the camera in a setting that objectified actors for profit, notwithstanding Emily Carman's revisionary consideration of the entrepreneurial independent female talent in classic Hollywood. In that same press release, Lupino comments on her "battle to untype [herself]." She remarks on the irony that she was cast as an "ingénue" when she first came to Hollywood in 1933, managing to escape being typecast for dramatic roles, only to wage "the battle all over again in reverse" a few years later as she sought a chance to play comic roles. Worn out by the *folie* of Hollywood, she said in 1942 that she would "prefer the producing and writing end of [her profession]. At this stage, I would like a long vacation to study and to write" ("Ida Wants to Be Herself").

Such thoughtfulness went along with a penchant for resisting studio claims on her acting and led eventually to her pursuit of filmmaking. But throughout her acting career, Lupino was ambivalent toward her role as performer and found the studio system unfulfilling, despite her success in transforming herself from nymphet to a fine dramatic actress by the end of the 1930s. In 1943, Hollywood columnist Hedda Hopper wrote that Lupino's "introspection . . . made an actress out of a blonde playgirl" ("Leap of Lupino").

Hopper took a particular interest in Lupino's ambition to alter her status as a glamorous star. In 1949, just as Lupino was establishing The Filmakers, the columnist applauded Lupino's courage in abandoning her studio contract with Paramount and the $1,750 per week salary she was paid. Hopper recalled acting with Lupino in *Artists and Models* (1939) and discussing Lupino's struggle to maintain a sense of artistic integrity inside the studio mill: "I told her," said Hopper, "'If you want to be an actress, throw your contract in the ash can and wait for the good parts. If you go on playing these blonde tramps for another year, you'll lose all that time and maybe the courage to battle for something better'" ("Ida's Ideals"). Years later, in 1965, Lupino expressed gratitude to Hopper for her encouragement,[2] and reflected on her decision, after her successes with films such as *They Drive by Night* (1940) and *The Hard Way* (1943), to refuse a lucrative studio deal when Warners offered her a seven-year contract. Lupino recalled, "I said I'd have to think that over. All I could think of was that seven years from that day, I'd be a movie star, but they'd be saying the same thing to another girl that in seven years she'd be another Ida Lupino. I decided there was something more for me in life other than being a big star. So I said no and walked out" ("Walk Back Rocky Road").

From early on, in other words, Lupino was aware of the commodification of the female star, a theme that would resonate in her work throughout her career. If she took charge in the 1930s to transform herself from a Hollywood baby doll with platinum blonde hair and sculpted eyebrows into a respected actress, she spent the rest of her career pursuing further creative opportunities, rejecting her objectification as part of the Hollywood spectacle. In fact, Hollywood became one of the grinding social institutions Lupino consistently criticized, since she knew well (as she said in 1949) that "Hollywood careers are perishable commodities" ("Lupino Legend") and sought to avoid such a fate for herself.

With a contract from Paramount awaiting her in Hollywood, fifteen-year-old Lupino emigrated from England with her mother in 1933; her father stayed in England to work and to take care of her sister Rita, who would later emigrate to the United States. Lupino grew up feeling pressured to become an actress, given that her father, Stanley Lupino, was a well-known stage comedian who was himself the heir to a legacy of performing Lupinos going back centuries (see Bubbeo 155). "I did what I thought would make my father proud of me," she said in an interview in 1976. "I knew it would break his heart if I didn't go into the business" (Galligan 10). She first stepped onto the stage for an audience at the age of seven, despite her aversion to performing. Interviewed by Morton Moss for the *Los Angeles Herald Examiner* in 1972, Lupino recalls, "I was the only one who didn't want to be part of it. I'd hide in the closet to avoid being forced to act. It was like pulling all your wisdom teeth. It was absolute, stark terror. That feeling never changed. . . . I was scared into being an actress, shoveled into it."

Lupino's initial film appearance was in England, in Allan Dwan's 1932 *Her First Affaire*, in which, at the age of fourteen, she played a seductive teenager who falls for an older, married writer. A short time afterward, she appeared with her godfather, matinee idol Ivor Novello, in a film in which she played his lover. The episode reveals much about Lupino's childhood: "So, there I was," she remembers in 1976, ". . . lying on a couch on top of my Godfather playing an eighteen-year-old hooker, saying: 'O my Gawd, ducks, I'm mad about you—I've got to have you'" (Galligan 10).

While Lupino still lived in England, Paramount Studios noticed her in a film called *Money for Speed* (1933). A small part of the film features her playing a sweet girl, on the basis of which Paramount brought her to Hollywood to star in *Alice in Wonderland*. When Lupino appeared at the studio in 1933 to read for the part of Alice, one of the executives commented that she sounded more like Mae West than Lewis Carroll's Victorian girl. Thus Lupino's career in Hollywood was stalled from the beginning because of her family's push for her to grow up at a very young age.

If the precocious Lupino was unsuited to play Alice, her roles as seductive young women were equally a mismatch, given Lupino's intellect. She was bored and insulted by the roles she was offered, culminating in 1934 in her suspension from Paramount after refusing a part in *Cleopatra*: "I was supposed to stand behind Claudette Colbert and wave a big palm frond. I said, 'No thanks'" ("Walk Back Rocky Road"). Spending the rest of the decade acting in insignificant films and doing radio work to supplement her income, Lupino received her big break in 1939 with *The Light That Failed*, adapted from Rudyard Kipling's novel about a blind painter whose working relationship with a destitute Cockney model named Bessie drives the model to madness. During the casting period, Lupino aggressively lobbied William Wellman, the film's director, to let her audition. He hired her on the spot after her impassioned impromptu reading of the part of Bessie Broke. Lupino earned rave reviews for her performance and, after another quiet period—"back into oblivion" in Lupino's words—she was asked by Warners to test for Raoul Walsh's *They Drive by Night* (1940). Lupino once again stole the film with a bravura performance that included going mad ("The doors made me do it. Yes, the doors made me do it!"). After the success of her collaboration with Walsh at Warner Bros., she was offered the seven-year contract that she would soon refuse.

Lupino Directs

Lupino resisted acting from the start because she found it to be too focused on spectacle and appearance. Even as a teenager in Hollywood, she rejected the film industry's commodification of talent, and soon began to search for a creative life away from the spotlight. She took a risky path by refusing Warners' lucrative contract in the 1940s, but she did so in order to choose her own roles, both on and off the screen. It is also worth noting that Lupino's childhood, during which she was thrust into mature and adult settings at a very early age, would inform the stories about lost innocence and the exploitation of youth she was drawn to throughout her filmmaking career.

Just as the stories she helped realize on the screen are rooted in Lupino's understanding of marginalization and alienation, her directing work is deeply attuned to the psychic experience of space and place. Her "poor bewildered people" (Lupino, qtd. in Parker 22) drift across a postwar American landscape where their isolation is distinctly connected to the social and gender roles Lupino saw as hostile to individual desire. Lupino's own role in Hollywood as an insider (an acclaimed actress) and outsider (a woman filmmaker) gave her a unique perspective on the theme of isolation, on the challenges her own creative force as a woman would pose to the status quo, and on the projects she undertook. Hollywood was only one of the modern social institutions she rebuffed. While throughout her life Lupino was eager to learn, her ambivalence toward formal education stemmed in part from her unhappy experiences in boarding school as a young child. As her daughter Bridget recalled, "She seemed to think school was a lot of suffering. She didn't feel like a duck in water with academia. She already had that artist's spirit" ("Ida Lupino: Through the Lens"). In her films, Lupino was especially critical of marriage, which she saw as failing those who entered into its contract, mainly because of the scripted roles it demanded that men and women play. These roles were disappointingly backward-looking in light of the modernity World War II was supposed to have ushered in, if we think of that modernity as a loosening of gender roles and the offer of more equitable gender relations. The government promulgated these roles in part by recruiting women to work in many different jobs and careers, as well as by encouraging women to stay single, even giving them communal housing, during the war. Postwar modernity was really a retrograde version of those gender roles and relations, a step backward.

In a radio interview with Anna Roosevelt in 1949 prior to the release of *Not Wanted*, Lupino spoke about the cultural habit of making pariahs of individuals who violate social norms: "Life doesn't give us the means of finding love within the bounds of our conventions and many of us will find it outside." Lupino here makes a plea for extending sympathy to unwed mothers and their children, rejecting, as Anna and her mother Eleanor Roosevelt did, not only the practice of "pointing the finger of blame at the girl or her family or any individual," but the prejudice implied in the rhetoric of "illegitimate children." Lupino's desire in *Not Wanted* to show "the heartbreak of the unwed mother" and the "difficulties of life, such as poverty, ignorance, overwork [that] are the underlying causes of girls becoming mothers outside of marriage" reflects her commitment to social change and her belief in the power of film to help bring about that change.

Lupino's work reveals modern institutional life, as it regulates personal and professional opportunities, to be oppressive, exploitative, and ultimately absurd. Her deep suspicion of cultural authority figures links her to Fritz Lang, Orson Welles, Nicholas Ray, Roberto Rossellini, and Alfred Hitchcock. Like these modernist filmmakers, Lupino sees human agency as often futile and desire as usually thwarted. In addition, like the celebrated male filmmakers who present us with the grand failures of their characters' strivings, Lupino's tone is ironic, repeatedly demonstrating the gap between desire and reality. Because Hollywood offered a particularly salient example of the failure of the American Dream for Lupino, it was a setting Lupino rejected, modeling her films instead after European-influenced documentary realism.

One theme we emphasize in these pages is Lupino's resilience—her courage to resist the status quo while using her considerable skills in diplomacy to achieve her ends. The difficulty of transgressing conventional boundaries may be seen in the anecdote Lupino told in 1972 about her aborted effort to help Claudette Colbert take up directing. Lupino noted that, for women, directing is "almost impossible to do . . . unless you are an actress or a writer with power." She enabled Colbert to direct by obtaining the property and consent for her to do so, but Colbert decided not to follow through with her plan. Lupino was steadfast, nevertheless, in her assertion that she "wouldn't hesitate right this minute to hire a talented woman if the subject matter were right" ("Coast to Coast"). The story, recalling Lupino's rejection of the decorative role she was asked to play in *Cleopatra*, is interesting because it indicates the psychosocial obstacles that stood in the way of female directorial entrepreneurship, as well as Lupino's willingness to help other women to achieve success in new roles.

As a woman in a field dominated by men and as an artist who wanted to make films about topics Hollywood wouldn't touch, Lupino had a gift for navigating professional obstacles. How she maneuvered in her film and television careers demonstrates the obvious challenges women faced, as well as more subtle forms of institutional sexism, all of which restricted women's prospects for creativity and success. Despite marked gains, women continue to confront such challenges well into the twenty-first century, a fact made abundantly clear in recent news reports about gender inequality in Hollywood.[3]

Lupino, Young, and writer Malvin Wald (nominated for an Academy Award for his screenplay for *The Naked City* [1948]) formed The Filmakers in 1949. Lupino and Young published their "Declaration of Independents" in *Variety* on 20 February 1950:

> We are deep in admiration for our fellow independent producers— men like Stanley Kramer, Robert Rossen and Louis de Rochemont. They are bringing a new power and excitement to the screen. We like independence. It's tough sometimes, but it's good for the initiative. The struggle to do something different is healthy in itself. We think it is healthy for our industry as well. That is why we independent producers must continue to explore new themes, try new ideas, discover new creative talents in all departments.When any one of us profits by these methods, there is bounty for us all—major or independent. We trust that our new Filmakers Production, NEVER FEAR, is worthy of the responsibilities, which we have assumed as independent producers. (12)

Kramer, Rossen, and de Rochemont, the men The Filmakers admired, all headed their own production companies at one time or another and were known as makers of semi-documentary, topical, and social problem films. By the time of the "Declaration," de Rochemont and Kramer had both produced dramas about race and postwar disability (de Rochemont's *Lost Boundaries* and Kramer's *Home of the Brave* [both 1949]; Kramer's *The Men* [1950]). Rossen, best known for directing *The Hustler* in 1961, was a particular favorite of Lupino's. In 1941, she starred in *The Sea Wolf*, for which Rossen wrote the script. Production of the film certainly habituated Lupino to being the only woman in an all-male cast. The film was a shipboard adventure drama, but its philosophical dialogue had Rossen's signature, especially the speech given by Dr. Prescott (Gene Lockhart) about the price of human dignity, just before he commits suicide. *The Sea Wolf* starred Edward G. Robinson but also featured John Garfield as Lupino's fellow down-and-outer and eventual lover. Lupino developed a close relationship with Garfield, who starred several years later in *Body and Soul*, also directed by Rossen. Rossen stopped making films in 1951 because he was blacklisted after refusing to name names for the House Un-American

Activities Committee, though he later recanted and did cooperate with HUAC in 1953.

Far from being just another independent production company of the time, The Filmakers was groundbreaking in its collaborative nature, in which the three founders took on all production tasks. Lupino is exemplary as a participant in this watershed moment in the history of American film; she is also formidable in that she shrewdly seized new opportunities despite the gender barriers she continually encountered. The Filmakers would go on to produce twelve feature films, six of which she directed or co-directed, five of which she wrote or co-wrote, three of which she acted in, and one of which she co-produced (see Hurd 9–13). Writing, producing, and directing, Lupino established herself as a filmmaker willing to cross boundaries by working inside an almost entirely male industry and making documentary-style films on daring topics impossible to produce in mainstream Hollywood.

Director Lupino and Colleagues

Lupino benefited as a director from having worked, throughout her career, with some of the top creative personnel in Hollywood: directors, camera operators, and editors whom she would approach for help from the beginning of her tenure as film director. In an interview in 1974, Lupino recalled this process as she stepped in to direct *Not Wanted* in 1949:

> Our editor on this picture [*Not Wanted*] happened to be Alfred Hitchcock's editor for *Rope*, William Ziegler. I would run to the phone every five minutes and say, 'Bill, listen, I want to dolly in and I think I'm reversing myself.' On the first picture he helped me out. He would come down to the set.
>
> On the second film we got Bill again. The picture, *The Young Lovers* [*Never Fear*], was based on my original story about a young woman dancer who contracts polio, and I cowrote the screenplay. I'd run to the phone again, but this time he'd say, 'Uh-uh, you're on your own. I'm cutting right behind you. You can't afford for me to come down on the set.' So that is how I became a director. (McGilligan and Weiner 222)

From the time she took over from Elmer Clifton on *Not Wanted*, in other words, Lupino learned directing hands-on, though she was already knowledgeable, having taken opportunities on set as an actress to find out about different facets of direction. Lupino recalls, for example, that Raoul Walsh "used to let me watch him in the cutting room. I wouldn't bother him, but I'd ask him certain things, you know, about 'lefts-to-rights' and 'rights-to-lefts' and 'over-the-shoulders.' As for splicing the thing, I didn't go into that" (McGilligan and Weiner 223).

While insisting that directors for whom she acted did not influence her own directorial style, she admitted she was influenced by their skills and abilities: "Certain directors, like Wellman, Charles Vidor, Walsh, or Michael Curtiz, couldn't help but rub off. And Robert Aldrich, God knows it was a delight to work for him in *The Big Knife*. He's not only a fine technician, but he certainly knows the actor. He digs down into your role and pulls things out you weren't aware were there" (McGilligan and Weiner 222–23). Lupino's experience as an actress clearly contributed immensely to her directorial skill at drawing out actors' performances. Her forte, in fact, was in eliciting the performances she wanted from her actors and knowing just what was needed technically to achieve the screen images she desired. Sally Forrest, whom Lupino directed in *Not Wanted*, *Never Fear*, and *Hard, Fast and Beautiful*, said of the director, "She was so knowledgeable in every area. . . . She was wonderful with actors. She was the best I ever worked with. She was completely understanding and knew exactly what she wanted and how to explain it" (King).

Archie Stout, Lupino's cinematographer on *Never Fear*, *Outrage*, and *Hard, Fast and Beautiful*, was best known as a second-unit photographer who mainly worked on B-pictures but was also closely associated with John Ford.[4] Stout was deeply impressed by Lupino as a director: "Ida has more knowledge of camera angles and lenses than any director I've ever worked with, with the exception of Victor Fleming. She knows how a woman looks on the screen and what light that woman should have, probably better than I do" (qtd. in Donati 164).

Interviewed in 2002, Mala Powers, whom Lupino directed in *Outrage* (and who remained a close friend until Lupino's death in 1995), described Lupino's transition from actress to director:

They would hand something to Ida she didn't want to play. So she would take a suspension—she couldn't work anywhere else during suspension, so she would go on the sets of movies. Most of the directors knew her and liked her, and she'd watch them direct. . . . She'd say, "Chum, I'd really like to learn about all of this." So she'd sit there and watch. And the cameraman would say, "Come over and look at this"—this is what the shot would be. So she learned to direct on her suspension times. (qtd. in King)

In her new career, Lupino continued to learn specific techniques and procedures from those more experienced than she. For instance, in pre-production on *Never Fear*, she consulted on directorial techniques, organization, and plotting with director Michael Gordon, known for his 1950 *Cyrano de Bergerac* starring José Ferrer and, after his career was interrupted because he was blacklisted, *Pillow Talk* in 1959. Stanford Tischler, too, whose first editing credit was for *The Bigamist*, praised Lupino for knowing exactly what she wanted:[5] "She wasn't the kind of director who would shoot something, then hope any flaws could be fixed in the cutting room. The acting was always there, to her credit" (qtd. in Donati 202). In an interview for the American Film Institute, Tischler noted how "Filmakers, out of necessity, was a very tight operation." He attributed its success to Lupino's leadership: "She was good, she was strong. She knew what she wanted. She knew what was good. She had a gut feeling. Ballsy gal. Everybody liked her, the whole crew. She wanted something? By god, they did it for her." Asked a question about her "battles" with director Don Siegel on *Private Hell 36*, Tischler says, "Ida didn't lose battles. She not only won the battles, she won the war." Like others, Tischler saw Lupino as "way ahead of her time."

The Filmakers' Films

In 1949, Lupino directed *Not Wanted*, the story of an unwed mother. Her directing work went uncredited: Elmer Clifton remained the director of record, although Lupino took over for Clifton after he suffered a heart attack just as filming was about to begin (Donati 150). In *Not Wanted*, the final sequence of the film, interestingly, shows the characters at their most desperate. Replacing a typical Hollywood conclusion with an open ending, Lupino has protagonist Sally Kelton (Sally Forrest) flee from Drew Baxter (Keefe Brasselle), the war veteran who loves her. Sally runs across the city while Drew chases her, but his prosthetic leg eventually gives out after he chases her across the city. On a bridge, he crumples to the ground, and Sally turns back toward him, full of sympathy. The camera records their final embrace without comment or dialogue. Sally and Drew are two lonely people finding solace together in an unnamed urban landscape. Lupino gives us no indication of what their future will be.

While Lupino always preferred writing, because of the success of *Not Wanted* at the box office, the company's backers insisted that she direct *Never Fear* (1949). This film, like *Not Wanted*, also deals with a female character under duress—in *Never Fear*, a young female dancer, Carol Williams (Sally Forrest), contracts polio.

FIGURE 2 The end of *Not Wanted*

Like its predecessor, the film employs a kind of documentary realism to convey the psychological effects of setting on characters who are already isolated because of their trauma. During Carol's first episode with the illness, she suffers utterly alone before Guy, her lover, turns from playing his piano and notices her behind him, stricken (figure 3). This dramatic irony—we know she is sick before Guy does—symbolizes her trauma and isolation, "underscoring her newborn awareness of being apart and excluded" (Scheib, in Kuhn 47).

As does *Not Wanted, Never Fear* highlights the environment. The Filmakers declared its intention to portray authentic experience in actual locations in its simple opening credits: "This is a true story. It is photographed where it happened." Lupino's own history with polio (she was stricken with the disease in 1934) was certainly one source of the project, as was the topicality of a film about polio at a time when there was as yet no vaccine, but The Filmakers also strove to situate in a real location the story of a young performer like Lupino herself when she contracted polio, though Carol is a dancer and not an actress. Much of the story was filmed at the Kabat-Kaiser Institute in Santa Monica, which simultaneously particularizes the story and also broadens its purview to evoke a larger problem in contemporary society.

The most affecting scene in *Never Fear* (which was later released as *The Young Lovers*) takes place at a party at the Institute, where patients maneuver their wheelchairs in a square dance. The lyrical realism of the sequence "packs a wallop," as *Variety* observed when the film came out (4 January 1950) (figure 4). Though a beautifully choreographed tribute, the dance is also an ironic counterpoint to Carol's dance routine pictured at the beginning of the film. Here, at the Kabat-Kaiser, Lupino captures a sense of the patients' escape from the difficulties of their illness into an art form whose vehicle (literally, the wheelchair) is humanized and indivisibly part of the

FIGURE 3 *Never Fear*: Carol (Sally Forrest) stricken, while Guy (Keefe Brasselle) plays the piano

FIGURE 4 *Never Fear*: the wheelchair square dance at the Kabat-Kaiser Institute

dance. It is cinematic poetry, "the wheelchair dance [seeking] to normalize the world of the paralyzed victims of polio . . ." (Georgakas 34).

While *Never Fear* shines a light on the traumas of sudden and profound illness, the critique in this film makes itself felt beyond the single social problem of polio. The film's emphasis on Carol and Guy's youthful optimism sets up the ironic anticlimax they experience as the story evolves. With little money and a dance act furnishing their version of the American Dream, Carol and Guy (whose name suggests that he is more generic than individual) are two in a line of Lupino characters fantasizing about their future success. "We're a sensation!" Guy gushes about a big break they have learned of, just before Carol becomes ill.

As Carol convalesces at the Institute, she suffers physical pain, as well as deep disappointment, internalized shame, and loneliness. Guy, his dance career sidelined, searches for work. He arrives at the Happy Homes, Inc. Real Estate agency, where Mr. Brownlee, the office manager, assumes Guy is looking to buy a house: "I suppose you want one of our happy homes. . . . A happy home is one of the wisest investments a man can make." Brownlee continues, "We mustn't forget what those boys did for us over there. . . . I didn't get into the struggle . . . punctured ear drum, you know, but c'est la guerre."

Brownlee, however, is a blowhard. When no one is listening, he talks about the "deadbeat" who doesn't meet his payments or take care of his lawn. "Friday is e-day. E is for eviction . . . out in the street. Out!" The scene paints a bleak picture of failed postwar idealism, as well as hypocrisy and exploitation. Brownlee articulates specifically the promise of the American Dream after the war, in which everyone was supposed to be able to buy a home. Eviction indicates very precisely the nature of this failed idealism and extends to the destruction of Carol's domestic ideals. Serving as a backdrop for Carol's own turn to cynicism, the sham display of the Happy Homes workplace gives the lie, on the eve of the 1950s (*Never Fear* was released on 29 December 1949), to the illusion of domestic contentment and meaningful work in the context of postwar capitalist America.

Never Fear didn't manage to pull in an audience, but The Filmakers was able to land a contract with RKO, then led by Howard Hughes, which would distribute the company's films and fund the social problem projects Lupino, Young, and Malvin Wald wanted to pursue. Indeed, The Filmakers' next venture, *Outrage* (1950), was about rape and a young woman's desperate psychosocial journey to cope with its devastating after-effects. After *Outrage*, in 1951, Lupino directed *Hard, Fast and Beautiful*, once again portraying a traumatized young woman, Florence Farley (Sally Forrest); however, this time the story is set in the field of competitive sports. Florence becomes a top amateur tennis player, ultimately co-opted by an exploitative manager and a stage mother who lives vicariously through her daughter's success.

All the films Lupino directed up to this point focus on women struggling with social expectations and psychological pain caused by the rift between their desires and their treatment by society or the limits they confront as they try to find fulfillment and happiness. The films are set in depressing postwar milieux—usually a generically named town or anonymous urban landscape that represents the narrow prospects offered to these women. The home, especially, becomes an active force revealing the perversity and destructiveness of family arrangements.

The two films Lupino directed in 1953, *The Hitch-Hiker* and *The Bigamist*, are also about a sense of being trapped, though male characters figure more prominently. In *The Hitch-Hiker*, two men on holiday (having lied to their wives about going on a fishing trip) are abducted by a serial killer (played by William Talman) and led across Southern Californian and Mexican landscapes by their brutal oppressor, who was based on

real-life murderer William "Billy" Cook. Cook's rampage in 1950 terror-
ized Americans and haunted U.S. roads. Lupino's portrait of America's
criminal underside was notably filmed on location (in the California
Alabama Hills by Lone Pine, where *High Sierra* had been filmed), adding, once again, a sense of place as an active force in her characters' fates.
In *The Hitch-Hiker*, complementing her location cinematography, Lupino did something else that was novel for the time in order to enhance
a sense of authenticity: without adding subtitles, she had Mexican actors
speak Spanish, prompting Carrie Rickey to say, "No other director of
her generation could shoot a movie on location in Mexico . . . and not
stereotype the Mexican actors" (44).[6]

The Hitch-Hiker portrays a society in crisis. Though Dan Georgakas
says that this suspense story is "largely devoid of social content" (34), other
critics have found deep significance in the fact that the male protagonists
flee from the demands of domestic life and lie about their destination to
their wives, as well as in killer Emmett Myers's monomania and fixation
on self-preservation, which can be seen as a noir parody of the American
Dream.[7] As David Greven observes, Emmett Myers "is an enemy of all of
the trappings of society at its most hopeful and normative."

The last film she directed for The Filmakers, *The Bigamist*, establishes
Los Angeles and San Francisco as recognizable places representing different
sides of American modernism. In these settings, Harry Graham (Edmond
O'Brien) is a lost soul, whose crisis about his own masculinity, brought on
by the reconfiguration of gender roles in the postwar period, leads him
to marry a second wife, Phyllis Martin (played by Lupino herself), while
remaining married to his successful first wife, Eve (Joan Fontaine). *The
Bigamist* is a moody film that surprisingly presents its male protagonist and
both of his wives in ways that allow and encourage viewers to empathize
with all three as they try desperately to attain happiness in an alienating
social world, particularly amid the detritus of failed dreams shown through
the carefully filmed details of the Los Angeles cityscape.

All the films Lupino directed for The Filmakers grew out of her and
Collier Young's desire to make independent films about ordinary people
traumatized in the postwar social environment, "films that had social
significance and yet were entertaining." In an interview in 1974, Lupino recalled, "The pictures were based on true stories, things the public could understand because they had happened or had been of news

value. Our little company became known for that type of production and for using unknown talent. Filmakers was an outlet specially [*sic*] for new people—actors, writers, young directors" (McGilligan and Weiner 224). In its emphasis on "newness," The Filmakers challenged the norm in Hollywood of investing in and promoting the star system. The Filmakers' projects were also very much ahead of the youth-culture curve, predating Nicholas Ray's *Rebel Without a Cause* by more than a decade but similarly confronting angst-ridden American youth, befuddled by the twin pressures of capitalism and conflicted notions of sexuality. In a newspaper ad for Lupino's second directed film, *Never Fear* (1949), the director comments on the success of *Not Wanted* (1949): "It proved to me that most people do want something different out of Hollywood."

Lupino and the Censors

Whether Hollywood was ready for The Filmakers' controversial social problem pictures, however, would be determined to a large extent by the often surprising communication between Lupino's company and the Production Code Administration (PCA). While almost all directors had to negotiate with the Breen office, they did so very differently from Lupino. For one thing, they had studio executives and producers fighting on their behalf. Collier Young and others also fought for Lupino's films, but as one of the producers at The Filmakers, she often negotiated with the censors herself. Further, as director and writer of the films she defended, she had a great creative investment in her projects. As the exceedingly rare woman in the roles she occupied, she knew it would be impossible to approach the PCA the way men did. As a woman, she couldn't use artistic privilege to sway the Breen office to her point of view. Instead, she knew she had to charm the censors, buttering them up.[8] Particularly illustrative of Lupino's savvy with the PCA are her correspondence and negotiations regarding *Not Wanted* and *The Hitch-Hiker*.

Not Wanted

In 1949, even before she became a director, Lupino led a savvy campaign on behalf of *Not Wanted* against the censorship office, then led by Joseph Breen. Before Emerald Productions (forerunner to The Filmakers) became involved with *Not Wanted*, the Production Code Administration had found the original script by Malvin Wald and Paul Jarrico, then called "Bad Company," "utterly impossible" (PCA Files).[9] Particularly unacceptable was the perceived representation of the young girl's parents as "incompetent ninnies," but the main objection to the script was linked to the film's basic motif: "The actual details of the girl's relationship with the boy, terminating in her pregnancy, are atrocious, having about them little more than the flavor of a main street sex problem drama" (PCA Files).

By the time Lupino, as producer and scriptwriter, was featured on George Fisher's syndicated radio show on 6 February 1949, she had already chosen to make changes to the script of *Not Wanted* so that it would pass muster with Breen and his colleagues, particularly Eric Johnston, who ran the Motion Picture Association of America (MPAA). The title's change from *Bad Company* to *Not Wanted* shifted the focus from a "main street sex problem drama" to unwanted children (a clever title that applies equally to Sally Kelton and her child). The most striking thing about Fisher's broadcast is the mock-heroic treatment of Lupino's dialogue with the Production Code censors:

> Something unheard of in Hollywood, Ida Lupino went out on the limb for the movie censors. [Lupino] amazed the Johnston office by showing up in person to settle the squabble of sex in her new movie. And she amazed reporters by stating that the movie censors aren't big, ugly beasts, after all, but nice, broadminded, human beings! It's the first time in my experience that anyone has ever had anything nice to say about the movie censors—or the Johnston office, for that matter.

Fisher went on to describe *Not Wanted* with a pointed emphasis on Lupino's success in gaining its approval from the PCA: "It's the kind of picture you suspect will be shown to adults only—in private roadshowings! But 'taint so—says Miss L, even tho any movie about unmarried mothers is dynamite in Hollywood. The censors actually coughed and acted embarrassed, when they asked Ida to delete a seduction scene. But when she agreed to make it beautiful, they okayed it." Fisher also alluded to Lupino's intention to show scenes of Sally in labor—"It's grim—but the censors decided maybe it's about time"—and ended his speech with a tribute to Lupino's strategies to disarm the PCA: "*Not Wanted* has earned the hearty approval of the so-called ogres of the censor board! How did Ida Lupino accomplish the feat? By charm and tact and the good old Lupino line of persuasion. What a girl!"

Fisher's celebration of Lupino's diplomatic prowess was undercut soon after the broadcast, when a United Press article by Hollywood correspondent Virginia McPherson was run in the *Ashland Daily Press*, whose editor, under the title of "A New Low in Vulgarity, Depravity and Viciousness," lambasted McPherson's report on Lupino's purported bamboozling of the PCA in order to slip *Not Wanted* by the censors. Breen wrote directly to Lupino asking her to respond. Lupino's response, found in her 9 February 1949 Western Union telegram to Breen, is worth quoting in full because it exemplifies the filmmaker's eloquence and gift for establishing a clever and persuasive tone of appeasement:

> I am shocked and incensed over handling by Virginia McPherson of United Press of interview with me on subject of censorship. Believe me the key note of my remarks was gratitude and appreciation for the constructive help of the Code administrators in trying to make my production NOT WANTED a picture both of truth and good taste. For your information the interview was arranged by our organization for just that purpose. Such irresponsible reporting is unforgiveable. Any protest you may wish to make will find me in hearty support. Hope you heard George Fisher over CBS last Sunday. Fisher got the facts straight and thus may have partially undone the damage. Because I am so deeply grateful for the aid of your office in treating a delicate subject we shall leave nothing undone to give the reading and listening public the correct impression.
>
> Kindest regards, Ida Lupino

The same day as Lupino sent this telegram, a story appeared in the *San Diego Tribune-Sun*, "Lupino Trying Low Budget 'Unwed Mother' Drama Film," by Bob Thomas, who comments in this piece on his interview with Lupino about her negotiations with the Breen office: "I expected a blast at the scene snippers. But no soap," Thomas says. He quotes Lupino's compliments to the PCA:

I found them amazingly helpful. . . . We went over the script with them and they pointed out what it must do. They virtually wrote the story for us. They showed that the story must be aimed at three classes:

TEEN-AGE GIRLS, since the majority of unwed mothers are between the ages of 11 and 18. Their emotions are immature and
their biggest fear is pain. Therefore, we must show as much of
Labor as we can.
OLDER GIRLS, whose emotions are more developed. They must
be shown the painfulness of having to give up their child, as
most unwed mothers must, for economic reasons.
PARENTS: We must show that because they have brought a daughter into the world, they must share the responsibility for her, no
matter what happens.

Lupino managed to defend the PCA and *Not Wanted*, and the compromises reached between the parties significantly favored production
of the film. For example, Joseph Breen wrote a letter to Anson Bond
(then the third member of The Filmakers) on 14 February 1949, in which
he approved the project provisionally. However, the letter details several points about the film that Lupino then deftly handled. First, the letter requests that Sally Kelton's age be increased to twenty, an insistence
muffled by the film's clear representation of *teen* pregnancy, though Sally
tells Steve coyly that she is "around twenty."[10] Another point of concern
remaining for the PCA was the film's depiction of labor. "Not only is this
an extremely delicate subject from the point of view of the Code," said
Breen, "but also it can prove a seriously embarrassing subject from the
point of view of audience reception. Actual delivery room scenes can be
carried only as far as very sensitive good taste will allow."
Lupino's clever means of dealing with Breen's fears was to film the
labor scene from Sally's point of view. Following her own dictate to show
"as much of Labor as we can," Lupino finesses the PCA restrictions by
using a subjective camera. Her perspective muddled, Sally is wheeled
down the hospital halls. Distorted images of the doctors and nurses give
us the young woman's subjective experience of pain and fear (figure 5).[11]
Breen had other concerns, including the off-the-shoulder dress Sally

FIGURE 5 Sally Kelton (Sally Forrest) and her POV during labor in *Not Wanted*

wears as she leaves home for the bar. Her dress remains in the final film, an important signal of her domestic life, since the dress occasions her mother to chastise her, calling it "disgusting." The exchange underscores the repressive family environment against which Sally rebels.

This same letter to Anson Bond also recounts the PCA's worry about how Sally and Steve's sexual encounters will be presented: "We pointed out to Miss Lupino that it was not good to indicate an acutal [*sic*] precise 'point of contact' between Steve and Sally, a point at which the audience will have it brought home to them that here our two young people indulge in an illicit sex affair." Breen refers in his written remarks to a telephone conversation with Lupino, the direct conversation a noteworthy element in these careful and protracted negotiations. But the demands here that the reference to sex "be considerably softened" are met in the finished film with Sally and Steve's encounter in the woods, where, after an embrace, the cutaway to a cigarette floating in the river unambiguously suggests an "[actual] precise 'point of contact.'"

On the same day, February 14, Joseph Breen wrote to "My dear Miss Lupino" to thank her for her "protest against the outrageous type of reporting—of which Miss McPherson's story is an example—which has done so much to degrade and misrepresent our industry in the minds of the American people." Breen concluded, "You are to be commended for your forthright indignation." Breen's effort to muffle or eliminate controversial elements of *Not Wanted* was clearly trumped by Lupino's communication strategy and material negotiations of his concerns in making the film.

It should be noted that others besides Breen who had a say in the production of *Not Wanted* put pressure on Lupino to censor the film's content. In a *New York Times* article in 1950, Lupino recalls her visits to homes for unwed mothers during her pre-production research. She had wanted to include women of color to represent "The Haven Hospital" so as to provide a "faithful presentation of life and to show the democracy of the home" (Colton). Lupino planned to include African American, Hispanic, and Asian women in the scenes at the home. Despite being prohibited from the multicultural casting by a financial backer (see Bubbeo; Waldman; Stewart), Lupino told the *Times* that she "sneaked in one Chinese girl." By the time the financial backer knew this, the film had already been released. This episode underscores Lupino's determination to bring a progressive agenda to the screen in a semi-documentary style to show "the way people actually live in the world and the problems they must meet and overcome" (Lupino, qtd. in Colton).

The Hitch-Hiker

In early 1951, Hedda Hopper reported that Lupino was in Palm Springs accepting an award for her filmmaking. "But not content to rest on her new laurels," Hopper states that Lupino met with Forrest Damron, one of the hunters (the other being Jim Burke) who had recently been kidnapped by notorious serial killer William "Billy" Cook.[12] The killer led the men on a terrifying trek through California and across the Mexican border to Santa Rosalia before his capture by authorities in Mexico. Cook was tried in California and sentenced to death. He was executed on 12 December 1952.

In 1952, The Filmakers undertook to film *The Cook Story*, a documentary-style film about Cook, whose rampage in the United States the year before was by that time legendary, and included the brutal murder of a family of five in Oklahoma and a motorist in California who had picked him up as a hitch-hiker. Collier Young was fully behind making the film, while Lupino was initially hesitant, fearing that controversy surrounding the film's production could ruin the company (Anderson, *Making of* 63). Lupino was especially worried because the story concentrated exclusively on male characters rather than on the lives of women, which up to that point had been Lupino's focus in the films she directed. Lupino's concern resonates with Karen Mahar's observations about the care Dorothy Arzner took not to jeopardize her career by innovating too much: "Arzner worked mightily to prove her competence; an effort that may have caused her to take few artistic risks. As Mayne suggests, Arzner's ability to bring in well-crafted films on time and under budget went far in securing her continued employment" (206). Mayne's and Mahar's analyses of Arzner are interesting as we consider Lupino's careful maneuvering between independence and conformity in the Hollywood system. As Donna Halper observes about women working in American media during the postwar period, "There were few rewards for women who were too different" (130).

Turning her critical eye on gender to what Lauren Rabinovitz calls a "*No Exit* of masculinity confronting its constituent parts" (92), Lupino conquered her fear that *The Hitch-Hiker* would undo The Filmakers, as well as her anxiety about working with an all-male cast and crew.[13] But in making *The Hitch-Hiker*, Lupino also grappled with a more material fear when she visited Cook in San Quentin:

I wanted to see Billy and tell him I was making a film about him. With special permission from my buddies at the FBI, I entered San Quentin under strict security. I was allowed to see Billy Cook briefly for safety issues. I found San Quentin to be cold, dark and a very scary place inside. In fact, I was told by Collie not to go; it was not safe.

I needed a release from Billy Cook to do our film about him. My company, Filmakers, paid $3,000.00 to his attorney for exclusive rights to his story. I found Billy to be cold and aloof. I was afraid of him. Billy Cook had 'Hard Luck' tattooed on the fingers of his left hand and a deformed right eyelid that would never close completely. I could not wait to get the hell out of San Quentin! (qtd. in Anderson, *Making of* 28)

Having secured and paid for the rights to film Cook's story, The Filmakers sent the script to the PCA. On 31 March 1952, the Department of Justice sent a letter of outrage that The Filmakers had meddled in a criminal case. James Bennett, then the director of the U.S. Department of Justice Bureau of Prisons, accused The Filmakers of damaging the case against Cook and also violating Cook's rights, since state and legal proceedings were still in process: "This underhanded trick, I think, is a sad commentary not only on the attorney but on Miss Lupino's organization, and I believe that the release is invalid." Sympathetic to Bennett's angry diatribe, Geoffrey Shurlock of the PCA wrote to The Filmakers on 8 April 1952 "that any such attempt to glorify this wholesale murderer could not receive Code approval." Shurlock subsequently wrote to Bennett at the Bureau of Prisons to reassure him that the film was in violation of the Production Code.

Against the charge of exploitation by the government, Lupino and Young responded to Bennett in a letter dated 10 April 1952: "I do modestly think we have made somewhat of a name for ourselves in the presentation of social problems which have been well received by critics and public alike. For this reason alone it would be folly for us to put our names on a cheap or sensational picture." They defended their script, reassuring Bennett that Cook would be a "symbol of evil—the enemy of society." "We at no time," they continued, "apologize for Cook's conduct, nor do we attempt at any point to glorify his criminal activity. The obvious reasons for portraying living people on the screen is that we specialize in the documentary film and have found that when dealing in facts we can produce pictures of greater import and impact."

Offering to visit Washington to discuss the matter and to "adhere to such suggestions as you may wish to make," Lupino and Young appeased the Department of Justice, but the MPAA continued to reject the project. On April 18, Breen wrote to RKO's publicist William Feeder that "this story is blatantly in violation of the Production Code, and could not be approved by us." The part of the Code being violated was Number 13 of the Special Regulations on Crime in Motion Pictures: "No picture shall be approved dealing with the life of a notorious criminal of current or recent times which uses the name, nickname or alias of such notorious criminal in the film, nor shall a picture be approved if based upon the life of such a notorious criminal unless the character shown in the film be punished for crimes shown in the film as committed by him." Breen further charged that the script violated the spirit as well as the letter of the Code in "capitalizing on the exploits and publicity of notorious criminals."

Following these exchanges, Young and Lupino revised the script, changing its title to *The Difference* (at different stages of its development, the film was known as "I Spoke to God," "The Difference," and "The Cook Story"), and fictionalizing the serial killer's story. The following month, Breen wrote to William Feeder again, saying that "this basic story seems acceptable under the provisions of the Production Code" (21 May 1952). However, Breen asked The Filmakers to address several issues, mainly relating to residual references to Cook that remained in the script, which now recounted the story of Emmett Myers. Like Cook, however (as Breen notes), Myers has a "paralyzed right eyelid." References to Oklahoma also associate Myers with Cook, and a line in the script, "Him and his wife and kids," was interpreted by Breen to allude to the family Cook brutally killed in the most infamous episode in his murder spree.

Breen was right to be suspicious of Lupino's resolve to reflect as much of the Cook case as The Filmakers could engineer and still be sure that *The Hitch-Hiker* would be distributed. Intent on keying the film to real life in America, Lupino portrays Cook's story in many obvious ways, but also more surreptitiously. For instance, at a filling station where the men stop for gas, a barking dog offscreen heightens the tension. Myers shoots the dog, a reference to the family dog that was murdered by Cook, along with all five members of the Mosser family.[14] Later in the film, the three men stop near a mine shaft, where the hostages, Roy and Gil, fear Myers will throw their bodies after he has killed them. This is a pointed reference to the well in which Cook disposed of the bodies of the Mosser family. Gwendolyn Audrey Foster makes clear how bold Lupino was to take on a gruesome contemporary serial murder case. Lupino's sly references to Cook's rampage further underscore the film's clear message that the horror portrayed in *The Hitch-Hiker* was no gothic fantasy. It was postwar America, its violence "remembered" from the war and permeating the boundaries that no longer divided embattlement from supposedly safe escapist activities and pastimes, such as fishing trips and family vacations:[15]

> Myers is anyone who is made pathological by the forced consensus and conservativism of the 1950s. He has developed a brutal, survivalist personality to cover up his own frail nature and insecurities, but the film is concerned with the broader picture of postwar America, a country that celebrated atomic weaponry, a country that tried to send women back to the kitchen, a country obsessed with the pleasure of excess consumption, and a country that felt it owned the world and that the world was for the taking. There is no way to miss the fact that Lupino adeptly dismantles the heterosexual white American Dream in *The Hitch-Hiker*. As audience members we are just as much hostages as Roy Collins and Gilbert Bowen, but we are also the perpetrator in this hellish nightmare, the tenth circle of hell as rendered by Ida Lupino. (Foster 47)

Like Greven and Rabinovitz (who identifies the "cultural crisis in masculinity" undergirding *The Hitch-Hiker* [92]), Foster recognizes the film's subversiveness in exposing the dark side of the American Dream. But she also links Lupino's themes of destabilization to the director's role as a woman in 1950s America:

> That Lupino is able to access the repressed and bring it out in the open is an act of feminist disruption, especially in the age of repression and the blacklist era. While many women were being domesticated and badgered into submission in the Eisenhower era 1950s, forced out of their war jobs to go back home and transform themselves into happy homemakers, Lupino was busy building an independent studio that made films about taboo subjects such as rape, polio, bigamy, having children out of wedlock, and an easily queered film based upon a real life serial killer strikes me as wildly ahead of her time and quite progressive. (50)

Lupino had just given birth to her daughter Bridget before going on location to film *The Hitch-Hiker*, which further highlights her resistance to gender conventions, especially when women in postwar America "had been taught repeatedly that their role in life was to make whatever sacrifices were needed to keep their home and their family running well" (Halper 130). Even today, women directors resort to hiding their pregnancies (or even their children) to land directing work in Hollywood.[16]

Lupino as Feminist Auteur

In 1980, three critical works were published that stand out for identifying Lupino as an auteur, or "auteuress," as Scheib calls Lupino in her title. Following the work of André Bazin, the "*politiques des auteurs*" by François Truffaut in *Cahiers du cinéma* in 1954 and Andrew Sarris's "auteur theory" in the United States in 1968 transformed film criticism. After its heyday in France and the United States from the 1950s through the 1970s, when male directors were hailed as preeminent film authors whose work expressed their distinct visions, preoccupations, and obsessions, auteurism fell out of favor as feminist scholars began to take issue with its masculinist bias that was blind to the collaborative nature of filmmaking and omitted the role of women in the history of film. Auteurism, feminists wrote, was preoccupied with "men at the top," and new models of criticism were needed that countered authorship as the all-important signifying practice in filmmaking. However, the problem with dismissing auteurism completely is that we close off an important way to recognize artistic contributions to society and film culture. In discussing the film authorship of Kathryn Bigelow, a filmmaker who owes much to the legacy of Lupino, Angela Martin has argued, "We need to find a way of recognizing this kind of conceptual and aesthetic work around the production of a film. We particularly need to do this for women filmmakers, and we need to do it for exactly the same reason as we need to claim women filmmakers as auteurs or to define and defend notions of female authorship" (132). Artists such as Lupino must be understood in terms of their unique visions and strategies for success, working from a marginalized position in the industry. As Aaron Meskin rightly suggests, a focus on authorship is only problematic when other contexts, such as industry conditions, economics, and collaborative forms of creativity are ignored for the sake of lauding the sole author, the idea that "authorship is the *only* thing worth studying when it comes to film" (15).

Lupino's success worked against the hierarchy embedded in the very notion of the classical auteur figure. Contesting the romanticization of the solitary genius film auteur—"One is always alone," Jean-Luc Godard famously averred—Lupino's creative work and her role as an industry leader exemplify one "special merit of the auteur theory," according to Bruce Kawin: "That it is *capable* of acknowledging the collaborative structure of the cinematic enterprise *and* the evidence of patterns of coherence that have the integrity of authorship" (192). To employ the orchestral metaphor for film authorship invoked by Kawin and others,[17] Lupino was an unusually fine "conductor," who fought some of the same battles as male directors of the period, as well as some very different ones unique to her situation as the only woman director in a male-dominated system. Reviewing Lupino's achievements within the context of socioindustrial change helps us to revise the concept of auteurism, which we see as an important, though not exclusive, model for understanding Lupino's work and the cultural forces that helped shape it and which it influenced.

Since the millennium, some scholars have sought to recover the idea of film authorship to account for women's agency in the history of film. Catherine Grant maps out the difficult theoretical terrain of a potential feminist auteurism, speculating that some form of directorial agency could conceivably be newly embraced: "If the theoretical pendulum has swung back, it has done so 'with a difference,' responding to the combined pull of post-structuralist and feminist forces." Borrowing from literary theorist Carol Watts, Grant discusses a "'reverse discourse' . . . enabling agency, after decades of embarrassed deconstruction" ("Secret Agents"). Approaches to female film authorship that assume a pluralist stance may be in a better position to recognize the richly varied history of women's roles in media and filmmaking.

In the 1970s, Claire Johnston explored the tensions between Lupino's films and conscious and unconscious cultural discourse about women and gender, though Johnston was more drawn to the work of Dorothy Arzner. Since then, Lupino's stature has been intermittently promoted then minimized, celebrated then castigated, ironically by auteur critics as well as anti-auteur critics, but also by feminists, all projecting a different set of values onto Lupino that often fail to register the presence of her deeply modernist, noir sensibility.

Francine Parker begins her landmark 1967 essay "Discovering Ida Lupino" by observing that as early as 1940, *Newsweek* claimed that "every so often Hollywood 'discovers' Ida Lupino. This time she will undoubtedly stay discovered!" Parker's prediction didn't quite prove true—it seems that fifty years after Parker wrote her essay and seventy-five years after *Newsweek*'s prediction, we are still discovering and rediscovering Ida Lupino. The present study seeks to participate in what we hope is a more fully sustained critical appreciation of Lupino's importance in film history.

Parker was the first of a number of eloquent appraisers of Lupino's role as a filmmaker. Her essay addresses Lupino's resistance to life as a Hollywood actress, "finding the glamour side of the acting life totally distressing." Parker also observes that Lupino's films reveal "the essential schizophrenia of woman's world" (23); her films are about the contradictory experience of women in the social world. After Parker's study of Lupino, however, in the 1970s and 1980s, feminist critics and scholars were not particularly kind to Lupino, with the exception of a small number who continued to find her films important as windows onto the world of postwar alienation in America.

Feminist ambivalence toward Lupino's films is complex yet, in many ways, understandable. It reveals a history of feminist efforts to identify and analyze sexist representations of women and to support empowering representations. However, Lupino's style and sensibility are feminist in ways that did not make sense to some second-wave feminists. Her films attack conventionality and the social institutions bent on maintaining norms at the expense of individual desire; those on the margins, because of their class or gender, pay most of the price. But Lupino's empathy for male characters, as well as female protagonists, drew the criticism that she was too forgiving of men and too invested in showing the victimization of women, or, in the case of *Hard, Fast and Beautiful*, women as predatory. In this context, Molly Haskell dismisses Lupino's representations as "conventional, even sexist." In her introduction to an interview with Lupino, Debra Weiner said in 1977, "Before feminists get too excited, it must be noted that the solutions to women's problems within [Lupino's] films are often conventional, even conservative, more reinforcing of 1950s ideology than undercutting it. A terse summation of Lupino might be to say that she dealt with feminist questions from an anti-feminist perspective. (Not that this summation necessarily would bear up under close scrutiny.)" (170).

Objections to Lupino's films usually focus on the victimization of female characters, or their "passivity," and on her "profound sympathy for men" (Quart 28). By far Lupino's harshest feminist critic is Barbara Koenig Quart, who wrote in 1988 that *Never Fear* is "yet another wounded woman melodrama" (27).[18] Quart is unwavering in her criticism: "If Lupino's first heroines are victims, vulnerable girls struck down, she moves on quickly to more assured and ambitious stronger women, whom she then finds it necessary to reproach and diminish. The anti-feminist content of her work becomes more explicit, and the gap between what Lupino herself did and the values she promulgated more dramatic" (27). These comments emphasize the trajectory of Lupino's stories, as if the films necessarily endorse what happens in their plots. Quart's problematic predisposition to judge stories that don't celebrate women or represent them transcending their oppression as unfeminist or antifeminist leads her to misread Lupino's intent to *show* the difficulties women face in finding fulfillment as an *endorsement* of their failure. Her anger about the fact that these characters aren't strong enough to rise above their bleak circumstances is revealed in a distinctly sarcastic tone. Feminist critics flummoxed by Lupino's bleak perspective have given short shrift to her films, placing Lupino in a double bind: Quart finds objectionable the "gap" between her representation of women and her own professional success—"But most striking is each film's repudiation of the values Lupino lived by in her own career." This suggests that Lupino had an obligation to represent in her films the successes that she experienced in her professional life, an obligation she did not live up to. This is an absurd requirement of any artist.[19]

Lupino was acutely aware of her reputation, as Marsha Orgeron suggests, but she certainly did transgress roles for women in the 1950s. She did what no other woman at the time was doing. In 1950, she was the only female member of the Director's Guild, where, according to Jeanine Basinger, "meetings she attended were often opened with the greeting: 'Gentlemen and Madam.'" Lupino manipulated gender and social roles, not by giving in to them or to a conventional set of expectations about what she ought to be doing. As we saw above, she had already abandoned the position of actress in a studio setting precisely because the commodification of women in Hollywood was so objectionable to her. While second-wave feminist critics didn't like what they perceived as Lupino favoring men, Gwendolyn Audrey Foster pinpoints the short-sightedness of this critique:

> In the 1970s Lupino was criticized for admitting that she preferred the company of men, but what on earth would she have in common with domesticated women in the 1950s, and why should either woman [Lupino or Arzner] be subject to such gender-based criticisms? Both women expressed quite a bit of frustration with the attention paid to them by feminist critics who rediscovered their work in the 1970s. Understandably, both wished to be taken seriously as directors, not as "female directors." (30)

We can only affirm, with emphasis, Sally Forrest's 2002 remark that "maybe she was too strong for those days" (King).

Antifeminist reactions to Lupino, stoked in part by the representation of the "ambitious mother" Millie Farley in *Hard, Fast and Beautiful*, were exacerbated for some critics by Lupino's adoption of the role of "Mother" on the set.[20] According to Peter Keogh, "Feminist film criticism in the 1970s did not like Ida Lupino, did not consider her a feminist, mainly on the basis of how she related to the male actors she gave direction to. She would play the part of the mother to humour them . . . giving herself the name 'mother' on set" (22). In fact, Lupino's nickname of "Mother" began because the young actors she worked with on her first films for The Film-akers saw her as a mother figure. Admittedly, as Lupino progressed in her career and gained more power in Hollywood, calling herself "Mother" on the set became more performative. It was a strategy to defuse anxiety about her role as director. By the time Lupino moved to television, she parodied the role of mother, commenting on her tactics in a short essay she wrote for *Action* in 1967: "You do not tell a man; you suggest to him. 'Darlings, mother has a problem. I'd love to do this. Can you do it? It sounds kooky but I want to do it. Now, can you do it for me?' And they do it—they just do it" (qtd. in Koszarski 372). While Lupino's directorial control may have been accepted by those working with her because she was seen as a reliable mother supporting her children, her nickname may also suggest more subversive elements of camp in her performances of gender in her professional life. Moreover, given the difficulties women face in establishing a credible tone as Hollywood directors because, to this day, the "clichéd paramilitary nature" of directing runs deep,[21] Lupino's knowledge of gender roles and her ability to "disarm" expectations regarding them to her advantage are striking and prescient.

It is clear that one reason Lupino's directorial career has been slighted in film scholarship is that intermittent readings of her films view her as antifeminist or, at least, favorable to male over female experience. In these pages, we oppose such readings of Lupino's film (and television) work. To respond to Debra Weiner, "close scrutiny" indeed reveals Lupino's feminism. Her approach to modern America assumes a traumatized point of view, one that is highly sensitive to the brutal realities facing men *and* women in the postwar period, but especially to the experiences of young women, who are systematically abused by institutionalizations of power.[22] For this reason, we find Lupino's work to be not only feminist, but often radically so, as she reveals and anatomizes the abject position to which individuals are brought as a result of social and gender rules that punish them for having desires that cannot be contained within conventional norms. The failure Quart and others object to reflects society's rejection of female desire and ambition, and not what these critics imagine to be Lupino's desire to see women fail. Instead of focusing on these female characters' success or failure, we believe that we learn more from looking at the trials Lupino's women endure throughout the films.

Critical consensus on Lupino has, however, clearly shifted, in part because even B-movies and independent films have become more accessible on DVD, and also in part because of more sympathetic analyses of Lupino's directing by critics such as Ronnie Scheib, whose 1980 essay suggests Lupino's exceptional role as a postwar American filmmaker. While other critics have often criticized Lupino for portraying women as "passive," Scheib contextualizes women's condition instead as part of a debilitating social network that drains individuals of their agency. Lupino's men and women are "sleepwalkers," trapped in the social roles they detest but inhabit by rote.[23]

In an essay she wrote for the *Village Voice* in 1980, Carrie Rickey also influenced later film scholars, stating that Lupino had a distinct vision in her films: "Not *film noir*, but Lupino *noir*: a dimly lit low-budget world in which everyone lives sadder-but-wiser ever after" (43). Rickey describes the tone and bleak postwar environment depicted in Lupino's films: their "bitter wisdom" and subtle analysis of the difficulty of human agency in a bleak social world—for women, in particular, the "huge gray area between independence and dependence" (44). Rickey is particularly good at identifying the noir tone of Lupino's films, as well as Lupino's clarity in representing the dark spaces of America: "No one films public spaces with Lupino's politesse and lack of condescension, that cue to the audience that this is squalor and the character wants better" (44). Indeed, Rickey argues that "Lupino rivals Nicholas Ray and Sam Fuller in her architecture of emotional space" (44). Rickey, like Scheib, saw a depth in Lupino's work that opposes the common consensus that her films were slight, dated, or antifeminist.

Only four scholarly books have been published that exclusively focus on Lupino,[24] but the films themselves have become more accessible and more frequently celebrated.[25] The sea change in attitudes toward Lupino may be the result of temporal distance. Jans Wager comments that Lupino's films are "remarkable in their complexity" ("Lupino" 225), which is a direct counter to the prevailing critical attitude that while her films are a curiosity (having been directed by the only woman director in the postwar period), she was "merely competent" (Haskell 33). Dan Georgakas explains Lupino's obscurity as a matter of her subjects being dated: "The cutting-edge issues of 1949 have become so much the norm that their once radical thrust now appears to be a weakness of vision" (33). We view, on the contrary, Lupino's treatment of social issues as a radical intervention in Hollywood film.

In 2009, Wheeler Winston Dixon surveyed Lupino's notable achievements in a comprehensive analysis of her film directing, including a discussion of her television work. Dixon highlighted Lupino's distinct style—her mobile camera, her use of noir lighting, and her signature talent for directing actors. He also inspired critical discourse when he stated that Lupino's last theatrical release, *The Trouble with Angels* (1966), was a "much-underrated" film (12). He ends his essay with an eloquent summary of Lupino's contributions to the history of film and media:

She was a woman working in Hollywood at a time when both the cultural climate and the incipient sexism of the industry mitigated against her efforts; she was an actress who turned to direction when her career in front of the camera failed to satisfy her needs as an artist; she directed films and television shows of a surprisingly violent nature during a period when television was known as the 'safe' medium, and she was unafraid to tackle impossible schedules and production budgets on a routine basis, creating work of dignity and originality under exceedingly difficult circumstances. Lupino's work is one of the most singular testaments of the 1950s, an era when women were still very much on the margins of cinematic practice. (13)

Martin Scorsese, too, used the term "singular" to describe Lupino's work when he praised her films. In 1995, Scorsese wrote an obituary for her in the *New York Times Magazine*, in which he called Lupino's films "remarkable chamber pieces that deal with challenging subjects in a clear, almost documentary fashion, and are a singular achievement in American cinema." Scorsese ends his piece with the following: "What is at stake in Lupino's films is the psyche of the victim. They addressed the wounded soul and traced the slow, painful process of women trying to wrestle with despair and reclaim their lives. Her work is resilient, with a remarkable empathy for the fragile and the heartbroken. It is essential" (43). Scorsese is attuned to her sensibility about marginal figures in a desolate postwar landscape, acknowledging Lupino's efforts to make women's plight visible: "In [*Not Wanted*] and later, far in advance of the feminist movement, she challenged the passive, often decorative women then common in Hollywood" (43).

It may seem ironic that one of the most celebrated auteurs in contemporary American cinema praises Lupino so highly, since many dismissive accounts of her directing were obviously influenced by auteur theory, nowhere more pointedly than in Andrew Sarris's *The American Cinema* in 1968: "Ida Lupino's directed films express much of the feeling if little of the skill which she has projected so admirably as an actress" (216).

Feminist ambivalence toward Lupino's directing was, indeed, exacerbated by the prominence of auteur ideology, even as auteurism was gradually dismantled by feminist discourse. As Annette Kuhn writes, "Skeptical about the very idea of authorship in the cinema, early feminist film criticism could clearly not admit to a wish for Lupino to be a Great Woman Artist, and was all too evidently dismayed by her failure to be an acceptably protofeminist one. And yet, such a judgment, in seizing Lupino's oeuvre out of its historical context and subjecting it to the political standards of a different era, is surely a little unfair" (5).

If feminist critics expressed disappointment that Lupino didn't champion female power directly in her films, more mainstream critics saw her failure in terms of auteurism. Fourteen years after Sarris's dismissive summary quoted above, we see the influence of auteurism in a 1982 article in *L.A. Weekly* written by Ginger Varney: "Now it needs to be said that I'm not making the case for Ida Lupino the neglected genius. Neglected she has been; a genius she's not." A defense of the notion of genius takes precedence here over the nature and content of Lupino's films. While we claim that Lupino was a film author, the very terms by which authorship have been defined have marginalized her. "Genius" is, of course, a limited category for understanding what is of value.

There are other ways to express value, such as bravery, or commitment to a vision; the ability to lead *and* collaborate effectively in a potentially hostile environment; doing something that has not been done before. These ways of understanding value constitute Lupino's distinct authorship and her importance as a filmmaker. Making a point of stating that Lupino was not a genius casts her work in terms of what it *lacks*, defined by the absence of something and not by what is present. Lupino's biographer William Donati makes this mistake, too, commenting that Lupino's films "fall short of being great films." Louise Heck-Rabi certainly damns with faint praise when she says, "Perhaps Lupino's approach was more *ad hoc* than aspiring, her works more crafted than created, more implemented than inspired, with sparse symbolism and absent imagery. But Lupino never reached for rainbows" (240). Such a claim undervalues Lupino's work, shifting emphasis from her unique contributions to evaluation of her work in terms that are unable to acknowledge its value.[26]

In many ways, there is hardly a better case for exploring constructive value in film authorship than Lupino's directing, since her work is characterized at once by a singular vision and a strong emphasis on the collaboration of many individuals who contribute to the production of a film. Her authorship is not about "men at the top"; rather, it is about creative and professional leadership in a community of artists. Indeed, Lupino's belief in the many creative roles necessary for making films was aptly expressed in an essay she wrote for *Films in Review* in December 1950. Her article, "New Faces in New Places: They Are Needed Behind the Camera, Too," was written a year after the "Declaration." In it, Lupino expanded on a crucial element in The Filmakers' venture: the desire to give young filmmakers, broadly construed, new opportunities. She wrote about The Filmakers' objective to give young unknown actors a chance to portray unique roles, and also its intent to give people working behind the camera new chances to work creatively together. While these goals would buck a Hollywood formula focused on entertaining audiences for high returns on investments, the subject matter of Lupino's films was, even today looking back, simply shocking. In our view, her projects not only "reached for rainbows," to take issue with Heck-Rabi, but also led to her determined negotiations with the MPAA's Production Code.

In her article, Lupino also emphasized the importance of the writer—for example, "It is easier by far to find a new acting talent than to find that rarest of all gems, a good, playable motion picture script" ("New Faces" 18). Lupino's versatility as a filmmaker—that she was a writer as well as an actor, and, by that time, a director and producer—made her sensitive to the importance of the script as a source of effective storytelling. Countering the popular view (even now) expressed by Joe Gillis in his voiceover in *Sunset Blvd.* (1950) that "audiences don't know somebody sits down and writes a picture. They think the actors make it up as they go along," Lupino foregrounded the scriptwriter and the dialogue director. She also discussed the importance of the production designer. Harry Horner, for example, "sketched out the entire narrative action for *Outrage*" (19).

The considerable effort Lupino took to highlight the contributions of her crew shows us that her idea of being a film author was based on collaboration. Mark Osteen captures Lupino's bold achievement with The Filmakers with his comment that "Ida Lupino and The Filmakers embody an alternative to a factory system that exploited writers and women. The Filmakers' approach to authorship endorsed collaboration over individualism, eschewed glamor in favor of social conscience, and abandoned moralizing for complexity" (218). Osteen's comments parallel

Amelie Hastie's claim that "Lupino does not simply exchange places with male directors of her era but actually helps to transform the very ways that we understand how films are created" (21). Hastie ultimately rejects the notion of authorship, although Lupino's vision of filmmaking and, indeed, her practice of it, must be understood as the expression of artistic choices. Lacking a version of authorship—one that strongly credits the role of collaboration—it is difficult to acknowledge Lupino's extraordinary vision and her remarkable professional life.

Postwar Hollywood, American Society and Culture
The Postwar Hollywood Industry

The story of Lupino's singular achievement behind the camera in the postwar years shows her ability to seize the opportune moment, using the cultural capital (and, often, money) she had amassed as an actress, to produce, write, and direct films as part of The Filmakers, Inc. Lupino's story would not be complete without including some of the important industrial, sociohistorical, and cultural contexts in which the members of The Filmakers were able to establish their company and produce twelve films between 1949 and 1954. Among these contexts is the upheaval the Hollywood industry underwent beginning in 1945, and how Hollywood studios ultimately reorganized themselves along new, and enduring, parameters. Had this reorganization not taken place, it is unlikely that The Filmakers would have survived as long as it did.

There are many factors involved in the reorganization of the studio system: union strikes in 1945, which raised salaries 25 percent for studio employees, added to postwar inflation; a sharp decline in box office profits after 1946, the last and most lucrative year for the industry; the Red Scare and the House Un-American Activities Committee (HUAC) investigations directly affecting Hollywood in 1947 and again in 1953; the creative stagnation that followed the blacklist, in which hundreds of Hollywood writers, directors, and actors were fired; a temporary (1947–48) 75 percent duty restricting the import of U.S. films in important foreign markets such as Italy and the United Kingdom; the beginnings of the white middle-class migration to the suburbs, resulting in box office losses from traditional urban venues; the rise of television; and, most important of all, the Supreme Court's Paramount consent decrees. The history of this decision is complex, but ultimately the Supreme Court ruled that block booking and ownership of theater chains by film studios constituted anticompetitive and monopolistic trade practices.[27] Not only had the Hollywood studios guaranteed their profits by showing their films in the theater chains they owned, but they muscled in on independent theaters as well. Block booking allowed them to rent multiple films to a theater as a unit. Independent theater owners suffered as a consequence, since they were forced to take studio pictures sight unseen (called blind bidding). In this way, the studios could add second-rate, cheaper pictures along with A-class features.

Now, without studio-owned theaters, and without block booking, the costs of production and distribution soared, the latter because the studios had to market their products film by film and theater by theater. Since the studios could no longer dominate the exhibition sector, they faced serious competition for the first time from independent and foreign filmmakers. Combined with the huge loss in numbers of moviegoers, inflation, and the costs to pay their union personnel, the Paramount consent decrees threw the Hollywood studios into crisis by 1948. The immediate response was to cut back on production and on the number of employees. Long-term contracts were eliminated, and many directors, screenwriters, and even actors became independent agents, no longer bound to work for one studio.

At that point, Hollywood studios welcomed independent productions, which saved them money, and contracted with production companies to distribute independently produced films.[28] This was the situation that Emerald Pictures and subsequently The Filmakers took advantage of, in order to "do something different," "explore new themes, try new ideas, discover new creative talents in all departments" ("Declaration of Independents").

Postwar American Society and Culture

At the end of the decade, the United States was no longer protected by the buffer of war against the effects of the Depression. Important, too, was the question of what it would be like to return to peacetime. Destroying Hiroshima and Nagasaki with the atomic bomb in 1945 was a major and unprecedented agent of destabilization. It is no wonder that

Americans' fears and anxieties found a place in film, mirrored in film noir, and a call for social change in the problem films produced later in the decade. Film noir questioned the ideals of American capitalism, the American Dream, and family and hearth that citizens had just fought to preserve, as well as the general trend to turn back the calendar on women's roles after the war, neither of which could but come under scrutiny during the instabilities of the postwar period.

It seems clear that the end of World War II substantially "upended the life of every American citizen," as Harry Benshoff and Sean Griffin write (37). On a brighter note, according to John Belton, "The workweek dropped from a wartime high of 48 hours to 40 hours in the postwar era and, for the first time in our nation's history, employers began to offer workers one- and two-week paid vacations. Indeed, the length of the average vacation doubled between 1941 and 1953. At the same time, wages increased: disposable personal income rose from $76.1 billion in 1940 to $207.1 billion in 1950, and then to $350 billion in 1960" (324). Given these changes in the structure of working life, with more money to spend and more leisure time in which to spend it, middle- and working-class men could devote larger amounts of time to recreation than had ever been possible before. Still, blocks of time for leisure were also regimented around work time, becoming part of the commodification of male domesticity. Belton continues, "The traditional six-day workweek encouraged the careful budgeting of leisure time, making an evening at the movies an ideal solution to consumers' short-term needs for inexpensive entertainment. However, the new five-day workweek and multiweek paid-vacation plans permitted people to spend weeks on vacation camping in the nation's public parks; to spend weekends hunting, fishing, and boating; to pass the day golfing, gardening, or puttering around the house, working on do-it-yourself home-repair projects" (324).

At the same time, the nature of work had changed for the middle class. With the postwar step-up in the production of commodities, such as automobiles, appliances for the home, and television sets, advertising expanded and studies of marketing began in a more formalized way than prior to the war. Jobs in sales and advertising increased, and working for a large corporation behind a desk in middle management became an expectation for white middle-class men. Magazines publishing articles with advertisement tie-ins were marketed to men in this new "leisure class." In fact, the first issue of Hugh Hefner's *Playboy* was published at the end of 1953, when Lupino directed both *The Hitch-Hiker* and *The Bigamist*. This is significant, because a male rebellion had been fomenting against the postwar changes in men's gender roles that had left men uneasy. From war veteran to office worker or salesman, white middle-class men struggled to conform to a postwar ideal that they be stable breadwinners, much as women were sent back from meaningful work to a life of domesticity.

Thus, Barbara Ehrenreich writes in *The Hearts of Men* that men in the 1950s were supposed to find fulfillment in marriage and fatherhood. Psychologists and psychoanalysts such as Hendrik Ruitenbeek, Therese Bendek, Erik Erikson, and R. J. Havinhurst popularized a notion of "maturity" that placed the role of breadwinner at the peak of male mental development and independence.[29] Popular sociological studies of the time attempted to define the "American character," addressing these changes for white-collar working men. They described a new type of man: the "gray flannel rebel" who outwardly "lived by the rules" of domesticity—married young, found a white-collar job, fit in at neighborhood gatherings—but feared the dullness of what was called "conformity" (29–30). David Riesman's best-selling 1950 book *The Lonely Crowd*, William F. Whyte's *The Organization Man* (1956), and Alan Harrington's *Life in the Crystal Palace* (1959) all describe, as Ehrenreich continues, "the masculine equivalent of what Betty Friedan would soon describe as 'the problem that has no name'" (30).

Ehrenreich writes that Hefner constructed his position as the champion of men oppressed by the obligation to marry, as the enemy not of "women," but of "wives" and "prospective wives." In an early issue of *Playboy*, Burt Zollo explained the magazine's vision of male liberation: "Take a good look at the sorry, regimented husbands trudging down every woman-dominated street in this woman-dominated land. Check what they're doing when you're out on the town with a different dish every night" (qtd. in Ehrenreich 47). The magazine and its readers believed in freedom from conforming to an idea of manhood whose apotheosis was marriage and work, and particularly making a commitment to the prevailing ideology of the American home. As a gauge of its appreciation by American men, in 1956 *Playboy* had a circulation of one million, and its founders were millionaires by 1960. The Beats, too, who got their start in the immediate postwar years, envisioned masculine liberation, but, unlike *Playboy*, attacked middle-class employment as well as middle-class marriage. Ehrenreich believes the fascination many "square" Americans had with Beat culture suggests that their critique touched a nerve.

Against this sociocultural backdrop, Lupino's *Hard, Fast and Beautiful*, *The Hitch-Hiker*, and *The Bigamist* take on even more profound meaning, since Roy and Gil in *The Hitch-Hiker* and Will Farley in *Hard, Fast and Beautiful* try to rebel against cloying ideas of mature masculinity as finding expression only in the roles of husbands and breadwinners, while Harry in *The Bigamist* identifies his manhood a little too strongly with fatherhood and breadwinning.

Close-up on *Outrage*

Late one night, the protagonist of *Outrage*, Ann Walton (Mala Powers), one of Lupino's true innocents, is raped on her way home from her workplace, the Bradshaw Milling Company in Capitol City, Lupino's version of a Midwestern "Hometown, USA." The rapist (Albert Mellen), who works at the food truck serving the mill's employees, lies in wait for Ann. Following the rape, Ann is encouraged to resume her normal life working, living with her parents, and preparing for her upcoming marriage to fiancé Jim Owens (Robert Clarke). However, the trauma she has suffered immediately isolates her from her previously comfortable and unquestioned life. Painful events subsequent to her rape cause Ann to flee her family and her hometown and board a bus for Los Angeles. Because she discovers the police are searching for her, Ann takes a detour on foot and never makes it to L.A., ending up instead near Santa Paula, where she is found and rescued by the Rev. Bruce Ferguson (Tod Andrews), who happens to be driving by and sees her collapsed at the side of a road. Ann and Bruce fortuitously make a good pair, since Bruce is a veteran of World War II, and as chaplain on board a navy ship has seen men wounded in combat first-hand. Their common experience is that of "shell-shock," which is today referred to as post-traumatic stress disorder. Bruce tells Ann he was healed from the crisis of faith he experienced during the war by communing with nature in a bucolic landscape, a safe haven, around Santa Paula's citrus groves. He is in a perfect position to empathize with Ann's trauma, to offer suggestions for healing, and eventually to become her advocate when she is jailed for assaulting a man from the town, Frank Marini (Jerry Paris), with a wrench when Marini, by all accounts a "nice guy," persists in sexually harassing her at an outdoor party. Ann relives her rape via this event (in a series of gorgeous subjective superimpositions); then, when Bruce advocates for her, she is released from jail and ordered to see a psychotherapist. After a year of psychotherapy, Ann is healed of her trauma. Bruce tells her it's time for her to return home to her parents and marry Jim. The film ends with her boarding a Continental bus for Los Angeles, where she is supposed to wait for her bus back to the Midwest. During the course of her stay, Ann also falls in love with Bruce and wants to remain with him, which he refuses, ostensibly because of his "calling," although, as Pam Cook points out, one of the last shots of the film shows us his regret at Ann's departure, a regret generated by the fact that "Bruce's 'faith,' which has been so important in the healing process, becomes the instrument of repression" (in Kuhn 60) when Bruce denies Ann's request to stay with him. It makes sense for Ann to fall in love with a minister, a "safe" man for her to associate with. It also makes sense that she doesn't want to return to Capitol City, because her past there is the source of her trauma. Moreover, when Bruce fails to acknowledge her desire to remain with him, he undermines her wish to make her own path. Her ability to assert her agency is left unresolved in the film.

The sociocultural context of the postwar years for women lends weight and deeper meaning to Ann's reactions to her rape. The trend to marry young and start a family was at its peak from 1950 to 1960. During the postwar years, as Elaine Tyler May writes in *Homeward Bound*, men and women were, overall, deeply committed to family life, from which they derived a sense of purpose, security, and success. For women, this commitment meant turning their sights and ambitions toward the home, even if they also held outside jobs. May continues,

> In spite of the power of the homemaker ideal, increasing numbers of married women worked outside the home in the postwar years. But their job opportunities were limited, and their wages were low. Employed women held jobs that were even more menial and subordinate than those of their male peers. Surveys of full-time

homemakers indicated that they appreciated their independence from supervision and control over their work; they had no desire to give up their autonomy in the home for wage labor. Educated middle-class women, whose career opportunities were severely limited, hoped that the home would become not a confining place of drudgery, but a liberating arena of fulfillment through professionalized homemaking, meaningful child rearing, and satisfying sexuality. (121)

Certainly, there was a confluence between wartime and postwar propaganda aimed at single women and exhibiting a fear that single women might not be willing to settle down into domesticity once the war ended. This fear likely arose precisely because women were working in jobs that had been reserved for men, and their competence showed that women could manage very well without men. Single women now became targets of government-sponsored campaigns urging them back into their domestic roles.

This turn toward marriage and the domestic is refracted by the lens of *Outrage*, in which a young woman's dreams of just such a life are violently shattered when she is raped. Her ambitions—to continue for a time working at her bookkeeping job while married to Jim, until Jim becomes the full-time breadwinner—are mirrored when Jim asks Mr. Walton for Ann's hand in marriage at a dinner organized by Mrs. Walton and Ann. Mr. Walton, a high school teacher, muses, before agreeing to Jim's request, that he had had ambitions for Ann to become a math teacher, like him. But Jim, faltering, counters, "But there's more! There's marriage." Viewed from the perspective of American social history, Ann is presented to us as an average white, middle-class young woman conforming to expectations that come from her surrounding culture, without considering for a moment her father's desire for her to have a career, since a career would automatically make her a single woman, and as the stereotype had it, a lonely "old maid." Twice in the film, the first time when Jim and Ann eat lunch outside at a park and again when Ann attends an outdoor party in California, elderly solitary women appear near Ann, as if to remind her and us of the loneliness of the "spinster," or Old Maid, the card no player has wanted to be stuck with since the game was invented in the early Victorian period.

FIGURE 6 Top, Ann (Mala Powers), Jim (Robert Clarke), and the old woman looking on, at the park, in *Outrage*; bottom, Ann and a "spinster" at the country dance

Even during wartime, women were cautioned by the government that they should keep their aspirations and behavior focused on the home. They were reminded, first, that they should not expect to keep their jobs or enter careers. Moreover, "experts urged women to remain 'pure' for the soon-to-be-returning men":

> At the same time, they warned men to avoid contact with single women for fear of catching venereal diseases. As historian Allan Brandt has shown, wartime purity crusades marked a revision of the germ theory: Germs were not responsible for spreading disease, "promiscuous" women were. Widely distributed posters warned soldiers that even the angelic "girl next door" might carry disease. "'She may look clean—but . . .'" read one caption next to a picture of everybody's sweetheart. (qtd. in May 121)

While the marriage rate soared after the war, many experts continued to worry about the new economic and sexual independence of women and its potential effect on the family. Wartime ushered in a fear of all forms of nonmarital sexuality and continued as a "national obsession" after the war (May 123). It was even believed, by high-ranking members of the Republican Party as well as those in the medical profession, psychology, and industry, that nonmarital sexual behavior (including homosexual behavior) would lead to the formation of "weak" and "immature" (that is, unmarried) men, who would fall prey to communist tactics, including being duped by seductive women working for the communists (May 157–58).

This atmosphere, in which women were held responsible for disease and duplicity, in concert with the silence about rape—a legacy of the Victorian period—and general ignorance surrounding the psychological effects of rape on the victim, informs the narrative of *Outrage*. Even the title of the film is highly ambiguous: yes, rape is an outrage, but what about those who stand by and do nothing, mired in ignorance about an act of violence whose psychological effects are the same as shell-shock for returning veterans? What of the audience members? Weren't they so thoroughly conditioned as a "society of masses," as C. Wright Mills wrote in a not-so-anachronistic 1956, the result of living in an age of the apex of industrialization and mechanization, in which a democratic "community of publics" became thoroughly atomized and transformed into a mass of passive recipients of media opinions and markets for selling toothpaste and automobiles? (300). This transformation of the public into the mass holds out a key to "the social and psychological life of modern America" (Mills 300). Had the audience, like the townspeople of Capitol City, lost any sense of community and responsibility to others? Lupino shows that the denizens of Capitol City are not simply ignorant; they actively want to know nothing about Ann's experience and how she feels. For example, the taxi driver on the deserted street drives on when Ann desperately hails him, leaving Ann to her pursuer; the apartment dweller near the scene of the rape shuts his window against the blast of the truck horn Ann leans on as a call for help; men thoughtlessly touch her body (an acquaintance boarding the same bus as she goes to work, a colleague at the mill, and, more disturbingly, Jim, who shakes her violently when she refuses to elope with him after she has been raped); young neighbor women giggle as she passes; her own parents barely ask her about her feelings: the entire town is complicit not only in ignoring her rape after the fact, but in the rape itself. The original titles of the film were "Nice Girl" and "Nobody's Safe," which definitively signal that rape can happen to anyone, and that the victim is not guilty for being raped. These ideas are still progressive in many quarters today.

Lupino said of *Outrage* in a 1974 interview, "I just felt it was a good thing to do at that time, without being too preachy. After all, it was not the girl's fault. I just thought that so many times the effect rape can have on a girl isn't easily brought out. The girl won't talk about it or tell the police. She is afraid she won't be believed" (McGilligan and Weiner 223). One major way in which Lupino "brings out" "the effect rape can have on a girl" is to keep visually close to Ann's perspective. Through her techniques, Lupino develops what we call her feminist and modernist "cinema of empathy."

Empathy and a Cinema of Engagement

Lupino's films fall squarely into the modernist tradition as outlined by R. Barton Palmer: "Arguably, one of the signal accomplishments of modernism in both its literary and cinematic forms (including . . . the neorealist movement) is its colonization of the unlimited terrain of life itself, its claiming of lived experience in all its forms as the object-ness proper to representation, dramatization, and performance" (110). Lupino clearly claims that the (vastly underrepresented) lived experience of traumatized women and men, whether the trauma is rape or gender trauma, is what she will represent in her films. The Filmakers' films were to be "message pictures," whose style was documentary realism, and they were also to be "entertaining." The Filmakers was formed at an exciting juncture in the history of genre and style in the American film industry, in which the social problem film and film noir came into their own. The notion of what is entertaining can certainly be debated, but one important feature of Lupino's films for The Filmakers is that they are socially engaged while also engaging viewers to connect emotionally with their protagonists, part of what Sarah Kozloff calls a "cinema of engagement."

According to Kozloff, engaged films "present their characters with a level gaze. The characters are neither exalted nor laughable. We respond to their common humanity. We feel as if the protagonist is one of us. The creators of the characters grant them essential dignity and ask viewers to feel compassion for their struggles" ("Empathy" 17). Lupino does not just reveal to us her protagonists' subjective sound and visual perspectives, although she makes use of both, especially in *Outrage*, to add to our understanding of Ann's traumatized state. She also gives us wider views of Ann's situation, as if we were sitting in the back of the room during the lineup at the police station, in which we see that Ann, sitting on a chair in the front row, is the only woman among men who are criminals, members of the police force, and onlookers such as Jim. The level gaze also places us as if we were sitting behind Ann in her bedroom as she looks out the window at Jim's approach, separated from her planned life with him by only a sheet of glass, to be sure, but a sheet of glass that absolutely prevents her from being touched by—or touching—a man, even her fiancé. Devices such as these do not set us above Ann, and they certainly don't exalt her, but they do give us an intimate view at her level that she does not have, in order to increase our empathy for her. We suffer for her and we root for her.

The many close-ups Lupino uses in *Outrage* also contribute to our empathic understanding of Ann's suffering and recovery. After being raped, Ann gazes out the window, and we understand immediately, through close-ups of her face and of the photo, that she now loathes herself. She smashes the image of herself that depicts her smiling innocence, thereby breaking definitively with her previous life. We don't need words to empathize with her feelings, though we do wish fervently that she wouldn't feel this way. Kozloff writes: "In forging connections with characters, close-ups and performance play special roles. When we study the face of an actor, we employ our skills at reading other people's thoughts and feelings; we practice what psychologists term 'theory of mind.' Close-ups make us believe that we are getting privileged information into the character(s)' thought processes" ("Empathy" 22). In other close-ups of Ann, such as when Frank Marini touches her hair and pulls her ribbon from it, we also feel Ann's anger, fear, and her rightful sense of being violated. Kozloff continues: "Moreover, because of the magic of 'emotional contagion,' close-ups can actually elicit similar emotions in viewers" (22).

As scholars such as Jeff Smith have indicated, because the musical track goes unnoticed, "and because music is hard-wired to our emotional systems, this track carries unique power" (Kozloff, "Empathy" 22). Lupino uses music sparingly in her films; when she does introduce it, it is quite subtle. In *Outrage*, non-diegetic music underscores mood. The few instances of diegetic music "tell" us of Ann's innocence. One instance occurs when Ann and Jim are happily lunching outside and discussing their plans to convince Mr. Walton to agree to their marriage. In the background, we hear a calliope playing "Johnny's Too Long at the Fair." A traditional song, this became a sort of lullaby for children. As Ann leaves the office late, in the prelude to the stalking scene, she whistles a tune that resembles the children's nursery rhyme and song "The Muffin Man," which is sharply punctuated by the rapist's raucous whistling. We may not note this music consciously, but we do take it in. Ann is a child wandering through a menacing landscape that will soon violently overpower her.

More generally, what we feel when watching Lupino's films and noting her refusal to vilify any of her named characters (excluding, therefore, "The Rapist" in *Outrage*, played by Albert Mellen, whom Malvin Wald said Lupino refused to interact with while shooting the film), men and women alike, has to do with devices such as the level gaze, the close-up, and the subtle use of non-diegetic and diegetic music. They give us a sense of Lupino's compassion, kindness, and her own humanity as an artist.

Italian Neorealism or American Realisms?

By the time Young and Lupino wrote their "Declaration of Independents," independent production and a new realism in film were making their mark on American cinema. Independently produced films had lower budgets than those produced by the studios, were shot mainly on location, and the strain of films Lupino and The Filmakers admired, particularly by Stanley Kramer and Robert Rossen, dealt with topical issues and social problems. The Filmakers also admired the semi-documentary newsreel *The March of Time*, produced by Louis de Rochemont. It can be said that the new realism, which many postwar American films had in common, was primarily defined by location shooting and emerged from war films during and just after the war, when many government projects and, later, semi-documentaries such as *The Big Lift* (1948) were being produced. A postwar audience accustomed to watching such films wanted to see more realism and grit, rather than glamor.

Many American scholars and critics attribute the American realism of postwar Hollywood and independent film, which had many strains, to the influence of Italian neorealism, which is actually a retrospective construction meant to give these postwar films cachet.[30] According to Robert Sklar, while "artists as disparate as Stan Brakhage and Robert Frank have acknowledged neorealism among their influences," more recently "commentators have begun retrospectively to assert that neorealism made an immediate impact on postwar mainstream U.S. moviemaking as well" (71). To give but one example among many, Sklar quotes Robert Osborne's history of the Oscars: "The gritty, realistic look of [*Shoeshine*], coming as it did on the heels of Rossellini's *Open City* and other post-war European pictures, was to have a major effect on altering the glossy, glamorized look of Hollywood movies in the next decade" (qtd. in Sklar 71).[31]

Regardless of the inaccurate identification of Italian neorealism as a project that informed many postwar American films, we contend that Lupino's semi-documentary style was indeed influenced and inspired by neorealism, an observation that has surprisingly never appeared in the critical literature on Lupino—yet that she herself expressed. Though not referring to what Palmer calls the "verist materialism" (110) of the neorealists, in which realism serves to articulate the necessity of a marxist political economy in order to build a viable future, Lupino acknowledged her debt to neorealist films:

> Ida declared that all the company's films will be semi-documentary about important topics. She said the company would avoid the lurid sensationalism of some films on controversial subjects. 'There's too much of that on the screen as it is,' she said.
>
> For support, Ida cited Roberto Rossellini, the great Italian director, now visiting Hollywood. At a party here, he complained: 'In Hollywood movies the star is going crazy, or drinks too much, or wants to kill his wife. When are you going to make pictures about ordinary people, in ordinary situations?' (Thomas)

And: "'What we're after,' she told me in her producer's office at California Studios, 'are pictures that look like $500,000 pictures but cost much less. After all, *Shoeshine* and *Open City*, the great Italian pictures cost as much as our budget.'" Cesare Zavattini, the screenwriter credited with writing a neorealist manifesto, lists the following as criteria for neorealist films: a preference for location, not backlot, shooting; the avoidance of a decorative and embellished mise-en-scène; the use of nonprofessional actors; the use of natural lighting; an unfettered documentary style of cinematography; an approach to directing with minimal intervention; and an avoidance of post-production and editing work that draws attention to the film image as a contrivance.[32] In the neorealist tradition, Lupino did little if any post-editing. Some of Lupino's colleagues, such as Archie Stout, quoted above, knew that Lupino was able to film performance brilliantly without having to resort to post-production to fix mistakes. In fact, Lupino's tiny budgets did not simply force her but enabled her to make use of locations in natural light that are more than pictorial backdrops; they are intrinsic to her narratives. In *Outrage*, for instance, Ann ends up, following her detour from the bus route to Los Angeles, in the area of the citrus groves of Southern California, the last innocent territory, or paradise, left in the United States—or so the myth went after the war. In addition, Bruce's bucolic mountain view is not just another lovely picture in paradise, but is significant as the exact place where he regained his faith in human goodness. Ann becomes determined to regain her faith in human goodness there, too. How the landscape functions subsequently—as the very place where Frank Marini preys on Ann—shows us that what is notable about it is that it is a safe haven for men only. We can also see, as Pam Cook does, that the theme of lost innocence "shifts onto a national level" in the context of America's postwar crisis of identity: "Ann's trauma and neurosis, and her flight from violent city to tranquil countryside, become symptomatic of the need for the United States to rediscover its lost innocence" (in Kuhn 62). On a different note, when Lupino wanted what she called a more "artsy" effect, she used deserted nighttime streets in a warehouse district of Los Angeles to simulate a set. We discuss this in conjunction with the relationship of *Outrage* to Fritz Lang's *M*, below.

Further, influenced by neorealism, Lupino used nonprofessional actors as well as unknown ones. Notably, in *Not Wanted*, her own doctor, Maurice Bernstein, appears as the obstetrician in the delivery room (Donati 151). The Filmakers was committed to discovering "new creative talents in all departments." This is probably not worded in such a way that Zavattini would have approved, but if he had learned that Lupino used her "houseman," John Franco, as music composer and arranger in *Outrage*, he surely would have been impressed (Donati 151).

Perhaps what made The Filmakers unique was the preponderance of films that Lupino directed for the company on the postwar experiences of ordinary young women. In neorealist terms, her stories are not just of individual plight but of larger social ills affecting many women in a patriarchal society and culture. This notion, that individual experience belongs to a larger collective experience of suffering, is intrinsic to the neorealist project. Where many postwar American realist films still retain the idea of an individual hero (one has only to think of Elia Kazan's *On the Waterfront*) saving the day, with some exceptions, notably *Marty* (Delbert Mann, 1955),[33] Lupino's protagonists represent those disenfranchised, without any heroics. "The true function of the arts," wrote Zavattini in "A Thesis on Neo-Realism," "has always been that of expressing the needs of the times; it is toward this function that we should redirect them" (72). Herein lies the power and urgency of Lupino's cinematic art.

In terms of the means by which this redirection should be accomplished, Zavattini wrote that neorealist films should "bring the audience to reflect . . . to think about reality precisely as it is" (68), which brings him close to Brecht on epic theater, in that Zavattini favors ideas over emotions as a means to arrive at the truth of experience. Roughly summarized, this notion involves the employment of devices that will distance the audience from the characters and plots of neorealist films. However, it has often been noted that neorealist films did not actually conform to Zavattini's formulas; even *Bicycle Thieves*, which Zavattini co-wrote in 1948, can be seen as part of a cinema of engagement as Kozloff defines it. Bruno, Antonio Ricci's son, registers emotionally his father's devastating and increasingly desperate experiences, which we see in close-ups of Bruno's face as he progressively internalizes the burdens he will have to face fully one day soon. We ache with empathy for the child, just as we ache for Ann in *Outrage*, who bears the burdens of simply being a woman in the United States in 1950.

The films that Lupino directed for The Filmakers are not inflected only by neorealism. The influences on them span a variety of styles, genres, and movements. *Outrage* is exemplary, in that it shows the influence of a very different movement and style from that of neorealism: German Expressionism.

Looking Backward? Outrage and M

Of *Outrage*, Lupino said in 1974, "I didn't think it was one of my better directorial efforts. There were certain things in it that I thought were rather touching and really true to life, but we tried to get artsy in places" (McGilligan and Weiner 224). This may be a disingenuous statement, since *Outrage* contains a scene that is a true tour de force, owing its ominous style to that of German Expressionism. Lupino's films are layered, with their more overt realist messages on the surface of the even more troubling noir backgrounds of town-, city-, and landscapes. Moreover, the films' influences are layered, too. Nowhere is this clearer than in *Outrage*, where Lupino's Italian neorealist–inflected style and German Expressionism meet.

In 1949, less than a year after production designer Harry Horner had won his Academy Award for *The Heiress* (winning his second Academy Award for *The Hustler* [Robert Rossen, 1961] with Paul Newman), Lupino asked him to design the production for *Outrage*. Horner and Lupino became friends, and The Filmakers produced *Beware, My Lovely* in 1952, one of the films Horner directed, starring Robert Ryan and Lupino herself.

On his design for *The Heiress* Horner commented, "It was a challenge—to inject the house with a personality of its own. Very often, houses that have a memory of one kind or another attached to them are able to dominate the inhabitants and mold them with a definite force of their own" ("Designing *The Heiress*" 181). For example, Dr. Sloper's space, his study, is patriarchally Victorian, while the space of his daughter Catherine's secret encounters with Morris, the mercenary suitor whom she eventually locks out of the home (as if the door were access to her body), is gothic, the scene of private, often women's, horror. Horner surrounds Morris with details of decor, such as gleaming, polished wood and glinting silverware and crystal. These details seduce Morris, expressing also his materialistic desires: he wants more than anything to become the future owner of the Sloper house. Further, Horner vividly shows Catherine as her father's helpless prisoner in the house by associating her

FIGURE 7 Above, Catherine Sloper (Olivia De Havilland), *The Heiress*; below, Mrs. Walton (Lillian Hamilton), *Outrage*

with the elaborate, cage-like, and much remarked-upon staircase. The wallpaper, with its pattern of diamond shapes, or latticing, reinforces the image of Catherine enclosed in this cage. As the narrative progresses, especially after Dr. Sloper's death, Catherine becomes more self-possessed. As she ascends the staircase at the end of the film while Morris continues to knock on the now-bolted front door, having finally imposed her will on Morris by denying him his dreams, she does so at the price of entombing herself in the house. This is illustrated again by the staircase, which is now viewed as a simpler enclosure: Catherine walks masterfully up the stairs between the latticed wallpaper and spindled banister, this time actively choosing to be no less a prisoner of the house than she was before. The very motif of latticed wallpaper and spindled banister is associated with Ann Walton's mother in Horner's production design for *Outrage*. Moreover, the cage motif of the famous staircase in *The Heiress* is transformed into a box-like trellis that encloses the Walton's house (see Part Two).

Horner had received his degree in architecture from the University of Vienna before becoming an actor with Max Reinhardt's troupe and subsequently apprenticing with Reinhardt as a set designer. He came to the United States in the mid-1930s, and by 1940 he was working in Hollywood. He met playwright Thornton Wilder and assisted production designer William Cameron Menzies on the film adaptation of *Our Town* (Sam Wood, 1940). Among other acclaimed film projects, he designed the sets for *The Little Foxes* (William Wyler, 1941), about which he said,

"I don't think a film should have too much 'locale,' it should not be the locale that one is attracted to primarily, but the characters, and how they fit into the landscape of the action" (Shorris 8). Edith C. Lee, author of the entry on Horner for *Film Reference*, writes, "In *The Little Foxes*, the sets were designed around Regina, a dominant and demonic character filled with greed and a lust for material pleasures. At one point she stands in front of a piece of furniture that actually gives her devil's horns! That this was indeed Horner's intent can be proved by referring to his still intact continuity sketches."

As the above examples illustrate, Horner's attention to architectural space and interior design exhibits a great sensitivity to how the spaces characters inhabit reflect the forces in and on those characters, many of them unconscious or determined from the outside. In other words, Horner invests his production design with psychosocial meaning. In neorealism, if we can put it this way, space demands a story and is as uncontrived as possible; in Expressionism, space exposes the workings of the psyche, whether collective or individual, and is highly worked or wrought. Having been born in the Austro-Hungarian Empire in 1910, in Bohemia, Horner was exceedingly familiar with German and Austrian Expressionist art and cinema, which influenced his choices as production designer as well as director.

In some very distinctive ways, the look and style of *Outrage* differs from the other films Lupino directed for The Filmakers. Her films after *Outrage* retain something of the look of *Outrage* in their noir styling—cast shadows reminiscent of nightmarish intent; attached shadows baring hidden meaning; staging, objects, and architectural and other forms that remind us of prisons and traps. While there are instances of noir style in Lupino's earlier films, *Not Wanted* and *Never Fear*, they are less elaborate than the ones in her films beginning with *Outrage*, which probably owe that style to her collaboration with Horner. But by far the most significant difference between *Outrage* and Lupino's other Filmakers films is its direct reflection of Fritz Lang's *M* (1931).[34]

After the family dinner scene in which Jim asks Mr. Walton for Ann's hand in marriage, we are ushered into the living nightmare Ann experiences by the stalking and rape scene. Shot on deserted nighttime streets in Los Angeles in a warehouse district, the look and feel of the scene is that of having been shot on an elaborately conceived set in

FIGURE 8 The *M*-like stalking scene in *Outrage*

Babelsberg—or at Staaken Studios, a large former zeppelin hangar outside Berlin where Lang filmed *M*. Filled with diagonal architectural frames, diagonally shot on silent streets illuminated only by the faint glimmer of street lamps, and shot often from above, *Outrage* compresses its visual citation of the earlier film into a taut, suspenseful scene culminating in Ann's rape. Because the Production Code explicitly stated that scenes of violence and sexual encounters could not be shown onscreen, *Outrage* could not show the rapist overcoming Ann. And Lupino was probably uninterested in showing such a scene, in any case. However, we can also look at the omission of the rape from the screen as a nod to *M*, in which most of the action takes place off-screen: we can hear it, but we cannot see it. The blaring truck horn, then, is not just Ann's desperate plea for someone to notice what's happening and to rescue her; its nearly intolerable noise serves as the aural dimension of the action of the rape itself.

Three of the visual elements Lupino cites from *M* are Elsie Beckmann's clown balloon as the symbol of her innocence, which floats free and and becomes caught on a telephone wire to signify her death, the child killer's shadow on the wanted poster, and his whistling before he murders his victim. In *Outrage*, we see these elements compressed into three shots: as the rapist follows Ann away from the sawmill, he whistles to catch her attention; as he stalks her, his shadow looms across old posters announcing a circus affixed to a wall; and, just after a shot of Ann banging on a door to alert people to her distress, Lupino continues to show the rapist following Ann. He violently tears a strip of paper from one of the posters, which depicts a clown. Ripping the poster for a spectacle that belongs to families and children quite clearly suggests that the rapist will tear Ann's innocence from her, and even suggests the violence he wishes to do by tearing her hymen. From time to time as he stalks her, the rapist whistles arhythmically, without pattern or melody.

Aside from these elements, *Outrage* is about how victims of rape internalize their abuse, becoming, in their own minds, filthy, "dirty" (as Ann tells Jim) perpetrators of harm to anyone close to them. Their worlds of human interaction shrink to nothing and they live in an isolating prison. That Ann lives in a psychic prison is articulated obsessively in the film, indicating that she is helplessly obsessed with her trauma, literalized by the boxes, squares, frames, and narrow architectural spaces that close in on her from right before her rape as she hides from the rapist and continuing throughout the film—easing up only during her stay in California.

But what does she have in common with serial child-murderer Hans Beckert, played so unnervingly by Peter Lorre? As we find out about Beckert's life, as he pleads with the kangaroo court, we discover that he, too, has suffered the trauma of abuse and internalized it, so that the only way to be rid of his nightmares and the pressure of his obsessions is to reenact even more definitively what was done to him as a child. "I can't help myself!" he pleads. We grow to have empathy for him, despite the fact that he kills children. Even though Ann kills a child—herself—in a purely symbolic way, we can see a shared self-image in Beckert and Ann. There is an aspect of each of them that makes us think of gendered reactions to abuse: while Ann takes her loathing out mainly on herself, steering clear of men, Beckert acts on his conditioned impulses, turning them outward. But is this wholly true? Doesn't Ann pick up a wrench with the intention of killing her rapist when Marini assaults her? We can even say that both reactions are intermingled, and victim and perpetrator roles are not clearly divided from each other. Horner and Lupino drew from *M* in part to complicate our ideas of victim and perpetrator.

The idea of the rescuer is also complicated in the film. Although Reverend Ferguson has essentially saved Ann by becoming her advocate, his voice and decisions stand in for Ann's own. Without consulting Ann about her feelings and desires, he becomes one of the characters complicit with the perpetrator by robbing her of any chance to develop her own agency, which of course is the central problematic of the film. The triangulation of victim-perpetrator-rescuer is a fluid model for these relationships, in which each role can become another given the right conditions. The inclusion of *M* as a subtext underscores that triangulation, which is likely to emerge pronouncedly (in dysfunctional families and societies) following crisis and trauma.

As we grow to empathize with Beckert, we begin to hate the denizens of Berlin for how they scapegoat him to keep from looking at their own corruption, bigotry, and murderousness. As to the public in Berlin, Inspector Karl Lohmann says, "Don't talk to me about collaboration with the public. Even hearing them talk disgusts me." Ann is also a scapegoat: the "mass society" of Capitol City coalesces around the spectacle of her misfortune and trauma, creating a temporary and ersatz community built on her suffering.

Critical-historical studies of and attitudes toward Lupino's role in film history have given short shrift to three central aspects of Lupino's filmmaking: her explorations, uniquely focused on the lives of women, of the dim possibilities for realizing desire in modern, late-capitalist America; her acumen as a director who found surprising visual and aural metaphors to represent thwarted ambition and failed social relations; and her innovative merging of classic Hollywood genres, notably film noir and women's melodrama, thus altering her social problem films. We turn next to Lupino's genre bending; as we conclude our discussion of feminist auteurism here, however, it is worth noting that Lupino's genre revisions paved the way for more contemporary female directors such as Kathryn Bigelow. Not only did Bigelow, like Lupino, learn to negotiate successfully with the Hollywood "boys' club," but she followed Lupino's lead in placing women protagonists in classically male genres. Related to this, Pam Cook has observed,

Like Ida Lupino almost fifty years before, Bigelow is a writer and producer as well as director, and interesting comparisons could be drawn between their production contexts and their work, particularly between Lupino's rape film *Outrage* and Bigelow's cop film *Blue Steel*, which includes a rape-revenge scenario. Such a comparison might suggest that the conjunction of post-1970s feminism and the entry of women film-makers at all levels of the industry with the greater visibility of graphic sex and violence, deplored by many, has had some beneficial effects for women, in that it has allowed feminism to move into a wider area. Women film-makers can, it seems, now use sexually explicit and violent material to confront issues of representation before much larger audiences. ("No Fixed Address" 162)

Lupino opened these areas for women filmmakers and feminists alike.

Shooting *The Hitch-Hiker* in 1952, William Talman, who played serial killer Emmett Myers, commented on Lupino's grace as director of an all-male cast and crew: "She was one of the gang; in fact, our leader, who met everything with an unbeatable—sense of humor. She set the pace for the seventy men who made up the troupe, and held it" (qtd. in *The Making of* 32). Lupino set the mold for Bigelow by appropriating crime and suspense conventions to create generic hybrids that explore gender and experiment with form. In Part Two, we explore the means by which Lupino ingeniously merges genres in the films she directed from 1949 to 1953.

PART TWO

LUPINO'S INGENIOUS GENRES

Early Films and *The Trouble with Angels* (1966)

In her essay "The Genius of Genre and the Ingenuity of Women," Jane Gaines locates the genius of films in "other texts as sources of meaning" (15) rather than in the auteur figure. She shifts critical emphasis away from isolated texts with single authors and toward considerations of form and style, social structures, history, and audience reception. For Gaines, "the genius of genre" offers a way to acknowledge women's innovations while "[praising] the ingenuity of the narrative and iconographic structure" (17).

Although Gaines employs a theoretical model that opposes auteurism at one level, her analysis helps explain the idea of authorship expressed in Lupino's work, where many distinct elements of Hollywood genres are merged to reveal psychosocial patterns in postwar American experience. Lupino's importance as a director lies in part in how she mixes genres while emphasizing women and gender. In her films, "ingenuity" is a feature of genre, which can allow discussions to center on the productive potential of genre—its "generative powers," in Richard Dyer's terms (176). These include not only a study of individual authorial agency, but also the social and industrial forces, historical contexts, and other formal, stylistic, and ideological factors that contribute to cultural production.[1] The "genius of genre" and Lupino's authorial identity are, in other words, mutually enhancing. Gaines elsewhere suggests a model of "the group of friends who shared the desire to make movies" (*Feminist Reader* 109), which is helpful in thinking about Lupino's approach to filmmaking. Gaines's concept of desire as a motivation that brings artistic filmmaking communities together is exemplified by Lupino's work as a director, producer, and screenwriter in an independent industrial context marked by a spirit of discovery, resistance to the norm, and commitment to collaboration. Similarly, Sarah Kozloff's discussion of collaborative filmmaking and a "plurality of voices" clarifies the idea of filmmaking communities, and helps define Lupino's authorship. In *The Life of the Author*, Kozloff argues that ideas of film authorship should not be abandoned, but refigured as inclusive, to reflect how films are really made: "Such approaches would be more accurate, less hierarchical and more truly democratic than standard auteurism . . . more grounded in the actualities of film production and infinitely more humanist than death-of-the-author, filmmakers-as-flotsam theories."

In Part Two, we look in depth at Lupino's early films from 1949 through 1953 in terms of their genre hybridity and explorations of postwar gender relations, and conclude with a discussion of Lupino's last-directed film, *The Trouble with Angels* (1966). In all of these works, Lupino brings an inclusive vision of gender to her directing across genres. While women are most frequently her central characters and women's issues the subjects of her films, male characters are not stereotypical and men's issues are understood non-judgmentally, sensitively, and comprehensively. In *The Bigamist*, for instance, Harry Graham's inability to adjust to the more flexible gender roles that emerged during the war is seen sympathetically, and Harry's bigamy more as a foolish act that only lands him, not his wives, in an untenable situation. Eve and Phyllis are perfectly capable of taking care of themselves. The unorthodox treatment of gender for the time period found in Lupino's films makes her narratives richer and more complex than critics have acknowledged.

Lupino's films are clearly allied with melodrama, as they excavate gendered spaces that extend from modern living rooms into the country landscape, fixed "by the claustrophobic atmosphere of the bourgeois home and/or the small-town setting" (Elsaesser 508). While melodrama, as scholars have noted repeatedly, is a broader generic construct, in film studies "women's melodrama" has typically referred to films from the 1930s through the 1950s that explore female subjectivity and desire as embattled or prohibited. Certainly, Lupino's films reveal the destructive suppression of creative energy in their portrayal of the domestic institutions of marriage and family relations, and so participate in the critique of modern social life so widely associated with women's melodrama, "the trials and discontents of maternity, threatened and disintegrating familial relations, the abuses of patriarchal power, marriage fatigue, class misalliance, and physical and psychic illness" (Landy 230).

While Lupino's films are allied with women's melodrama, they are more fundamentally shaped by the social problem film and film noir. There is much to say about Lupino and film noir, since her style (including chiaroscuro lighting and an emphasis on authentic locales) and thematic preoccupations put her at the center of this series or genre. As in the most celebrated noir films, Lupino's work offers a bitter vision of wounded, alienated men and women in postwar America. If film noir criticizes modern America, "Lupino noir," to borrow Carrie Rickey's phrase, exposes social institutions as profoundly damaging, even traumatic, especially for women.

Thus, it shouldn't surprise us that the classic noir films that most resonate with Lupino's work are woman-centered noir films, such as *Leave Her to Heaven*, *Mildred Pierce*, *The Strange Affair of Uncle Harry*, *The Spiral Staircase*, and *The Reckless Moment*. These films, like Lupino's, depict domestic space as stifling, even inimical. To account for this quality, we introduce the concept of "home noir," which reveals the forces at work in these films' domestic spaces, where the ambitions and desires of both women and men intersect. The films we highlight in Part Two are *Hard, Fast and Beautiful* (1951), *The Bigamist* (1953), and *Outrage* (1950). We return to these films more than once because of their visual richness and thematic diversity.

The Social Problem Film and Film Noir

In 1949, Malvin Wald declared that The Filmakers was founded to "tackle serious themes and problem dramas" (qtd. in Donati 156). Participating in postwar social-minded cinema, The Filmakers' films were at odds with conventional formulas for success in American filmmaking. In 1948 in the *Nation*, James Agee predicted that only "problem dramas" would supply the means for achieving great film art: "It is hard to believe that absolutely first-rate works of art can ever again be made in Hollywood, but it would be idiotic to assume that flatly. If they are to be made there, they will most probably develop along the directions worked out during the past year or two; they will be journalistic, semi-documentary, and 'social minded,' or will start that way and transcend those levels" (*Agee on Film* 286). Lupino's films engaged in the "quest for authenticity" (Schatz, *Boom* 392), like other films of the period, such as *The Naked City*. Her films also expose social evils without having the budgets afforded Elia Kazan's and others' films with their male directors' imprimatur.[2] By the time Lupino started making "problem dramas," there was already a backlash against the "political liability and [potential to] fragment the audience" in these films' provocations (Balio 281; qtd. in Stanfield 223). The conservative backlash is best represented by the MPAA's Eric Johnston's oft-quoted declaration in 1947, "We'll have no more *Grapes of Wrath*, we'll have no more *Tobacco Roads....* We'll have no more films that show the seamy side of American life" (qtd. in Schatz, *Boom* 382). In the tense HUAC postwar cultural environment, Johnston's scorn for films with social or political messages helped to undermine the desire and ability to make "problem dramas." According to Schatz, "In 1950, Hollywood went into a full-scale retreat from message pictures and prestige-level social problem drama" (386). As Peter Lev notes, "Even sympathy for the underdog was problematic" (11). Lupino once again went against the grain, pursuing problem films in this environment and focusing them on women.

The problem drama, according to Jackie Byars and Thomas Schatz, "is distinctly male—white male; although female characters may play crucial roles in solving the problem, the problem is rarely theirs" (Byars 115). For Schatz, "issues are treated from a distinctly male viewpoint" (370). Aside from *The Lost Weekend* (1945), *The Best Years of Our Lives* (1946), *Crossfire* (1947), and *Gentleman's Agreement* (1947), however, other postwar social problem films did focus on women, such as *The Snake Pit* (1948) and *Pinky* (1949), as Kozloff observes; in fact a "notable feature of social-problem films [is] the number of women protagonists" (in Friedman 461). The films Lupino produced, directed, and co-wrote for The Filmakers fall into this latter grouping in that they deal with women's issues, but more than this, Lupino stretched the problem drama's conventions to encompass film noir. Lupino's films merge these generic traits as does a film like Edward Dmytryk's *Crossfire* (a problem-drama film noir about postwar veterans and antisemitism). Problem dramas are typically distinguished by the way their subject carries as much—or more—weight as their stars or story. This is certainly true of The Filmakers' films, in which, often, "unknowns" play the protagonists, such as Mala Powers, whose first big break came when she read for the part of Ann Walton in *Outrage*, or Sally Forrest, originally a dancer, who broke into acting because Lupino hired her in the lead role in *Not Wanted, Never Fear*, and *Hard, Fast and Beautiful*. In an AFI interview, another Lupino discovery, Hugh O'Brian, recalls that Lupino gave him his "real beginning." He auditioned for the role of Len Randall in *Never Fear* on an empty stomach with a dollar and a half in his pocket.

Problem films use individual dramas to present morality tales with wider social implications. Indeed, in Lupino's problem dramas, such as *Outrage* and *The Bigamist*, choruses of lawyers, judges, priests, psychiatrists, and detectives provide the moral of the story: women have not been well served by the lessons of the war, they say; we need to become aware of what they suffer and change our institutions accordingly. Lupino is unique in the postwar American film industry for calling public attention to women's traumas and their repercussions in a society unready and unwilling to address them openly. These traumas include unwanted pregnancy, rape, the pressure to become successful through accepting favors and ruthlessly competing at sports, illness, and betrayal by bigamy. Domestic spaces become the theater of war for Lupino, rather than military battlegrounds or their postwar concomitants. In *Outrage*, for example, Lupino responds to problem films depicting postwar trauma, such as *The Best Years of Our Lives*, by seeming to ask, "What about women?" The shell-shock of a rape victim on domestic ground is no less than that of a war veteran who has fought overseas. In fact, it is uncanny how Lupino captures in her protagonist Ann Walton what today we call post-traumatic stress disorder, which is, as Judith Herman observed in her ground-breaking study *Trauma and Recovery*, much the same for soldiers as for victims of child abuse or sexual abuse and refugees from war-torn countries.

Lupino's early films examine women's disappointments in the wake of World War II and the modernity it ostensibly ushered in, which included more flexible gender constructions, the right of all people to realize the American Dream, and the waning Victorian legacy of silence and shame around women's traumatic experiences. Concisely stated, Lupino's problem dramas focus on the failure of America to provide the benefits of wartime modernity to women after the war.

In addition, by focusing on failed gender relations and social institutions, Lupino's films not only represent the social problem film's "[combination of] realism and melodrama" (Kozloff, in Friedman 459), but carry on an important legacy from silent film left to us by Lois Weber. Like Alice Guy, who directed the first fiction film in 1896, *The Cabbage Fairy*, Weber had a remarkable career. In 1916, she became "the highest-paid director of Universal Studios and the highest-paid woman director of the silent era" (Seger 3). Guy and Weber became filmmakers "before [the industry] had time to shape itself into a male enterprise. Movies were not born gender specific."[3] Lois Weber's legacy, however, is important not only because Weber was a successful female director in early Hollywood. Her forgotten story of female artistic and industrial achievement also recalls the 1940s *Newsweek* article (discussed in Part One) proclaiming that "every so often Hollywood 'discovers' Ida Lupino." Weber brought social issues to the screen, setting a precedent for Lupino in a different postwar era. Weber's problem films, about birth control, abortion, poverty, and capital punishment, rebelled against Hollywood's "easy pleasures" (Palmer 106). Indeed, Weber herself predicted that "the frothy, unreal picture is doomed"; her films realized a desire to "make constructive pictures of real ideas which shall have some intimate bearing on the lives of the people who see them" (qtd. in Mahar 141). Weber paved the way for Lupino in her willingness to address controversial subject matter that had a particular impact on women. As Shelley Stamp observes, "[Weber] recognized that her films might intervene in contemporary debates, not only through on-screen stories depicting social problems like poverty, criminality, and addiction, but also by featuring female characters in complex leading parts that resisted two-dimensional stereotypes like 'ingenue,' 'flapper,' or 'wife'" (*Lois Weber in Early Hollywood* 5). Stamp's description of Weber's revolutionary vision strongly resonates with Lupino's films, which similarly intervened creatively in serious topics of the day. In a noteworthy illustration of the cyclical nature of American cultural trends, Weber's idealistic prediction that there would be no more froth prefigures Agee's conviction quoted above that "first-rate works of art" would be "social minded."

Anthony Slide calls *The Blot* (1921), perhaps Weber's best-known movie about the ills of poverty, "a film without delineated villains or heroes, but rather a story of ordinary, *real* people" (17). Lupino always opted for description and revelation over moralizing judgment, leading her, like Weber, to avoid tidy conclusions. Weber's narratives were open-ended, as in *Where Are My Children?* about birth control and abortion, which leaves viewers with the "disturbing effect" (Brownlow 53) of an unresolved domestic portrait of husband and wife mired in mutual resentment.

Working for Universal Film Manufacturing Company, Weber began making one-reel films in 1907 with her husband, Phillips Smalley. In 1914, she was the first American woman to direct a feature film, *The Merchant of Venice*. As her career blossomed, she became as powerful in Hollywood as D. W. Griffith and Cecil B. DeMille (see Stamp, *Women's Film Pioneers Project*). Weber was a woman of diverse talents, who rejected the glamor of onscreen performance, and preferred writing, directing, and producing to acting. She developed her own style of creative leadership in filmmaking, which, shockingly, made little material impact on the role of women behind the scenes from the beginning of the twentieth century to this day.[4] Weber struggled, as Lupino did, with a "celebrity persona." She worked, as Stamp tells us, to "smooth the bold image of a woman filmmaker" (285) in an environment in which she collaborated but also met with resistance.

Lupino's contributions should be seen as part of the feminist lineage Weber inaugurated that includes many other women working behind the scenes. The fascinating stories of these women fall outside the scope of this study, but include the career of Dorothy Arzner, which has been documented by scholars such as Judith Mayne and Claire Johnston.[5] Thinking about Weber's legacy alongside Lupino's achievements, as well as the limits placed on these women's professional lives, underscores the relevance of such stories to contemporary discussions of women, gender, film, and media. As Stamp concisely observes about the history of damaging gender constructions in the lives and careers of women in film, "These fictions have a long tail" (*Lois Weber in Early Hollywood* 285).

Lupino's films are important not only to the history of the problem drama and its focus on gender but also to a revisionary look at film noir. Film noir has been fused to gender since the 1940s, when Nino Frank first coined the phrase. In the immediate postwar period, French critics discovered the "hardboiled" precursors of film noir in the American novels of Dashiell Hammett and Raymond Chandler. While the work that noir films do to shore up conventional masculinity may seem obvious (one thinks here of Chandler's ideal detective: "Down these mean streets a man must go who is not himself mean, who is neither tarnished nor afraid"), critics have over time discovered the more complicated issues these movies address in connection with masculinity. They show portraits of a teetering postwar male identity in the face of historical change and cultural shifts in gender roles. More recently, film noir has also been explored as a series of films and a tone equally invested in men's and women's experience, not the exclusively male sphere with which it has conventionally been associated. The knee-jerk association of film noir with the centrality of hardboiled male experience has been questioned by feminist critics, such as Elizabeth Cowie, Philippa Gates, Julie Grossman, Helen Hanson, and Jans Wager, among others, who have shifted critical attention to female subjectivity and the feminist critique embedded in film noir.[6] In this context, Ida Lupino's protagonists can be seen as yearning, vibrant noir women whose prospects for fulfillment in postwar America are bleak or thwarted.

Lupino's films—in Jans Wager's words "remarkable for their complexity" ("Lupino" 225)—are central to the classical noir period (usually designated as extending from 1941 [*The Maltese Falcon*] through 1958 [*Touch of Evil*]). Indeed, film noir itself is a more complex mix of genres than common fixations with character patterns generally allow. Viewers may focus on the femme fatale and the hardboiled detective as two of the defining character types of film noir; but such movies are more invested in a critique of the myths undergirding American society and culture. Linking film noir to Lupino's social critique, Mark Osteen observes that the "Filmmakers offered an alternative to the patriarchal Hollywood system, making progressive films that examined women's issues and questioned the American pursuit of wealth and happiness at any cost" (216). Indeed, Lupino's films are a compendium of noir themes; they also criticize social institutions and individualist conceptions of selfhood held sacred in American culture.

Lupino's noir reveals that the American Dream has failed women. Her noir motifs—a powerful sense of belatedness and the inability to escape the past; modern social institutions that thwart the desires of individuals; and figures cast adrift in an alienating American landscape—relate to the failure of postwar America to deliver on its promise of success and happiness to striving individuals. The hopes for modernity in relation to patriotism, productivity, and more flexible gender roles (including expanded fields for female work and agency) led to disappointment in the postwar period, especially for women, who bore the heavier burden of these failures.

Lupino's perversely gendered family and social roles are accompanied by a fatalism linked to human error, bad judgment, and the tough choices that haunt her protagonists. One might think here of adoption investigator Mr. Jordan and his fear of "making the same mistake twice" in *The Bigamist* (1953). Of course, in *The Bigamist*, Harry Graham leaves his San Francisco home to escape his feelings of inadequacy as a man in the face of his wife's success in business, only to find himself in Los Angeles caring for a baby and doing housework while his "other wife" goes to work. From *Out of the Past* (Jacques Tourneur, 1947) to *Chinatown* (Roman Polanski, 1974), this "compulsion to repeat," or never becoming free of the past, is a quintessential noir theme, here beautifully expressed in Harry's bigamy and in the fact that he duplicates his unhappiness, finding even less of what he wants in his second marriage. It should also be noted that just as Jake Gittes's seeming existential lesson in *Chinatown* about traumatic repetition is in fact a result of misreading Evelyn Mulwray as a femme fatale, so, too, *The Bigamist* is mainly about misapprehension related to gender.

Lupino's noir is deeply connected to the theme of a gendered landscape—for example, a landscape that purports to offer male escape from female domesticity in *The Hitch-Hiker* (1953), or from responsibility and commitment for Steve Ryan (Leo Penn) in *Not Wanted* (1949). Ironically, these escapes are often revealed to contain as many traps as home, giving the lie to a conventional gendering of space in American culture. The spaces in America that are supposed to be sites of excitement, hope, and comfort are revealed to be empty or profoundly dangerous; marriage, family, and work, and the cultural spaces that express these social institutions, are oppressive. There are no real "safe" zones in Lupino's films. Through her rendering of space, Lupino shows how close perverse behavior and violence are to "normal" domestic life: rape, serial killers, traumas of various sorts beset Lupino's characters, and, true to classic noir, these traumas portray "a riposte, a sour disenchanted flip side," in Philip Kemp's words about noir generally, "to the brittle optimism and flag-waving piety of much of Hollywood's 'official' output of the period" (86). In Lupino's noir view of America, desire is thwarted or channeled into capitalistic exploitation.

Despite film titles that are blunt (*Not Wanted*), melodramatic (*Never Fear*), or titillating (*Hard, Fast and Beautiful*), Lupino's films explore the complicated relationship between desire and disappointment, a double view similar to film noir's twin fascination with American idealism and American cynicism. Lupino is deeply critical of American fantasies of radical selfhood, dismantling the myth of "rising up," or transcending class identities. Noir films sympathize with down-and-outers struggling with the stark limits social standards impose on individuals. This noir theme pervades Lupino's films.

In Lupino's America, the portraits of youth are grim. In *Not Wanted*, the first film Lupino directed, Sally Kelton (Sally Forrest) pursues her lover to Capitol City, where she meets "kind and cheerful" Drew Baxter (Keefe Brasselle), who falls in love with her. The noir contrast of innocence and experience in this film associates Drew with childlikeness, when, for example, he plays with his electric train set. Ignorant of her former steamy relationship with bounder Steve, Drew continues to court Sally, rubbing her feet when she is tired and taking her on dates to the playground where they ride the carousel.[7] In a scene that anticipates the chaotic merry-go-round two years later in Alfred Hitchcock's *Strangers on a Train* (1951), Lupino uses a subjective camera when Sally's vision of the carousel becomes distorted and the merry-go-round metamorphoses into spinning images of chaos, uncontrolled fear, and horror. As a noir stylist, Lupino thus explores expressionistic means of communicating the tormented "inner life" of her characters, quite aside from the symptoms of early pregnancy that Sally is experiencing—a realm belonging only to women. Throughout *Not Wanted*, in fact, Lupino shows Sally's suffering through a subjective use of music and camera work. While Sally "plays" with Drew and his toy trains, she begins to hear Steve's piano refrains. Later in the film, in the labor scene, Sally hears Steve playing the piano as she is taken to the operating room to have her baby. As we discussed in Part One, Lupino uses a subjective camera, employing point-of-view shots as Sally is wheeled down the hall to give birth. Sally sees shadows on the walls and blurred images of doctors and nurses, suggesting her disorientation and distress.

The sequence with Drew in Capitol City also strongly expresses the noir theme of belatedness. Sally's prospects with Drew have been ruined because of her affair with Steve. As Tana says to Hank Quinlan in an important moment in *Touch of Evil*, "Your future's all used up." Sally's fate has been determined, but this fatedness is, as Lupino's film demonstrates, inextricably linked to the narrow paths available to women who have unexpressed passion and whose yearning may cause them to make mistakes.

While Lupino is most interested in Sally's journey from adolescent fantasy to adult disillusionment, *Not Wanted* refuses to judge Sally. Instead, the film sets Sally's actions within the overarching structure of the failed American Dream. While Steve is, in reductionistic terms, the cause of Sally's downfall, he too is caught in a web of confused hopes and disappointments that, for Lupino, seems to characterize the idea of America. Steve's appealing piano riffs (fun for viewers today to watch, since Leo Penn bears a striking resemblance to his actor son, Sean Penn) only barely disguise his limited prospects: with no money, Steve bounces from one music gig to another, his travels across the country and then to South America symbolizing the life of a drifter who nevertheless has talent and charisma. Steve is "stir-crazy," as he says, and his affect of repressed anger is a symptom of the impossibility of getting ahead. He registers his failure to settle down as "a sickness with me. I don't know. I've got to keep going until I find some place where I belong." Like the "detours" that fill the noir landscape, Steve's future is also "used up." Even Drew, the "nicest, sweetest person in the world," as Sally calls him, is broken. His "girl" leaves him after he returns from the war with a prosthetic leg. Drew lives a lonely yet cheerful existence running the gaseteria where he hires Sally to work. When Sally learns of her pregnancy, she abandons Drew and the gaseteria, landing finally in an urban home for unwed mothers.

At the film's conclusion, Lupino opts for a sober, non-Hollywood ending. After giving up her baby for adoption, Sally tries to steal a baby from its carriage and is put in jail. Upon her release, she seems to be in a trance, but she panics and flees from Drew when he comes looking for her. The final extended chase scene is suspenseful and visually arresting. Drew stumbles after Sally because of his prosthetic leg and finally falls. She turns back toward him, overcome with sympathy. The film ends, as we noted in Part One, without any audio recording of their exchange, with an image of two marginalized figures finding solace with each other in an indifferent urban landscape.

If Sally's affair with Steve is a trap for her, marriage is equally a trap. Sally's mother (Dorothy Adams), shown in one scene as stricken with a headache, is burdened and miserable: "If I nag at you, it's for your own good because I don't want you to have to slave around a kitchen for the rest of your life like I do." (Sally's father, played by Wheaton Chambers, is shown as likable enough but ineffectual.) In Lupino's films, the critique of gender roles is clear. Women are exploited, and men are desperate in their search to confirm their masculinity. Predation in these films is directly linked to a distorted postwar world in which rigid, conventional gender roles have not been given up, in spite of being "used up."

In *The Bigamist* (1953), Harry Graham (Edmond O'Brien) is indecisively caught between two women he loves. One, his wife, Eve (Joan Fontaine), threatens his masculinity as she becomes professionally successful. Harry seems disappointed by not having an Angel in the House, his wife's name perhaps signifying his repressed feeling about such betrayal; "marriage," for Harry, we learn in his voiceover, had "became a business partnership." In his voiceover confession to Mr. Jordan

FIGURE 9 Harry and his new appliance, the deep freezer, in *The Bigamist*

FIGURE 10 Exterior of the restaurant where Phyllis works, a cultural pastiche, in *The Bigamist*

(Edmund Gwenn), Harry recounts Eve's success in their "deep freeze" sales business: "She caught on [to the business] fast, so fast that she doubled our sales in no time."

At one point, a disillusioned Harry describes Eve as being in "one of her executive moods." Eve is a "modern" woman. The Grahams discover that Eve cannot have a baby the "natural" way, which is how they meet Mr. Jordan, who ultimately learns of Harry's bigamy. However, Eve is a "natural" at business. Her failure to fit into a conventional gender role and her business acumen are the twin sources of Harry's sense of failure as a man and drive him into the arms of the more traditionally loving Phyllis, the other woman Harry marries (played by Lupino, making her the first woman in the post-silent era to direct herself).

Phyllis is also a noir figure, cynical and disappointed with life, abandoned by a lover during the war, and now working as a waitress at an unsuccessful Chinese restaurant. Indeed, the Chinese restaurant seems a symbol of failed American ideals, the hope for a melting pot of diverse identities bottoming out in anonymous locales and barren eateries. "Where are all the people?" Harry asks. "Sundays are quiet, and all the rest of the week," replies Phyllis. Harry is obviously enamored of Phyllis, though the noir setting defines the tone of their "romance" as bleak and ironic. The restaurant, whose storefront is flanked by a flashing neon image of a cowboy lassoing a horse, reflects an incoherent cultural pastiche.

Phyllis introduces the restaurant to Harry as "early American Chinese." Later, Phyllis tells Harry about the Chinese restaurant's manager, Hannigan, who used to manage a hot dog stand. Phyllis describes the food as inauthentic but recommends the egg soup, "the only genuine Chinese dish we serve here." Earlier in this scene, Collier Young, the film's producer and Lupino's ex-husband, appears in a cameo as one of the silent barflies in this noirish restaurant. Lupino films Young's face to emphasize the scar across his cheek, and the cigarette smoke that blankets the shot reflects a murky social environment in which individuals appear as fixtures in this gloomy late-capitalist mise-en-scène.

The Los Angeles setting of Harry and Phyllis's relationship is also a noir extension of modern alienation. Like many of Lupino's other characters, Harry wanders the city streets. The ironic contrast between Los Angeles as a city of dreams and the actual lives of its inhabitants is especially marked in the film in the irony of Harry and Phyllis's loneliness and the Hollywood bus tour of the stars, where they meet. Buses figure prominently in Lupino's films; here, Phyllis and Harry meet on a "homes of the rich and famous" bus tour. Harry tries to strike up a conversation with Phyllis, and the dialogue presages his future bigamy: he asks her, "Haven't you any interest in how the other half lives?" More important here, the idea of the double life invokes a Hollywood fantasy of "going places," an alternate life of fulfilled dreams that contrasts with Harry's own physical and psychological drifting. In his voiceover commentary as he mounts the celebrity tour bus, Harry says, "I liked movies though

FIGURE 11 A barfly (Collier Young) in *The Bigamist*

I really didn't care where Clark Gable lived, but here were people going someplace, and I went around with them." Paradoxically, these tourists imagine "going someplace," though after they go "around," they will end where they began. Some have commented on the in-joke during the bus scene, when the driver notes the Hollywood house of actor Edmund Gwenn (who plays Mr. Jordan). That the film refers to Gwenn and his most famous role as Santa Claus in *Miracle on 34th Street* (which it has already referenced when Eve says that Mr. Jordan looks like Santa Claus) offers ironic commentary on the landscape of Lupino's Los Angeles. This Los Angeles landscape is neither magical nor charming.

The *Bigamist*'s noir reflection on the failure of the American Dream can also be seen in its treatment of the idea of freedom. *The Bigamist* shows this myth to be bound up with gender fantasies. Phyllis says to Harry, "You're free, as you've always been," but Harry feels trapped. Though Harry has pursued a transgressive, individualist life by having two wives, his outlaw status is undercut by the domesticity of both his homes. With Eve, he hosts dinners for clients; with Phyllis, he takes care of the baby. Harry's confused desire for fulfillment is ultimately about being needed, people depending on him. When Eve's father dies, she is once again dependent on Harry, and when Phyllis falls sick after giving birth to her and Harry's child, she depends on him too. That Harry is in over his head now is a comment on how his desperate bid for masculine validation has backfired.

The Hitch-Hiker, lauded as a noir classic, is also a portrait of failed gender roles. As others have noted, the masculine fantasy of escaping domestic obligations is radically undercut when draftsman Gil (Frank Lovejoy) and mechanic Roy (Edmond O'Brien) are mentally tortured by "Kansas desperado" Emmett Myers (William Talman), whom they pick up on the road. Trying to escape the country after a serial killing spree, Myers at one point forces Roy to exchange his clothes with him, which symbolizes the potential violence in Roy himself. The scene in which Gil is asked to shoot a can from Roy's hand shows the closeness of traumatic crime to the normal state of things in this vision of America. Lupino's mise-en-scène, the wide-open southwestern and Mexican land-scape that signifies freedom, becomes the site of the violent identity of modern experience and its potential for crime and transgression. The fantasy of freedom and self-fulfillment that motivates Gil and Roy's road trip is parodied when Myers, the "consummate individualist" (Osteen 145), brags about having made his "own way." While we learn early on that Gil and Roy's trip is the first time Gil has been away from his family "except for the war," Myers shows his contempt for Gil and Roy's domestic lives: "You guys are soft. You know what makes you that way? You're up to your neck in IOU's. You're suckers! You're scared to get out on your own. You've always had it good, so you're soft. Well, not me! Nobody ever gave me anything, so I don't owe nobody! . . . My folks were tough. When I was born, they took one good look at this puss of mine and told me to get lost. I didn't need 'em. Didn't need any of 'em." Myers's speech is a parody of self-determination and radical individualism, but his role in the film also serves as a check on smug masculinity, a rejoinder to the belief in freedom, control, and an ability to escape from conventions felt to be stifling, especially in the postwar years when men's leisure was domesticated. Myers's afflicted eye is described as partially paralyzed, which indicates a deeper paralysis. Moreover, the bum eye that won't close "paralyzes" Gil and Roy: unable to tell if Myers is awake or asleep, they are prevented from nighttime escape by their sense of Myers's uncanny surveillance. Myers is a masculine monstrosity—or, in David Greven's words, a "cinematic Cyclops."

Hard, Fast and Beautiful, based on the short story "Mother of a Champion" by John Tunis that first appeared in *Harper's Monthly Magazine* in 1929, is a film equally invested in depicting postwar gender trauma, but it focuses on women instead: a young tennis prodigy, Florence Farley (Sally Forrest), and her mother, Millie (Claire Trevor), who is obsessed with her daughter's fame and success. As a film about the limitations of prospects for ambitious women, a fundamental noir theme that provides a crucial postwar context for the so-called femme fatale, *Hard, Fast and Beautiful* illustrates Janey Place's description of the noir female figure, the "independent, ambitious woman who feels confined within a marriage." Like Mildred Pierce, Millie Farley expresses her desire and ambition vicariously, through her daughter. Both *Mildred Pierce* and *Hard, Fast and Beautiful* employ hybrid genres to expose the desperate position of women in postwar America wanting more than domestic gender roles allow them. Writing about late 1940s and 1950s maternal melodrama, E. Ann Kaplan comments, "Mothers in these films are blatantly monstrous, deliberately victimizing their children for sadistic and narcissistic ends, and thereby producing criminals" (134). While it may be tempting to read Millie Farley this way, Lupino's tone is more sympathetic, which we see in how she renders the traps laid for ambitious women. Millie and Florence's stories, tracked through Lupino's symbolic mise-en-scène, reveal a strongly feminist critique of marriage, in particular, but also of sports. In *Hard, Fast and Beautiful*, sports are appropriated by capitalist exploitation.

Uninterested in her husband, Will, an ineffectual character much like Sally's father in *Not Wanted*, Millie turns her attention to Florence's prospects. "From the very moment you were born, I knew you were different. I could see things in you that no one else could and I knew that somehow," she says in her initial voiceover, "I was going to get the very best out of life for you." Having married young and become disappointed in Will (whose passivity is ironically connoted in his given name, which differs from that of the character in Tunis's source text), Millie takes over in the family and manipulates everyone to ensure that Florence becomes a tennis star. Millie is the stage mom translated into the sports arena as the "Queen Bee Mom," a syndrome in which parents use "their children's lives as an arena to enhance their own popularity, prestige, sense of self-esteem, and entitlement—to their children's detriment" (Wiseman 6).[8] However, Millie's obsession with Florence becoming "somebody" is also a fundamental noir theme, one that applies to female and male experience. From the enterprising appeal Laura Hunt makes to Waldo Lydecker to endorse a product for her advertising agency in *Laura* (Otto Preminger, 1944), Mildred Pierce building an empire from the humble beginnings of baking pies in her home, to the hopes of Cora Smith in *The Postman Always Rings Twice* for expanding the diner on a dusty road in modern California ("I want to be somebody," Cora tells Frank Chambers), film noir's strong women aren't merely deadly seductresses. They are representations of wartime and postwar female desire and ambition. Millie and Florence, too, seek fulfillment beyond a dull bedroom and the backyard garage.

Millie's role as manipulative stage mother thus only barely covers a wellspring of loss and desire central to Lupino's vision. Lupino's modernist sensibility interprets postwar American social and family roles as damaging and traumatic, in which individuals struggle to escape their entrapment. While ambition with little outlet in an unresponsive social

FIGURE 12 A triangle in *Hard, Fast and Beautiful*: Millie, ineffectual husband Will, and Fletcher, the exploitative agent

world often fuels noir "darkness," Lupino's mise-en-scène also reveals the claustrophobia of psychosocial space in the domestic sphere, as we see in Millie and Will's home. For example, in one scene Will watches the predatory agent Fletcher Locke (Carleton Young) looking offscreen at Florence. Will is dwarfed between Fletcher and Millie. Here, he is shown as ineffectual, standing behind Fletcher's threatening figure, while Millie, in her own world of desire and longing, finds her husband irrelevant (see figure 12).

By the time this movie was made, sports writers and enthusiasts were decrying what they called "shamateurism," tennis amateurs living well, taking in-kind gifts—travel and stays at ritzy hotels—instead of cash for playing tournaments, since the top players were prohibited from making profits from playing tennis until the Open era in the late 1960s. As Millie and Florence come to rely on the glamor of "shamateurism," their world darkens. A noir vision of corruption permeates sports "play," and Florence herself grows cynical. Infected by the exploitative landscape of a corrupt tennis world and angry at her mother for embracing that world, Florence psychologically abandons her mother. Millie's tangle of confused feelings, which she represses as her daughter retreats, explodes in the home noir-styled burst of light and shadow in a European hotel room (see figure 13 and the discussion of home noir below). Florence having turned away from her, Millie is now vulnerable, her hopes for controlling the terms of Florence's success dashed by her daughter's withdrawal. At the same time, the previously passive Will has mustered

FIGURE 13 *Hard, Fast and Beautiful*: Noir interior landscape, a European hotel room

the energy from his hospital bed to reject Millie for her narcissism and contempt for their marriage. Will, sick nearly "to death" of Millie's domination, tells her in tough-speak to "beat it, Millie." Rejected by both her daughter and her husband, Millie slinks off, shoulders down, in defeat.

In the final scenes of the film, Florence wins the Forest Hills tournament. Despairing at the emptiness of her "success," and her full realization that she has been betrayed, she abandons the court and flees into marriage with "good-guy" Gordon McKay (Robert Clarke), while Millie is handed the trophy, now a symbol of her and Florence's defeat. Wrapped around the pole, clinging to an object now symbolizing her failed ambition (see the third image in figure 14), Millie is left alone in the stands. Lupino moves in succession to longer and longer shots of Millie sitting by herself in the darkening stadium. Drifting papers and tournament programs represent the detritus resulting from women's ambitions. While some have argued that the film shows Millie's aloneness as the just deserts of her ambition,[9] the film presents a sympathetic view of her downfall, tracking her increasingly desperate isolation with pathos clear in Lupino's mise-en-scène.

FIGURE 14 The ending of *Hard, Fast and Beautiful*: Florence and Millie's bleak future

Although Pam Cook has called Lupino "technically unsophisticated" (in Kuhn 58), screen shots from this film go a long way toward showing Lupino's stylistic virtuosity. Shot analysis reveals her acumen as a director who created visual metaphors and mise-en-scène to suggest themes of privation, postwar alienation, and gender trauma born of changing conceptions of male and female social power and roles. Indeed, Florence's traumatic journey can also be traced through Lupino's mise-en-scène. Through low-angle shots, we observe her gritty determination as she plays matches. As the film progresses and Florence becomes a diva, she moves from idealism to cynicism. Florence lives her life increasingly in the shadows, which Lupino shows in an intriguing noir image: Florence practicing her backhand under the nasty tutelage of the exploitative Fletcher Locke (see figure 15).[10] Florence's shadow wields the tennis racket as a weapon aimed at bludgeoning Fletcher. Florence and Millie's American Dream has collapsed, the noir shadow world enveloping these two women as their fates close in on them.

In *Hard, Fast and Beautiful*, desiring women are offered two bitter paths. One is to succumb in the end to domestic roles, as when

FIGURE 15 Florence's shadow wielding a tennis racquet as weapon in *Hard, Fast and Beautiful*

Florence, having given up tennis, is folded into the arms of her future husband, Gordon. Florence is less relieved than confused and unhappy. Depressed and disoriented, Florence is presented in Lupino's mise-en-scène as entering yet another socially sanctioned prison, the face of the tennis racket providing a symbolic view of the next frame that will determine Florence's life and future: marriage (see the first two images of figure 14).

Even bleaker, however, is Millie's used-up future, shown in the trash swirling around her in the stadium. Florence bids her mother goodbye. In the end, Lupino positions us as viewers to empathize with both Florence and Millie. As Mandy Merck notes, "Far from representing some happy domesticity, the film's final shots stay in the stadium, where the abandoned Millie sits in the gathering darkness" (83–84).

Some have read Millie's acquisitiveness as a warning against female ambition (Dozoretz focuses, for example, on the film's portrait of women as "greedy" and "deceitful" [55]). In contrast, we find that the film shows the tragedy of limited possibilities for women who wanted more than what postwar gender conventions allowed them and who wanted to break apart the social institutions that constrained them, as Lupino herself knew well. Millie's ambition is portrayed in the context of failed gender roles, desperation born of painful desire, and a powerful sense of loss. Millie's forlornness, as is clear in Lupino's mise-en-scène, works to align us with the character.

Home Noir

Lupino addresses specific social problems in her films, but she reaches beyond message pictures. Of especial interest is her nuanced critique of modernity and of the ways that women are left out of its promises for success, advancement, and happiness. The locus of that critique is the home, where women, for Lupino, are trapped within a psychic space that has become malevolent in postwar America. Studies in film noir have acknowledged the "female stories" that disrupt the supposedly "male sphere" of the genre or series. One strain of this submerged feminist energy in film noir can be seen in connection with Lupino's yearning yet bewildered young women. In film noir more generally, some women characters are sidelined by the male protagonist and the dynamic figure conventionally referred to as the femme fatale. While the latter often has a story of her own that complicates her presence as the fatal woman, other women who are distinctly related to Lupino's female characters haunt the margins of film noir. Here, we discuss those "minor" women left behind in classic film noir, such as Ann Miller in *Out of the Past*, Lola Dietrichson in *Double Indemnity*, Diane Redfern in *Laura*, and Emma Newton in *Shadow of a Doubt* (Alfred Hitchcock, 1943). All of these women live with the legacy of Victorianism and are lost in a desolate modern world. Lupino's merging of film noir and the social problem film can be seen as drawing attention to these quieter figures of despair. Cast in the shadows by the more active and dynamic dangerous women who seduce the male protagonist, these women who stand on the sidelines are brought onto center stage by Lupino in her female noir films.

Though marginalized in criticism on *Out of the Past*, Ann Miller nevertheless plays an important role in the film. A blond inversion of the dark fatal woman Kathie Moffat, Ann represents the yearning Kathie acts out. In figures 16, 17, and 18, we see a visual representation of Ann's traumatized presence in Bridgeport. Ann longs to escape the town in which everyone knows everyone else's business, as town maven Marnie reminds Jim in her café at the beginning of the film— "Nothing can happen in this town that I don't hear about it across this counter."

Meanwhile, Ann sits by the lake with Jeff Bailey, looking to the clouds, an objective correlative of her desire to move and be free of Bridgeport. Envious, she asks Jeff about his travels: "You've been a lot of places, haven't you?" "One too many," he responds, his urban past leaving him cynical about that world beyond Bridgeport.

But the two share a moment of hope focused on the house Jeff proposes to build, there on the lake, "by the cove." This idyllic house is imagined as an escape not just for Jeff, a refuge from his guilty past, but for Ann, as well, a haven away from the re-

FIGURE 16 By the lake in *Out of the Past*

pressive Victorian home the film subsequently alludes to (see figure 17). Here, later in the film, Ann stands outside the kitchen, in the liminal space of the hallway. She watches her parents, who seem utterly unrelated to her; rather, they look more like two Victorian servants gossiping together downstairs. She listens to her parents' self-righteous vindication of their disapproval of Jeff, as they read in the newspaper that Jeff is accused of a double murder. The news item confirms for them that he is, indeed, "no good." Mrs. Miller's summary judgment of Jeff Bailey also echoes a postwar political climate sullied with Cold War hysteria about outsiders. One might recall that the Waldorf Statement announcing the MPAA's intent to expel communist threats from Hollywood was made in 1947, the year *Out of the Past* was released. In this scene in the film, Mrs. Miller sanctimoniously adds, "I said all along there's a man who should be run out of town."

Suffocated by her parents' small-mindedness and quickness to judge, Ann literally runs from the house. She temporarily escapes to the outdoors, where she is further subjugated by the patriarchal Jim, who has "loved her ever since I fixed her roller skates." Jim lambastes Jeff further and insists that Ann belongs with him. Ann resists her friends' and family's warnings and advice until she has nowhere to turn except back to the blinding convention from which she sought to escape. In the second shot below, Ann turns away from the deaf boy, The Kid, who has just told her that Jeff was running away with Kathie Moffat. While The Kid wants to free Ann from her desire for Jeff, Ann appears devastated. As she walks toward the car, whose label "State of California" announces Ann's retreat into a life governed by institutions, a chapel is seen in the background, the place where she will presumably marry the hometown boy Jim and spend the rest of her life entombed in Bridgeport.

In her films, Lupino focuses on this strain of female trauma borne of being trapped in the confined domestic spaces of family. Other women in noir echo Ann's failed efforts to escape conformity. Lola Dietrichson in *Double Indemnity* also yearns to escape a hothouse domestic environment defined by hostile authority figures. She, like Ann Miller, is drawn to a seemingly dangerous man, Nino Zachetti. In *Laura*, viewers might wonder about the untold story of Diane Redfern, mistakenly killed by Lydecker in place of Laura. In Vera Caspary's source novel, Detective Mark McPherson describes the tragedy of Redfern's short life. Her real name was Jennie Swobodo. She worked as a model in advertising, spending her days in "expensive settings" and "[dreaming] of Hollywood." "At night," McPherson speculates as he visits her apartment, "she came home to this cell" (136). Despite the counterexample of Laura as a successful working woman in advertising, Jennie/Diane is lost, part of the waste of modern capitalism, scaling the steps of her dilapidated apartment, her "suicide staircase" (135). If this is urban life for modern women, years earlier Hitchcock had predicted in *Shadow of a Doubt* (1943) a similarly darkened interior landscape in small-town America. Like Ann Miller, by the end of Hitchcock's film young Charlie (Teresa Wright) will marry a man of law, Jack Graham, but her frantic and unsatisfied mother, Emma Newton, will remain in Santa Rosa. Emma is unaware that her beloved brother, Uncle Charlie, is a sociopathic murderer. She is bereft when he leaves. "I can't bear it if you go," she says, since her life will return to what young Charlie described at the beginning of the film: "Poor mother. She works like a dog. Just like a dog. . . . Dinner then dishes, then bed. I don't see how she stands it."

Another in a list of unfulfilled women in *Shadow of a Doubt*, Louise Finch was Charlie's school peer, but now she is a down-and-out barmaid whose voice and demeanor reflect her despair. One of the gloomiest portraits of the fate of women in modern America in wartime and postwar film, Louise Finch has worked "in half the restaurants in town" and unknowingly predicts a dark fate for her own future when she moons over the spoils of Uncle Charlie's murder, the ill-gotten ring: "Ain't it beautiful. I'd just die for a ring like that. Yes sir, for a ring like that, I'd just about die."

In contrast to the depictions of postwar gender roles described above, Lupino places centerstage those women who typically exist only in the margins of film noir. Her stories explore what happens when, as Uncle Charlie says, "you rip the fronts off houses." Like Hitchcock and other noir filmmakers, Lupino reveals the darkened space within the postwar American house, particularly as it expresses the damaged psychic state of the women who inhabit it.

FIGURE 17 *Out of the Past*: Stifling kitchen

FIGURE 18 *Out of the Past*: Street with chapel

FIGURE 19 Desolate woman Emma Newton in *Shadow of a Doubt*

FIGURE 20 Louise Finch, another desolate woman in *Shadow of a Doubt*

Home Is Where the Noir Is

In all of her early films, Lupino investigates the double-bind of individuals who escape their antagonistic homes, often driven by American myths of the new freedom of the road, only to be forced back into the "real world" of home—or suffer the realities of the road. We propose that Lupino's "home noir" provides not only a means of understanding her synthesis of film noir and domestic melodrama, but a critical lens that illuminates the home as an inimical site and site of rebellion. The architecture, design, and decor of the postwar home and household social arrangements become active forces in Lupino's home noir; objects, light and shadow, and architectural forms and frames in domestic space, as extensions of character and conflict, destabilize conventional associations and connect with sociocultural forms beyond their mere presence as backdrop, representation, metaphor, or symbol. Unlike classical Hollywood's mise-en-scène, the considerable forces of home noir are often activated by states that disrupt the home and household.[11] Significantly, in Lupino's early films and television episodes, these are traumatic states, keyed to the social rules and structures against which objects rebel and for which they are touchstones. Moving beyond the opposition of domestic melodrama and film noir, with their inevitable gendering of place and genre, Lupino's home noir opens up a way of conceptualizing her "ungendering" of genre and gives us deeper critical access to her iconoclastic vision of gender roles and the institutions that bind men and women to them.

Home noir tells us about both women's and men's relationships to postwar modernity. It is a way of viewing the home spheres in these films as indices, expressions, and revisions of wider sociocultural transformations and meanings. From the perspective of its relationship with discourses and practices outside film, home noir becomes a larger field than that of film's formal structures, particularly its mise-en-scène. The modern American home in film—in this instance that in the immediate postwar era—exists in a reciprocal relationship with the modern home in American life. Developments in architecture, interior design, interior decoration, and the spread of household commodities were popularized in Hollywood movies and in magazines and advertising. They were also influenced by the movies. As we have stated, home, with reference to films of the late 1940s and early 1950s, is usually thought of as a woman's extension of herself, her domain, her power, and her ability to act on the world of gendered space; however, it is often through the home that the seamy, dysfunctional underside of the American Dream is exposed, its noir side. The home sphere is heavily inflected by the burgeoning technological and commodity culture belonging to late capitalism, as well as being laden with patriarchal values and myths. In fact, our commonly held idea that the domestic sphere is exclusively "feminine" (private, etc.) is a relatively new one. Kathleen Anne McHugh's study of two centuries of discourses on the home in the United States, *American Domesticity: From How-to Manual to Hollywood Melodrama*, demonstrates that domestic discourse established the terms within which the most crucial national issues, such as the market economy, consumerism, spectatorship, and desire, were conceived, assimilated, and understood. Thus, the domestic is hardly the antithesis of the public sphere. The image we have of it became so in the nineteenth century with the various discourses that sentimentalized women and domestic space.

Domestic architecture, interior design (its spaces and the movements it facilitates or prevents), and decorative and utilitarian objects exist in part as indicators of the relationships of gender and the modern.[12] After World War II, with the ideology of the American Dream more firmly in place than during the Depression and the war, the domestic arena assumes certain relationships to late capitalism and an economy of assembly-line production: the stepped-up production of modern mass-produced consumer and household items such as furniture, appliances, and knick-knacks; cars for the expanding highway system; and homes themselves. We see examples of the burgeoning economy in Lupino's films: in *Outrage*, lumberyards and trucking companies in Capitol City, as well as the fruit-packing plant in Southern California, form not only the settings where Ann works, but are also showcased as meaningful parts of the landscape of California, with its vast citrus groves, and that of the Midwestern Capitol City, with the housing construction industry booming. In *The Bigamist*, Harry and Eve sell home freezers, a new domestic commodity. Reinforced by what was then held to be ubiquitous advertising (on radio and television, often incorporated into the content of programs, and in magazines for both men and women that extended their feature stories through advertisements), the home and what pertains to it are of central importance generally in postwar Hollywood cinema.

The modern home, as opposed to the Victorian one, shares in the American Dream in part through its industrialized construction. The shift in concepts of home architecture began in the 1890s.[13] It involved envisioning a home that opened out immediately into nature, opposing the private, walled garden of the Victorian home and promoting new doctrines of health. Plans for the modern house did away with the parlor and the library, replacing them with the living room and built-in bookshelves on which knick-knacks could also be displayed. The modern home rejected the ornate ornamentation of the Victorian house. It envisioned a plain, streamlined home without servants, whose design made the housewife's tasks easier by drawing the kitchen and dining room closer together. Beginning in the Progressive Era, affordable commodities such as the vacuum cleaner and washing machine became available to support this vision. For those with more modest incomes, bungalows were built, beginning in the 1910s, and kit houses became available from Sears beginning in 1908. A Sears kit house arrived with plans and a seventy-five-page instruction booklet for do-it-yourselfers. Kit houses spread from the East Coast to the West Coast, designed by a number of different companies.

In the noir of home noir, falling along a continuum with the gothic and horror film, the home and its objects rapidly become forces that unsettle the home's safety and familiarity, threatening danger, imprisonment, and chaos. Sometimes, they act of their own accord. A film that lends itself as an excellent example of a classic interpretation of mise-en-scène, on one hand, and a home-noir approach to homes and their objects, on the other, is Max Ophuls's *The Reckless Moment* (1949), which deals with housewife and mother Lucia Harper's struggles to maintain her household and family in the direct postwar period while her husband is absent, at work in the U.S. efforts to rebuild Europe. To take but one example, that of the anchor attached to the boathouse, an interpretation based on mise-en-scène might view this inert object symbolically, even ironically, when Beatrice's erstwhile lover and present blackmailer Ted Darby falls on it and is killed. In our reading through the lens of home noir, the anchor is an active force: as a noir object activated by Lucia's uncommon trials, it "defends" Lucia by stabbing and killing Darby, only thereby to usher in the multiple dangers from the outside world that beset and attack her. It is at once murder weapon and murderer.

Similarly, while we have discussed Florence practicing her backhand as Fletcher Locke sits in an armchair and criticizes her in *Hard, Fast and Beautiful*, the Florence emerging from the shadows—disavowed in the "real" world of student-teacher decorum—wields her shadow-racket as a weapon aimed at Locke. In true noir fashion, the shadow-Florence reveals an unconscious intention, cast by a homely object, that later becomes meaningful in the narrative.

In Lupino's early films, home and its objects are transformed into noir spaces and things especially through traumatic experience, in which an image of the world as a safe, known place changes in an instant. Notably, these traumas are exerted on individuals from the outside: from the gendered contours of the American Dream; the dislocations of gender roles and relations; and life-altering events befalling women. When these traumas occur, the protagonists of Lupino's films immediately metamorphose into outsiders, whose view of the society around them, most particularly seen in their over-normalized home lives and households, becomes radically transformed. By "over-normalized," we mean that the façades covering the dysfunctional, retrograde, and nightmarish truths of the social arrangements pervading the home sphere are at first lived as customary. Characters function quite well in them. Trauma rips away these façades through its activation of familiar objects and spaces that suddenly become menacing. In order to show how the noir aspects of home function in Lupino's postwar films, we revisit *Hard, Fast and Beautiful* and *The Bigamist*, and make another foray into *Outrage*, which we discussed in Part One in terms of the influence of Fritz Lang's *M* and themes of guilt and innocence, victim, rescuer, and perpetrator. To do so reveals the less obvious elements of Lupino's artistry, which have not yet been written about by film critics, in which subterranean forces of rebellion exceeding conscious individual striving and struggle overwhelm individuals as they attempt to cope with a society and its laws now pitted against them.

Doubled Dreams in *Hard, Fast and Beautiful*

As we suggested above, Lupino's *Hard, Fast and Beautiful* portrays the impossibility of female ambition in modern American capitalist culture, set in the context of the values of capitalism more generally as part of the

American Dream. Both mother and daughter long to participate directly in the American Dream. But, while men's ambitions are expected, Millie's and Florence's are transgressive.

James Truslow Adams popularized the term the "American Dream" in his 1931 book, *The Epic of America*, defining it as follows:

> The American dream that has lured tens of millions of all nations to our shores in the past century has not been a dream of merely material plenty, though that has doubtlessly counted heavily. It has been much more than that. It has been a dream of being able to grow to fullest development as man and woman, unhampered by the barriers which had slowly been erected in the older civilizations, unrepressed by social orders which had developed for the benefit of classes rather than for the simple human being of any and every class. (404)

The ethos of the American Dream in the postwar period belongs to a society of material abundance, and intimately involves the notion that determined individuals who persevere can achieve material success and upward mobility. Ironically, these notions of individual striving and success were given a jumpstart by Franklin D. Roosevelt's National Housing Act of 1934 and the 1944 G.I. Bill, which guaranteed home ownership and access to higher education to returning servicemen, who were arriving in the United States in huge numbers after the war. Despite Adams's clause about "material plenty" counting "heavily" but diminished in importance by the "fullest development as man and woman," in the postwar era a culture of material production and consumption equated with individual development arose as never before. Moreover, actual class, race, and gender experiences in the United States played no part in the formulation of the American Dream. These experiences of inequality were in large measure due to the barriers erected in history and by capitalism itself. From the viewpoint of gaining material plenty—in order, presumably, to develop spiritual potential—in a society that at the same time promotes gender arrangements in which women do not have equal access to capital, equality is impossible to achieve.

For our discussion of home noir in *Hard, Fast and Beautiful*, it is useful to bear in mind that excelling in sports represents the fulfillment of

FIGURE 21 The Farleys' garage, in *Hard, Fast and Beautiful*

the American Dream. Specifically, competitive sports highlight the elements of determination, perseverance, and winning by dint of one's superior skill. Florence—although Will reminds her to remember always that tennis is "just a game"—is from the very first scene determined to perfect her skill and win competitively.

The Farleys' driveway and garage become an important site of female defiance, where Florence's agency is paradoxically expressed both within and outside of the terms established by the Farley home. Florence is an energetic tennis player pushing herself to improve her skills in the backyard of her parents' house. But her limited prospects can be seen in the fact that she plays tennis with herself within the confines of the garage driveway. The exterior of the house unsettles conventional domestic arrangements as Florence invents a makeshift workplace in which to practice. She has painted large numbers in side-by-side squares on the garage door, and calls out the numbers as she hits the proper box with her forehand, symbolizing the ambitious drive toward eventual competing. Boxed within middle-class Chatsworth (see our discussion below), Florence rebels against her "place" by occupying the side of the house, which means the garage door must stay closed, and the driveway, which typically would provide entrance to and exit from the home for "the man of the house," is blocked by Florence's raid on the space. Even in the opening scene, we see that Will is stymied in the familial competition for access to the American Dream.

However, Florence has, unwittingly, also drawn an image of her inevitable failure as a woman with an ambitious dream. The boxes, as elements of home noir, intervene in the smooth functioning of her pursuit of that dream: no matter how good she is at the control and direction of her swing, she is doomed to fail, either one way (by becoming a success, thereby exploited by the capitalist machinery at work in competitive sports), or another (by fleeing to marriage with Gordon, which she doesn't want). She is boxed in. As Lupino reiterates in her early films, in the postwar period, these are the twin options available to women, for whom avenues for expression and empowerment are limited. That evening, Florence tells her parents, "I must have hit holes into the garage door." Her boxes, then, serve two functions in their noir aspect: to rebel against and destroy a family order that reins her in; and to box her into inevitable failure in pursuing her dream.

Along the borders of the driveway is a picket fence, another way Lupino establishes the frames of Florence's experience; here, through the openings in the fence (see figure 22), she looks at Gordon, her love interest and liaison to the tennis club. Interestingly, while most viewers focus on the obsessive ambitions of Millie as the exploitative Queen Bee Mom, the plucky Florence thinks when she's invited to play with Gordon at the club, "Maybe I can beat him." The fence pickets imprison Florence in a dream bound to fail, and punctuate her separation from Gordon—their spikes like knives, moreover pointing at her own face—whom she now views as a competitor. Later, when she has become a tennis star and Gordon is left behind, the contest between the two culminates in Gordon's

FIGURE 22 The Farleys' fence, in *Hard, Fast and Beautiful*

rejection of a plan that he travel with Florence to Europe to write press articles about her athletic success. Tantamount to Gordon being "aced" by Florence, this proposal upsets him. Resentful of being asked to promote Florence on the tour, Gordon doesn't want to be a "ghost-writer" ("Do I look like a ghost?" he asks). Gordon fears and is angered by the prospect of becoming a feminized helpmate behind the scenes. No longer about tennis but about gendered social roles, the competition is won by Gordon in the end when Florence abandons sports and submits to conventional marriage.

Twinned with Florence's desire to participate in the American Dream is Millie's. For Millie, participation means upward mobility, an idea that pervades the beginning of the film with the Farleys' initial discussion about their home. In the second scene, Millie sits at the open bedroom window and paints her nails while Will makes tentative sexual advances toward her, kissing her neck and touching her hair. But immediately, we note the contentiousness between them:

MILLIE: Will, couldn't we look for another house? Maybe something on the Palisades. . . . You don't care if we rot in a place like this!

WILL: What's wrong with a place like this? I remember when you thought Raymond Street was the top of the world.

MILLIE: I was seventeen then! And, oh, I had to push you for everything we've got!

This discussion sets the Farley home in Chatsworth, a neighborhood of Los Angeles in the Northwest San Fernando Valley not far from the movie studios. Of course, we might think Lupino chose this location because she had to work with low budgets. However, there are even more compelling reasons for her to choose Chatsworth: it had belonged to the City of Los Angeles as a neighborhood for quite a long time by 1951 (since 1915), making it clear that the film is not a suburban tale. Only in the 1960s did Chatsworth contain the subdivisions we associate with early suburbia, when an industrial tract was under construction. The neighborhood was the site of famous directors' and stars' homes, such as Josef von Sternberg's avant-garde modernist house, designed by Richard Neutra; Lucille Ball and Desi Arnaz's home, called "Desilu"; Roy Rogers and Dale Evans's home, as well as that of Errol Flynn. This location lends the "star-struck" Millie's dream credence and weight. Chatsworth was an affluent community nevertheless divided into middle-class and very rich inhabitants, in which the Farley home, inside and out, is an example of modernist middle-class domestic space. Millie and Florence's plans are therefore consonant with the postwar American Dream in a society of abundance. Yet, as women, they will inevitably fail to realize their dreams.

The Farleys' division of labor mirrors that of many middle-class white Americans in this period: Will is the breadwinner and Millie the unpaid housewife. At the outset of *Hard, Fast and Beautiful*, Millie has already decided to pursue her dream "on her own," in spite of the fact that she has no job, no career to provide her with the capital she needs. In Millie's dream of upward mobility, she has lighted on Florence, whose competitive spirit, grit, and determination seem most likely to make her dream a reality. As has been shown, Florence is far from averse to the idea of competing and winning at sports. To be sure, the mother in maternal melodramas lives out her disappointed or unfulfilled dreams for herself through her daughter in one way or another. Millie seems to be one of these mothers. However, she is not a static character. Recognizing that she and Florence share a desire to "win," though the meaning of winning is slightly different for each, Millie begins as a mother "proud" of her daughter's successes, and progresses to partake in those successes by sharing Florence's limelight. Finally, she is corrupted by the demands of capitalist exploitation, beguiled by Fletcher Locke. From that time forward, Millie will be Florence's manager and promoter, using Florence's success as a proxy for her own success. Her dream of a new home is a surrogate for her share of the self-development promised by the American Dream.

Between 1931 and 1956, the Production Code of the Motion Picture Industry did not stipulate that married couples sleep in separate beds, contrary to widely held belief. Under "Particular Applications," Article IX, "Locations," states, "The treatment of bedrooms must be governed by good taste and delicacy." Why, then, did Lupino choose to arrange Millie's and Will's beds in the odd and much remarked-upon way she does in *Hard, Fast and Beautiful*? (see figure 23).[14] The audacity of her choice is at once obvious and not so obvious. Looking at the whole of her work from this period, it is quite clear that Lupino is interested in rendering visually what separates people from each other (and from themselves) in more than a symbolic way. Dividing lines constitute a diagram of relations that belong to larger social relations. Here, Millie and Will are not only separated from each other, or divided as husband and wife, but are opposed to each other; in fact, they compete in a domestic arena in which world views and dreams clash diametrically. The outrageous positioning of the headboards is the most graphic signal of this more-than-dysfunctional couple's most intimate life together, in which the bedroom is a battleground where Millie and Will go head to head. In the bedroom scene, sex is an active subtext. Millie waggles her freshly painted nails in Will's nearby face. It is hard to imagine that Will would hope to have sexual relations with a woman whose headboard faces his, and yet his hope persists. Unlike the war of the sexes belonging to screwball comedy, in the Farleys' war, neither side balances the other, neither side will compromise, and neither side grows to appreciate the other. If we as viewers find Millie's desire for upward mobility repugnant, Will's values seem to reinforce our view. In fact, for every shot of Millie scheming, there is a shot to follow of Will—or Will is included in the shot as an onlooker—listening to, watching, and judging Millie (see figure 12, where Will, frowning, is positioned in the background between Millie and Fletcher Locke in the foreground). The shots and edits suggest that Will's is the definitive view, aligned with Lupino's. But is Will a reliable spectator/auditor? He never takes action against Millie until he is safely on his deathbed. Ultimately Will, though a sympathetic character, is one of Lupino's cowardly, passive husbands, who even believes himself to be a failure, bound, as he says, to "disappoint" his family. It is therefore difficult to take his perspective as narratively reliable. We would suggest, instead, that the shots and edits joining Millie's schemes and Will's passive evaluations of her function in much the same way as do the headboards: to oppose wife and husband in a contest. Moreover, the more active Millie becomes, the more Will slumps into inactivity and inertia. Will already slumps in disappointment and consternation on his side of the headboard. Moreover, Millie takes over the family room by placing her office there. The American home is the battleground, and in the "war of the wills," Millie wins—to be halted by the gender inequality that trips up women in their pursuit of the American Dream.

In *Hard, Fast and Beautiful,* Lupino reveals the many exploitative facets of promotion involved in competitive sports for women, such as the

FIGURE 23 The Farleys' notable bed arrangement, in *Hard, Fast and Beautiful*

instrumentalization, commodification, and exploitation of the bodies of others. Millie's gravest mistake is to treat the body of her daughter in these ways, thereby herself becoming the chief agent of the destruction of her family, a piece of the architecture of modernist home noir itself, since the one thing that sets Millie apart from Fletcher Locke is that she is Florence's mother. She embodies a noir vision of the family order, in which the last safe place for Florence becomes her parents' home. This fact alone propels Florence into marriage with Gordon. *Hard, Fast and Beautiful* shows us once again Lupino's trenchant critique of the options for women in postwar America, which shuttle between work and marriage, neither one a fulfilling choice, and, more important, neither one a true choice, since powers beyond women's control determine their decisions and their fates.

Doubled Domesticity in *The Bigamist*

We have mentioned that Lupino's early films focus on her protagonists' trials rather than on outcomes. Unlike many noir films, Lupino's films

insist on the potential or opportunities for change, which her protagonists miss. In this respect, Lupino's films can be drawn into the purview
of women's melodrama, in which a key trope is that individuals miss
opportunities, usually for love. In Lupino's early films, however, everyone misses these opportunities, establishing the individual as part of a
conformist collective.

As part of her commitment to making social problem films, Lupino's
aim is to call for social change. As stated above, hearings in which detectives, pastors, and doctors, among others, debate (in dialogue often
dismissed as corny and implausible, or derided as masculinist and au-
thoritarian), represent an ideal state set against reality. Thus, the hearings do not operate as they would in the real world, and what various
judges say is not what they would say in an actual courtroom. The scenes
are high artifice, artifacts of melodrama, motivated by Lupino's artistic
goal to encourage social change. In *The Bigamist*, one of her strongest
films in this regard, the potential for change becomes palpable, although
the ending of the film leaves matters unresolved. Harry may be given a
second chance to become a man in his own right.

Harry is only traumatized by Eve's business acumen because he is
boxed into a rigid definition of manhood, whereas Eve's talents call
for a more fluid definition of gender roles than Harry is prepared to
accept. Lupino implies that just as women should be lauded for their
ambitions, they should also be praised for their talents. Yet in social
arrangements—a legacy of the Victorian era rather than the fulfillment
of the promise of wartime modernity—that preclude fluid gender roles,
her success is bound to initiate crisis. Harry's conformism leads him to
repeat his perceived marriage scenario of emasculation with Phyllis in
less ambiguous terms. Harry falsely believes that Phyllis's working-class
status will allow him to have a more traditional marriage. He bumbles
into fatherhood with Phyllis, who for her part had no intention to become a wife and mother.

The Bigamist, more than any of Lupino's other early films, offers us
a comprehensive visual sense of "California modern," through its shots
on location and through its visual irony about Los Angeles as the "City
of the Future." If so, it is an already failed city in its promise of postwar
largesse and gender equality. Indeed, the setting for the hope of gender equality lies outside Los Angeles, in San Francisco. In *The Bigamist*,

FIGURE 24 *The Bigamist*: Top, exterior of Harry and Eve's building; bottom, interior of their apartment

FIGURE 25 *The Bigamist*: Phyllis and Harry's bungalow

Lupino specifies through architectural space the two worlds Harry inhabits. Two very different American modernist styles of architecture appear in the film, both from the same era, 1925 through the early 1940s. The first is the high-modernist building in San Francisco where Harry and Eve live, its décor that of California modern inflected by chinoiserie; the second is a Los Angeles bungalow where bigamist Harry lives with Phyllis. These styles can be seen as class indicators, certainly: Harry and Eve's apartment is downtown, swank and expensive, whereas the bungalow Harry shares with Phyllis embodies the guarantee of modestly priced homes for the working class to enable their participation in the American Dream.

In keeping with the key noir theme of the inability to escape the past, Harry is compelled to repeat his unhappy marriage to Eve. By marrying Phyllis, he believes, at last he can ascend to the status of breadwinner, enjoying the ease and leisure of home accorded to a married man and father—depended on by wife and child. But money is tight because of his two households, and it becomes increasingly difficult for him to make excuses that he is spending long periods of time away from home on business. More important, the repair Harry has hoped for in marriage and parenthood with Phyllis is immediately dashed: no sooner does he return home in the evenings from work than he has to take over household and parenting duties while Phyllis goes to work the dinner and night shifts at the Chinese restaurant.

FIGURE 26 *The Bigamist*: interior of the Chinese restaurant

As elements of home noir, Eve's and Phyllis's spaces are mutually permeable: the decor of the Chinese restaurant where Phyllis works has infiltrated Eve and Harry's home through chinoiserie already in the opening minutes of the film. Viewed from the perspective of Harry's voiceover narration, which begins when Mr. Jordan finds him minding the baby at his and Phyllis's bungalow, the chinoiserie highlights the tainted space of Eve and Harry's living room.

Likewise from this perspective, the rooming house where Phyllis lived before moving in with Harry, through its staircase and elongated noir shadows, can be pinpointed as the portal into Harry's crime, the passage to his private hell as he "ascends" to his fate. The bungalow, with its division of space designed for

FIGURE 27 Phyllis's rooming house (top) and Harry's private portal to hell (bottom) in *The Bigamist*

FIGURE 28 *The Bigamist*: Above and below, Harry harassed with work and minding the baby when Mr. Jordan visits

housewives *sans* servants—compact and accessible—becomes a clutter of toys and essential baby things that deluge Harry with the knowledge that he has only gotten himself deeper into the quagmire of his failure to free himself. Harry resembles nothing so much as an exhausted mother and wife when he answers the door to Mr. Jordan one night after work as the baby cries and Phyllis sleeps.

Like so many characters who attempt to extricate themselves from extortion, blackmail, and a criminal past in film noir, Harry falls victim to (internalized) gender conventions, and his quest fails. He cannot stand up to the challenge posed by gender equality, as embodied in the modern building in which he lives with Eve. This is the very vision of modernity that Lupino endorses, and which none of her characters even ambiguously achieves. But here, at the end of the film, Eve, the "first woman," lingers in the courtroom after Phyllis decisively walks out. The potential for Harry to return to Eve and live a more equitable life with her is present. Harry may be given another chance. And this is where Lupino ends the film.

Doubled Trauma: *Outrage*

In some films of the direct postwar period, home noir involves the refusal to confront, engage with, or enter into the changed world belonging to the wartime promise of a new modernity. This is demonstrated first by the house itself, which clings to retrograde styles. It involves men and women who refuse to work and build careers as much as it does men and women who refuse to marry. In *The Strange Affair of Uncle Harry* (Robert Siodmak, 1946), for example, while even the infantile Harry can be coaxed from his Victorian family house by a career woman who wants to marry him, his sister Letty is unwilling to leave home. When encouraged to work or marry, she refuses both. To demonstrate her predicament—of being stuck in the past of her childhood and unwilling to confront a world that is passing her by—shadows cast on the walls of her bedroom appear, from the first shot of her in bed with one of her "sick headaches," as prison bars. In *Sorry, Wrong Number* (Anatole Litvak, 1948), Leona's father, James Cottrell, inhabits the only Victorian space in the film, a large library packed with hunting and other trophies. He wants Leona to divorce her husband, Henry. When Henry has a chance to interview for a position, Cottrell sabotages the interview. There is more than a hint of Cottrell's incestuous desire for, as well as his ownership of, his daughter in the film: among his many trophies is a portrait of his daughter, sitting prominently on the mantelpiece. Moreover, Leona suffers from "heart attacks," psychosomatic symptoms of her felt knowledge that her father boxes her in and desires her sexually, as well as her inability to separate from him. These symptoms are similar to Letty's contrived illnesses, which stay her confrontation with her desire for Harry. In both films, the Victorian signals not just the inability to confront the modern, but a degenerate sickness at the heart of the old order. In contradistinction, in *Mildred Pierce* (Michael Curtiz, 1946), the beach house (which belonged to Anatole Litvak) is the site of noir's elongated shadows, housing Monte and Veda's affair—and murder. Its architecture and interior space are too modern, too sleek, and too refined. A Victorian space may signal a recalcitrant patriarchy and a refusal to enter into the promise for postwar modernity, but an ultra-modern space can be a façade concealing a heart of corruption.

As we suggested earlier, *Out of the Past* also illustrates the use of home noir in its subplot about Ann Miller, giving force to her desire to marry Jeff, which otherwise would be naïve: "Everything you say, I believe," she tells him as he begins to recount the story of his tainted past. She knows that in order to escape her small-minded parents and their home—figured in stagnant, Victorian images of darkness, long hallways, crowded walls, an obsolete kitchen—as well as Jimmy, the hometown boy who loves her, she has only one choice, to marry the intriguing outsider Jeff, in whom she places all her hope. In Tourneur's film, women only have one path available to them, to align themselves with men who will improve their lot in life. This is as true for Kathie Moffat as it is for Ann. One can say of Kathie that at least her goal is to become independent, while Ann sees marriage as her final goal.

Outrage, too, explores the tension between the modernity of the postwar period and the legacy of Victorianism. While war trauma for men had been recognized at least since World War I and was accorded medical treatment, albeit inadequate and often damaging to soldiers returning home from war, the traumas suffered by women on domestic ground, such as rape, largely went unrecognized, and worse, became stigmas for women to bear hidden away and in silence. Co-written by Lupino, Wald, and Young, *Outrage* was the second Hollywood film after 1933 to deal with the issue of rape. *Johnny Belinda* (Jean Negulesco, 1948) was the other. Harry Horner, who had recently won an Academy Award for his art direction of William Wyler's 1949 film *The Heiress* (which can also be thought of in terms of home noir), is credited as the production designer for *Outrage*. Unfortunately, there is little original information available about Horner's role in the production of the film, but we suspect that his influence was great.

"Home" extends from protagonist Ann Walton's claustrophobic home, workplace, and hometown of Capitol City to America's agoraphobic highway system and interstate bus routes, Southern California and its healing landscape amid citrus groves, and all of the United States as domestic ground. Therefore, in *Outrage*, in the context of the uneasy relationship of gender to postwar American modernity, "home" requires an expansive definition.

In nearly all of Lupino's early films, home is a prison. It cannot accommodate unwanted pregnancy, illness, unhappiness in marriage, a failed marriage, the aftermath of rape, or female ambition. Leaving home is, therefore, a motif across these films. If the act of leaving home, however, results in disaster, the home itself provides the impetus for flight. In *Outrage*, in particular, the home reveals its inner workings after Ann is raped. Ann's parents (played by Lillian Hamilton and Raymond Bond) exhibit, like the townspeople, an incapacity to consider how Ann must feel. Ann overhears her father tell her mother that his students

FIGURE 29 The *Leave It to Beaver* house, seen after Ann is raped, in *Outrage*

now scrutinize him and gossip about Ann at the school where he teaches, which he considers, narcissistically, as damaging to his image. In addition to feeling guilty of her rape, Ann is made to feel guilty for causing suffering to her parents. She also feels imprisoned at home.

The Waltons' wooden clapboard house is in the style of the popular Colonial Revival, standing out from the others in the neighborhood, which are brick. Essentially it is designed as two-and-a-half stories of rectangular boxes built on top of each other. It is composed of four large, boxy rooms on each floor, with bedrooms upstairs, and a large front porch with wide stairs. The first floor contains a living room and dining room on one side that open onto each other through an archway.

The Colonial Revival was initially presented at the 1876 U.S. Centennial Exposition, a modern yet traditional alternative to the fussy Victorian Queen Anne style, reflecting American patriotism and a desire for simplicity (Wlodarczyk). Between World Wars I and II, Colonial Revival was the most popular historic revival house style in the United States. In the media, it represented the wholesome, patriotic American "nuclear" family, a term first used in this context in the 1950s (Coontz 26).

The Waltons' house stands out from its neighbors not only because of its wooden siding, but because of its stretched horizontal plane and a cage-like trellis, which covers half of the front porch, leaving the entranceway open, and surrounds the windows on the first floor. With the yard enclosed by a white picket fence complementing the lattice-work of the trellis, the Waltons' house reminds viewers of a prison, especially through the eye of the camera after Ann's rape when she returns to the house. Judging from Harry Horner's production design for other films, we surmise that the trellis and the dramatically ironic white picket fence are his contributions to the production design of the exterior of the house, borrowed from the idea of the elaborate cage-like staircase in *The Heiress.*

The trellis and fence have the look of contraptions from which the house itself can't escape, signaling that the seemingly wholesome nuclear family house is a trap. This image contrasts sharply with that of the Paramount house at Universal studios, the second and most famous of the Cleavers' houses in *Leave It to Beaver* and the other Colonial Revival styles in 1950s and 1960s TV family comedies, where the period is shown as a successful, distinctively American, effort to fulfill family members' desires and needs through personal life.

The Colonial Revival style marked the end of the Victorian period in architecture, based loosely on Federal and Georgian house styles, and was a clear reaction against excessively elaborate Victorian Queen Anne architecture. But, while the Waltons' house reflects this reaction in style, as well as the modern turn to the industrialization of house-building, the interior of the home is a throwback to the Victorian era, stuffed with ornate furniture, doilies, oval paintings in gilded frames, and family mementos. It compromises its modernity through its Victorian interior, the lived spaces of the home.

Details beyond those of interior decoration support the idea that wartime modernity has passed the Waltons by. Ann's father, Eric Walton, remains a patriarch, though seemingly benign. The entire after-dinner scene, when Jim asks Mr. Walton for Ann's hand in marriage—a legacy of the nineteenth century when daughters were passed from fathers to successful suitors—is framed by the Victorian setting. In this

family world, Ann's only possible rebellion against the "over-
normalized" Victorian order is to
ignore her father's desire for her
to become a math teacher (like
him), take a bookkeeping job instead, and then marry Jim.

The division of space in the
Waltons' home tells us that the
family is separated by gendered
activity. Jim and Eric sit together
on the couch near the book-
case. The women sit apart, Ann's
mother on her rocking chair and
Ann on the floor helping her
mother wind yarn for knitting
and crocheting. In other words,
the division of after-dinner space
in this modern house is the same
as that after dinner in a Victorian
household, when men retire to the
library to smoke and discuss matters of importance, and women

FIGURE 30 *Outrage*: Top, the interior of the
Waltons' Victorian home; bottom, the gendered
space of the living room

move to the sitting room to engage in domestic activities and to chat.
Ultimately, the contrast between the house and the family life within it
sets the stage for the rest of the narrative, in which, while appearing gentle, understanding, and benign, men at best speak for Ann and decide
her fate, and, at worst, physically assault her. While rape and attempted
rape are overtly violent acts toward women, which leave emotional
and physical wounds, the kindness and false benignity of men expose
the overarching patriarchal structure of the society shown in *Outrage*,
leaving women no place at all within it to speak or act for themselves.
Ann's is the story of a woman without ambition—unlike the women in
Hard, Fast and Beautiful—who has been spoken for, in all senses, her
whole life by men, beginning with her father. In the web woven around
her by well-meaning men, she is trapped. Around her are the signs and
symbols of postwar modernity: the economy of the immediate postwar

period is booming; bus culture promises freedom; and Los Angeles, where all can make a new start, beckons. Yet, beginning with her noir family home, Ann is and will be boxed in—scrutinized, pigeonholed, excluded, spoken for, imprisoned. The obsessive framing of the film in portraits of entrapment reinforces these ideas, overwhelming the viewer with its malignant force.

Beginning with the stalking and rape scene, boxes and prison bars become ubiquitous, as if emerging into reality from a nightmare of the safety of the workplace, home, everyday activities, and the nuclear family. While her rapist stalks her, they appear on the deserted streets of Capitol City. After the rape, they appear at her parents' house and at her workplace.

As Ann enters the gate to her parents' yard, the pickets of the fence and the lattice on the porch effectively reproduce prison bars and boxes (see the bottom of figure 29). When she enters the house, her mother descends the staircase to meet her (see figure 7, bottom). The figure of her mother casts a shadow on the wall revealing the identical elements of bars and boxes—the mother is trapped behind the bar-shadows from the staircase spindles cast on the wall, overlaid on the wallpaper's latticing. It is as if Mrs. Walton's shadow-self, her unacknowledged self, is trapped in the home, briefly suggesting a link between mother and daughter, which is reiterated in other Lupino films, such as *Not Wanted* and *Hard, Fast and Beautiful*. Moreover, her real self becomes menacing, as if she were Ann's warden, not her mother, advancing along the corridor between prison cells toward her daughter. This concise and harrowing portrait of her mother forms the unconscious motive for Ann to flee. Home noir here radically defamiliarizes the image of the comfortable mother and wife to whom Ann is both helpmate and co-conspirator in her aspiration to marry Jim. Mrs. Walton is trapped in domestic arrangements. Further, she becomes an antagonistic agent of Ann's fate if Ann is to remain at home, her jailer, trapping Ann into domestic life as wife and mother. This portrait of Mrs. Walton, seen from Ann's perspective in a state of trauma, connects with the portrait of Ann and Jim formed by the windshield of Jim's car, another box, when Ann exercises her only definitive choice in the film, which is to say "No!" to his proposal that they elope and marry immediately. To say yes or no to a proposal by a suitor had long been one of the few privileges accorded to women, so

even here, Ann is shown to conform to social convention. Yet her
decision is also informed by her
profound self-loathing and determination not to inflict herself on
her parents or Jim, not to mention her queasiness at being in the
presence of any man with sexual
intentions toward her.

Ann's confirmation photo-
graph, a vehicle for our empathy
with Ann, as mentioned in Part
One, becomes the emblematic
object inside the Waltons' house

FIGURE 31 Ann is framed by the windshield of Jim's
car in *Outrage*; moreover, all the spaces that concern
her are framed and ultimately defined by men

in terms of home noir. It is displayed on the mantelpiece, introduced
to us in a corner between Detective Sergeant Hendrix (Hal March) and
Mr. Walton, demonstrating that Ann is cornered between the wills and
desires of men.

In this photograph, Ann is smiling, radiant, wearing white. After the
rape, the photo is a reminder of her lost innocence. But more than this,
it becomes her double, or she becomes its dark double: she looks at it
as if into a mirror and finds another self there, one she can no longer
identify with, let alone abide. As she gazes at the photo, she experiences
a profound dissociation: she is utterly estranged from her past. Proof
that she has internalized a sense of culpability for her rape and its at-
tending feelings of defilement and
unworthiness is that she angrily
throws the framed photo onto
the floor, where it shatters. Even
though she is the victim of rape,
her self-image has changed to become everything the photo was
not. Here, in effect, she breaks, or
kills, her own innocence, her self.
She can no longer accept that she
is innocent of anything that happens to her.

FIGURE 32 Ann's confirmation photograph
between her father and the police detective in
Outrage

FIGURE 33 *Outrage*: Top, the lineup; bottom, Ann's hearing

Linked to the notion of home are the ideas of the road and the countryside—pointedly, in Southern California and its citrus groves. In film noir, drifters are almost always men. The road belongs to men and their cars, which Lupino, a few years later, exploited in *The Hitch-Hiker*. The road signifies to Ann freedom from her prison at home. However, her flight is not a well thought out plan. She walks by the bus station, and the idea of leaving occurs to her after she reads a bus destination, "To Denver." After Jim grabs her and shakes her violently subsequent to her refusal to marry him, Ann takes off for Los Angeles, the capital city of the mythic land of opportunity. Though Ann is unaware of it, flight is her attempt to escape all contact with men, as well as with her internalized image of herself. Even when, later in the film, she wants to stay with the Rev. Bruce Ferguson, she does so patently because Ferguson does not belong to that world of men. For instance, twice in the film, Lupino draws our attention to the fact that Bruce sucks and chews on a pipe with no tobacco in it, about which Pam Cook writes that "the character's emasculated status" is suggested by his having "'no lead in his pencil'" (62).

Thus far, every space in the film has been defined patriarchally: her home, workplace, the town's streets, the police investigation, interrogation, and line-up (see figure 33). After Ann's detour on foot from the bus headed for Los Angeles, space seems to open up. But her journey through that space is grueling. When she eventually collapses by the side of a dirt road, the long shot of her lying under trees swaying in the wind shows us only that she is a "lost soul," wandering in the agoraphobic forests and hilly terrain of Southern California.

The second half of the film, which takes place among Southern California's orchards, fruit-packing and shipping plants, ranches, and healing landscape, almost exactly reproduces the first half. As Cook observes, "The city/country division dissolves in Lupino's film as the heroine finds herself victimized in both places" (in Kuhn 65). At the country dance, stylized to duplicate any city or town nightclub or dancehall, Frank Marini, reminiscent of the rapist, sexually assaults Ann. Further dissolving the city/country division, Ferguson's mountain view is notable for the fact that it heals only men. In addition, in the Southern California landscape, when she is given a job as a fruit packer, we see that the motif of Ann being boxed in continues. The remainder of the film highlights the inescapability of the past found in many noir films. Every scene that takes place in the California landscape doubles the previous scenes in Capitol City, showing that Ann is effectively trapped in the repetition of her earlier trauma, now in the setting of bucolic California, finally fleeing a literal jail cell into post-traumatic psychosis.

The first and second parts of the film are punctuated by Ann's bus journeys. At the end of the film, after one year of psychotherapy, Ann is shown about to board a Continental bus moving in the same direction as the bus she took on her way to California—toward Los Angeles. This subtly suggests that she may not return to her family, her home town, and Jim. Moreover, if she does return home, she will do so deeply marked and changed by her experiences. It is difficult to imagine that she will still fit into the environment of her home town. (And something in us does not want her to return to that horrible place and its people.) Lupino suggests the question of what it might mean for a young woman to take off on her own on America's bus routes, after a profound trauma that alters her forever. As we have seen elsewhere, in Edgar Ulmer's *Detour* (1945), to give but one example, it takes a hard, determined, and ambitious woman to survive in these male spaces—for time enough to steal from men, blackmail them, and murder them in desperate bids for self-sufficiency. Ann is not such a woman. She may not have the relative good fortune of meeting another Bruce Ferguson next time around. It is a windy day when Ann catches her bus, just as it was when she arrived. She blows into and out of a landscape that means her ill. *Outrage* represents, as do Lupino's other early films, "the product of a postwar consciousness, left, in the disjunctive transition between trauma and a possibly even more traumatic return to normality, to reconstruct or re-destruct the suddenly tenuous connections between an alienated subjectivity and the too-stable structures through which it can no longer define itself" (Scheib, "Auteuress" 55).

Outrage details the traps set for women in a world that refuses to confront the modernity offered during wartime and snatched back in the postwar period. Recognizing war trauma for veterans, this world does not recognize, much less deal with, women's trauma, nor does it see a need to empower women to speak for themselves, make decisions about their lives that may fall outside the box, that is, the choice between marriage and work, and to act on their own behalf. The stubborn recalcitrance of patriarchy, which has simply been refigured after the war as kindly or well meaning, Lupino shows to have its roots in an abiding Victorianism.

A Mighty Girl: Lupino and *The Trouble with Angels*

The Trouble with Angels (1966),[15] writes Wheeler Winston Dixon, is a "much-underrated" film, one that "was almost universally dismissed upon its initial release, and yet Lupino orchestrated a beautifully restrained performance from Rosalind Russell as the Mother Superior, and created a work of considerable depth and feeling within the confines of a rather blandly modern Columbia program picture." He continues: "Even when constrained to direct 'treacle'" (as Dixon calls Jane Strahey's memoir, *Life with Mother Superior* [1962], on which *The Trouble with Angels* is based), Lupino had the uncanny ability "to make a personal statement within the confines of a decidedly commercial enterprise."

It is highly likely that William Frye of Columbia approached Lupino to direct *The Trouble with Angels* because an all-women spectacle would be a selling point for the film. It is a woman-centered film based on a book by a woman, from a screenplay by a woman, Blanche Hanalis, and with a nearly all-woman cast—including newcomers such as June Harding, veterans such as Rosalind Russell as Mother Superior and supporting character actresses Mary Wickes and Marge Redmond as nuns, and Gypsy Rose Lee as a teacher. And of course, its main draw, Hayley Mills, whose British accent and costuming in what American girls from ages nine through thirteen thought of as "mod" fashions, brought something of "Swinging London" to the screen. Who better to direct than one of the few woman directors in Hollywood, Ida Lupino?

The film's critical dismissal at its release had to do with the fact that it is a formula film, coming as part of a spate of "fun-nun" movies in the 1960s following Vatican II.[16] At that time, the power of nun-themed movies was so great that Sister Luc-Gabrielle's ("The Singing Nun") "Dominique" topped the charts, outselling The Beatles in 1963. In 1965, Julie Andrews and the clever Nazi-trouncing nuns of *The Sound of Music* broke box office records; 1966 brought *The Singing Nun* to the screen, starring Debbie Reynolds; and in 1969, Elvis Presley courted an inner-city nun played by Mary Tyler Moore in *Change of Habit*. The television series *The Flying Nun* made a big splash the year after *Angels* was released, lasting from 1967 to 1970, starring Sally Field. It is also likely that critics dismissed the film because it is a girls' coming-of-age story, not exactly a staple of Hollywood genre films, then or now. And yet, the film was so popular that Columbia went on to produce a sequel, *Where Angels Go, Trouble Follows*, directed by James Neilson in 1968.

Concurrent with the release of funny nun and family films, at a time when features had been distinguishing themselves markedly from television through the use of color and wide-screen formats in order to reintroduce the element of the spectacular to films that television did not yet have, the Production Code was challenged, and in 1968, finally gave way to the MPAA ratings system. Hollywood had been successfully ignoring the women's movement and became an agent in propagating "the sexual revolution" as a substitute for "women's liberation," in which the political agenda of the latter was translated into a series of superficial changes in sexual attitudes. In 1960s films, John Belton succinctly observes,

> Women were depicted as sexually liberated or aggressive. But Hollywood's women were modeled less after the revolutionary women who fought for equal rights in NOW [the National Organization for Women] than after the centerfolds found in the misogynistic pages of *Playboy*. *Lolita* (1962) and *Cleopatra* and *Irma la Douce* (both 1963) celebrate the sexual power of the new woman, as does *Barbarella* (1968), the futuristic film in which Jane Fonda revolutionizes life in the forty-first century by making love "the old-fashioned way." James Bond films introduced a host of sexually

available women, including Pussy Galore (Honor Blackman) in *Goldfinger* (1964). The sexual revolution culminated (for men, at least) in the wife-swapping craze celebrated in *Bob & Carol & Ted & Alice* (1969). (345–46)

Further, women in middle-class society, while being offered university educations and jobs as never before, remained subjugated by the sexual revolution. Radical feminists argued that the sexual revolution benefited men, making women into victims of sexual exploitation. "Nor was the trade-in of unpaid domestic drudgery as a home-maker for a 40-hour workweek necessarily liberating, especially when men began to expect women to be breadwinners and lovers as well as homemakers" (Belton 347). Lupino turned her analytical eye to this era of change and saw that its troubles for women had not diminished.

Despite the commercial nature of the project at Columbia, *Angels* represents the culmination of Lupino's feminist sensibility found in her films for The Filmakers. The film, to put it another way, gives us the flip-side of the trouble with patriarchy women endured in the postwar period, and offers a vision of a possible way out, through empowering girls and young women. In Lupino's earlier films, young women find temporary respite from a larger, often dangerous, society they are too naïve to size up, in which their painful difficulties are neglected and ignored, in all-too-rare institutions, such as the home for unwed mothers in *Not Wanted*, the sanitarium in *Never Fear*, and, less physically contained but just as regimented and firmly overseen, the psychotherapy Ann is court-ordered to receive for one year in *Outrage*. In a world inimical to women, places and programs such as these are essential, functioning as safe havens. Lupino does not criticize these institutions as much as ruefully admit that they are necessary in a patriarchal world, and wish that there were more of them. Seen from this perspective, the most tragic figure in Lupino's early films is Florence in *Hard, Fast and Beautiful* because the pain of being betrayed by her intimates—her mother and her coach—forces her, without any guidance and anywhere to turn, into a marriage she doesn't want. She flees into marriage and domesticity, intending them to become her safe harbor, but given her mother's disillusionment, boredom, and disappointment as wife and mother, Florence's solution is at best deeply flawed. Like her mother, Millie, many

middle-class women experienced such unhappiness—famously commented on by Betty Friedan in 1963.

In *Angels*, the spirit of St. Francis Academy is closer to radical feminist Shulamith Firestone's notion of a communal "household" than it is
to the nuclear family or a Catholic convent school. Firestone saw this
new kind of household as a "liberating social form," correcting the nuclear family's patriarchal inclination toward ownership and the objectification of human beings (208). Men would not be heads of household
nor would women bear children. In short, Firestone's vision is akin to
Lupino's vision of the convent in *Angels*—a radical feminist commune.

The Saint Francis Academy, where most of the action occurs, was
filmed on location at Saint Mary's Home for Children in Ambler, Penn-
sylvania. Because *Angels* takes place at a Catholic girls' school, the men
who appear in it are of necessity incidental (indeed, in the credits, male
characters are listed among "The Outsiders," a wonderful twist on the
many outsider women in Lupino's early films). Moreover, the fact that
it takes place at a Catholic girls' school and convent is also incidental:
Lupino removes almost every religious reference from the film; her convent school is nothing like convent schools in 1966; and she makes no
reference to the patriarchal structure of the Church. Instead, Lupino's
convent functions as a protective world for girls, a "room of their own."
Saint Francis, the saint who watches over the poor and sick, preached
sermons to animals, and praised all creatures as brothers and sisters, is
known as the patron saint of animals and ecology, a lovely metaphor
for an inclusive vision of the world. Girls can only assume their rightful
place in the world as strong adults, knowing what they want, and initi-
ating change, if they first live in an environment that will protect them
from the injustice of the world.

In their essay on *Angels*, Mary Beth Haralovich, Janet Jakobsen, and
Susan White view the film through the lens of queer theory, stating un-
equivocally that it is "a film about woman-woman identification and
the attractions of a community of women" (119). This is certainly a valid
way to interpret the film, particularly since the convent setting and its
all-female denizens invite a lesbian rereading. But the argument is more
polemical than apt, as if a film, simply because it is about nuns and initi-
ates, *ought* to be read as queer. The essay is gleefully subversive. It evokes
our collective fascination with nuns' sexuality, which in a convent can

only take a few forms for straight women (aside from autoeroticism): the mystical ecstasies of a Saint Teresa of Avila; occasional encounters with male clergy; or successful repression and sublimation. It comes as no surprise that we can more easily imagine lesbian sexualities in the perfectly cloistered world of the convent, perhaps because then sexual expression would, at least, be more convenient.

While fascination with lesbian sexualities in the convent has found its way into many film narratives, as well as having spawned the pulpy "nunsploitation" genre, we set it aside for *The Trouble with Angels*. As Tyler Coates writes,

> [W]hat makes nuns so worthy of artistic portrayal? There's certainly a gendered aspect to our collective fascination with them (or at least, those of us who were not raised Catholic and have little experience with nuns in real life). There's something that seems very extreme about a woman giving up the opportunity for love, marriage, children, etc., in order to devote herself completely to God—even more so than for priests, as there's the sense that the men of the Catholic Church have much more power. But it's also worth considering the freedom that being a nun brings—the ability to live life on a woman's own terms, and to live within a matriarchal society.

Our sense of *Angels* begins with the context Coates outlines, which returns us also to Lupino as a feminist author.

In 2015, the Melbourne International Film Festival celebrated Lupino's films and television episodes. The program notes state that "much of *Angels* unfolds along a complex vertical seer/seen axis quite unique in Lupino's films (although extensively explored in much of her TV work)." As part of Lupino's complex visual economy, we, the viewers, are positioned "in the shot" as active onlookers, which is consonant with Lupino's cinema of empathy. As in her Filmakers' films, we are positioned so as to have a "level gaze." Quite literally in the diegesis, Mary and Rachel are often voyeurs looking at private scenes of life among the sisters and Mother Superior; however, they are not Hitchcockian voyeurs, in which the camera-eye objectifies what it sees, emphasizing the gendered object's "to-be-looked-atedness" (Mulvey). In other words, the gaze in these instances does not equate the Freudian POV shot with voyeurism/objectification and reaction shot with narcissism/identification that forms part of Laura Mulvey's analysis of the male gaze. Rather, we can call the gaze in *Angels* a female gaze, which has many variants in the film. Through spying, Mary and Rachel learn to surrender their understandable antagonism to parental and authority figures and come to see their elders as human beings who have feelings with which the girls can empathize. Rachel actively turns away from this process of increasing empathy, which is precisely the measure of adulthood, thereby articulating that she is not yet ready to grow up.

The presence of well-known stripper Gypsy Rose Lee reworks the idea of an objectifying male gaze into one variant of the film's female gaze, a blatantly admiring one. Of Lee's Mrs. Mabel Dowling Phipps, the "interpretive dance instructor," Rachel says, "She's a blast!" We can even say that adopting Mrs. Phipps as a role model is part of Lupino's empathic cinema, because by doing so, the girls "feel their way into" a potential future version of themselves, regardless of whether or not they actually become those selves. The girls at Saint Francis receive diverse opportunities to play, in a safe environment, with possibilities for their respective futures. Lupino decisively diverges from the male gaze that Michael Powell anatomizes so well in *Peeping Tom* (1960), in which Mark murders women to punish them when he perceives their desire to be filmed and to become objects of that gaze. Such exhibitionistic women appear in various guises in *Peeping Tom*. As a stripper, Gypsy Rose Lee could very well play one of these female personae. However, *Angels* emphasizes Phipps's dance à la Isadora Duncan as she teaches the girls grace in movement, imitating a willow in the wind. The girls try to imitate her; the result is comic.[17]

As viewers, in our often larger view when we see what Mary does not, we empathize with both Mary and Mother Superior rather than identify with them. Lupino's Filmakers productions had begun this empathic filmmaking, but here it is more elaborately developed, employing more mobile framing and other techniques that Lupino used in her television episodes. For instance, when Mary watches Mother Superior privately mourn the death of her friend, after publicly showing little emotion, the camera slowly descends as Mother Superior bends over the coffin and embraces it, bringing her down to earth from her exalted position in

FIGURE 34 *The Trouble with Angels*: Mary (Hayley Mills, top) gazes at Mother Superior (Rosalind Russell), who registers the girl's anger and misery without reacting to them

Mary's view. Mary may not note this change in her perception, but we do. Secret looking is also the provenance of the nuns and Mother Superior, such as when Mother Superior glances at the girls out of the corner of her eye to see how they feel. Here, the female gaze is maternal, as well as empathic, sometimes generating Mother Superior's satisfaction, and sometimes giving her information she stores away as food for thought about how to raise these girls.

Last, in gazes exchanged between Mary, Rachel, and the nuns, we see something of object-relations theory at work, as explored by Heinz Kohut, Alice Miller, and others. Object-relations theory emphasizes inner images of self and other and how they manifest themselves in

interpersonal relationships, primarily in the family and especially between mother and child. The "object" is the significant person who is the
focus of another's feelings or intentions. "Relations" refers to interpersonal relationships and suggests the residues of past relationships that
affect a person in the present. In this theory, it is important to note that a
person's mental representations and memories of significant objects are
crucial for development and change, called "internal objects." "External
objects," on the other hand, are actual people (or places or things). An
external object can trigger an internal object, because it is someone or
something that reminds the person of an object invested with that person's emotional energy. Lupino seems to have had a deep understanding of the ways in which internal objects affect our interpersonal lives
and the formation of our "self," a conscious and unconscious mental
representation of ourselves. One essential example of an internal object
we see at play in *Angels* is that of the internal mother and how it affects
the child's way of relating to the external object of mother and subsequent mother figures. We see this best in those shots of Mary looking
angrily and resentfully at Mother Superior. For instance, when Mary
watches out her window as Mother Superior takes a solitary walk on the
grounds, we see her in close-up, disheveled and angry, framed by her
cage-like window and surrounded by ragged bits of snow clinging to
the windowsill. This image contrasts sharply with the open space of the
outdoor world, and the peace of Mother Superior's figure as she walks,
lost in her thoughts. However, Mother Superior notices Mary looking
at her and returns Mary's gaze, mirroring it in such a way as to defuse
the girl's anger and resentment, which we can see, from Mother Superior's perspective, contains a fundamental sadness (see figure 34). Mary
is miserable. Mother Superior looks up and leans slightly backward, con-
veying the sense that she is surprised by Mary looking down at her, but
the sweet composure of her facial expression does not react to Mary's
gaze in kind. Rather, it reassures Mary that Mother Superior is strong
and patient. Therefore, in object-relations terms, Mother Superior's mirroring is that of a good mother. During Mary's ascent to maturity, she
also learns of Mother Superior's humanity—her flaws, her background
as a rebel herself, and so on. This knowledge serves to transform Mary's
internal mother into one in which "good" and "bad" mother are min-
gled, no longer separate constructs of white and black (like the very

habit Mother Superior wears, a façade covering her humanity), but as one whole, in a nuanced spectrum of grays. This type of internal object marks healthy development into adulthood. The relay of gazes between the two characters can be understood more profoundly in light of the fact that Mary is an orphan who lost her mother at a young age, consequently experiencing abiding feelings of abandonment. She acts out against her guardian, a lascivious uncle who chases young women, and who patently finds her an unwanted burden. And she has missed out on crucial developmental stages. Mother Superior then functions to mirror Mary's feelings maternally, nurturing her, so that Mary becomes increasingly able to internalize that mirroring as her self-image. In this way, Mary's sense of self is given a chance to flourish, and it is no surprise that she becomes attached to the place of her growing up, which marks one step on the path to her decision to become a nun.

PART THREE

LUPINO MOVES TO TELEVISION

Industrial Contexts: Film to Television

In 1949–1950, the number of moviegoers in the United States dropped drastically from 90 to 60 million. But as John Belton writes, the rise of television had little to do with this drastic decline in movie theater attendance, since "during those two years, there were only a handful of television stations and relatively few families owned television sets" (323). Television was, nevertheless, on the rise: in 1951, the number of television sets jumped to 10.3 million and in 1953 to 20.4 million. In 1956, just as Ida Lupino was settling in to a new career in television writing, producing, and directing, the number increased markedly, to 34.9 million. By 1960, television sets had penetrated 90 percent of the American home market (Belton 323). This dramatic rise was due in part to the lifting in 1952 of the FCC's freeze on licensing new stations during the completion of the network of coaxial cable and microwave links, which allowed the broadcast range of television transmission to expand from cities into the suburbs and rural America (Belton 323–24).

Between 1950 and 1956, the spread of television certainly affected how the film industry sought to distinguish itself from the small screen. But it wasn't the numbers of television sets sold or the new broadcast capabilities of network television that made the small screen a perceived threat to the survival of the silver screen. Rather, as Belton notes, "television was merely a highly visible, superficial symptom of a much more profound change in postwar entertainment patterns rather than the direct cause of the movies' downfall; the source of the problem lay elsewhere—in the economic and sociocultural transformation of blue- and white-collar Americans during the postwar period into the 'leisured masses'" (323–24). The first television programs, before the requisite cable links allowed television to proliferate across the country and then to become integrated into the ways the "leisured masses" lived their daily lives, were broadcast live from New York. In 1949, urban Americans who lived within range of television stations could watch *The Texaco Star Theater* (1948), starring Milton Berle, or the children's program *Howdy Doody* (1947–1960). They could also choose between two fifteen-minute newscasts, CBS's *TV News* (1948) with Douglas Edwards and NBC's *Camel News Caravan* (1948) with John Cameron Swayze. To reach more far-flung television audiences in range of local stations, these shows were filmed and immediately flown to locations where the film could be screened and rebroadcast.

As television became central to the new leisure culture, The Filmakers' social problem films and their "look" (in black-and-white and Academy ratio) would have seemed antiquated; film became a new CinemaScope world, in which the film industry experimented with ways to create a full-immersion theatrical experience to draw audiences back to the movies. Not only were 60 percent of all Hollywood films released in color by 1956, but other cinematographic processes in the early 1950s, such as Cinerama, followed by widescreen technologies such as CinemaScope and Todd-AO, were implemented. These processes changed the dimensions and shape of the screen so that viewers found themselves in the midst of a spectacular cinematic experience, enhanced by multi-track sound. Indeed, these processes were very popular among audiences; today, updated versions of these widescreen and sound processes still endure as integral parts of our theater-going experience. Added to these processes were other experiments to enhance moviegoers' immersion in the world of cinema, such as 3D, which at the time was short-lived because of technical problems and its relegation to effects in thriller and horror movies, with which audiences soon became bored. The less-than-successful 3D notwithstanding, The Filmakers' bankruptcy was due not only to its principals' unfortunate decision to distribute films, but also to a changing culture and expectations.

Despite technical and other innovations, such as the drive-in for a fast-growing suburban population, movie theaters never again made profits as they once had, nor did they regain their influence. Audiences continued to dwindle. Added to this, film personnel, such as directors and actors, including Lupino, also turned their sights to television and exited Hollywood for the new medium, seeing in it opportunities for work that Hollywood was unable or unwilling to give them.

For instance, blacklisted actors, directors, and screenwriters were given a second chance by the television industry and were accorded proper credit for their work. Lupino's close bond with John Garfield and her marriage to Howard Duff, both part of a large group of men and women tarnished by anticommunist zealots, attuned her very personally to changes taking place throughout the fifties and sixties in the politics of the entertainment industries. As part of the transition from postwar Hollywood's collusion with HUAC to the new era ushered in by television, cracks in the blacklist finally began to appear: the first of these came in 1957, when Alfred Hitchcock hired blacklisted actor Norman Lloyd as an associate producer for his CBS anthology series *Alfred Hitchcock Presents*, which was then entering its third season; Lupino directed episodes of the show three seasons later.

Certainly, there was much crossover between film and television, and in both directions. For instance, Charlton Heston, who began acting in theater, starred in episodes of *Studio One*, an anthology drama on CBS, where he was scouted for film. *Dragnet* (1954), starring Jack Webb, was the first film based on a television show (1950–1959). In 1953, Delbert Mann directed *Marty*, based on a script by Paddy Chayefsky and produced for NBC's *Philco Television Playhouse*. It starred Rod Steiger as a thirty-six-year-old decent but insecure and lonely working-class man who lives with his immigrant mother in the Bronx. He and his friends want to meet women and get married, but their prospects seem dim. Finally, Marty meets a "plain-looking" woman, Clara (Nancy Marchand). The plot hinges on whether he will go through with plans to see her again. Mann and Chayevsky also worked on the film version of *Marty* (1955), shot on location in the Bronx rather than on a sound stage, giving it a realism that the television drama did not have. The film version starred Ernest Borgnine, who would win the Academy Award for Best Actor, and the film won as well for Best Picture. *Marty* was also the first American film to win the Palme d'Or at the Cannes Film Festival, making Mann one of only three directors to win both the Oscar and the Palme d'Or (the other two are Billy Wilder and Roman Polanski). *Marty* displays the mutually enhancing relationship between the television and film industries, and is a wonderful instance of postwar realism in film.

Finally, Hollywood studio heads had acknowledged that cooperating with the television industry would be far more lucrative than trying to compete with it. Television production began relocating to Hollywood and environs; film studios converted sound stages for television production and rented out their backlots to television production companies; studios signed over their pre-1948 theatrical rights to allow television networks to air their films; and film studios began to produce their own programs for television. Warner Bros. was the first of these, with its series *Warner Brothers Presents* premiering in the 1955–56 season. Subsequently, the studio produced the hit series *Cheyenne* (1955–1963), *Maverick* (1957–1962), and *77 Sunset Strip* (1958–1964).

Lupino overcame an initial trepidation about working in television— "this new medium," as Thomas Schatz calls television of the period, "with its insatiable appetite for product" ("*Desilu*" 121)—after she saw first-hand that television offered her greater opportunities than the film industry. The fast pace of television production matched her high energy, and its team orientation fit her penchant for collaboration. While a number of stars eschewed what was perceived by some at the time as a "step down" (Becker 26–31), others, such as Dick Powell, David Niven, and Charles Boyer, embraced television.[1] As Becker notes, the three actors "had each bristled under or completely avoided studio control over their careers in the 1940s; through the new opportunities for independent production, however, they became media moguls in television" (11). It was one of Lupino's collaborators in filmmaking, cinematographer George Diskant (who had helped make *The Bigamist*), who urged her to move to television, as Lupino recalled in "Me, Mother Directress":

[Diskant] said, "Ida, I'm in with a group called 'Four Star' with some old buddies of yours, David Niven, Charles Boyer and Dick Powell. Why don't you come over and go into television?" "Television," I screamed, "Really George, you're out of your mind." Well, the next thing I knew, David Niven called me up and said, "Lupy

Kupy, I know you're against television, but come over and do a guest spot on our show anyway." I said, "Oh, Niv, I can't. The whole thing scares me." He said, "Come and do just one." So I went over and did this one shot. And the next thing I knew Dick and David said, "Now, look, you must be the guest who came to dinner—stay with us." So I stayed with them for two years. I was the guest who never left and became the fourth star of "Four Star Playhouse" and loved every minute of it—and never missed directing.[2]

Lupino began performing on *Four Star Playhouse* at the end of 1953, the year, according to Thomas Schatz, "the 'TV boom' hit the country in full force" (*"Desilu"* 119). By 1956, when Lupino began her television career writing and directing "No. 5 Checked Out" for the anthology series *Screen Directors Playhouse*, television was well underway as a new medium. Early television broadcasts such as *Amos 'n' Andy* (1951–1953), *The Goldbergs* (1949–1956), and *The Jack Benny Show* (1950–1965) based themselves on radio programs. Radio genres—news, variety shows, dramas, thrillers, and situation comedies—were imported into television, which then, like film, worked flexibly with generic hybrids. From 1955 to 1956, Hal Roach Studios broadcast original television drama through *Screen Directors Playhouse*, which had previously been a popular 1949–1951 radio drama series. Each of the television episodes was directed by a well-known Hollywood director, including John Ford, Fred Zinnemann, Leo McCarey, and Frank Borzage. About halfway through the series, Lupino directed "No. 5 Checked Out," bringing home noir to the small screen. Willard Weiner penned the script based on Lupino's original story. Exemplifying the crossover of film and television in the 1950s and the aspiration of anthology drama to film art, the episode featured two actors well known from their film careers, Teresa Wright in the lead and Peter Lorre as part of the supporting cast. William Talman, whom Lupino had directed in *The Hitch-Hiker*, also appeared in the episode.

Directing for Television

"Largely, I hate doing television," Jacques Tourneur once commented; "it's horrible. It's against everything I believe in; if you don't bring some of your individuality and some of your experience and sensitivity to bear on a subject, you don't get more than a mechanical result" (qtd. in Guinle and Mizrahi 82). Lupino's experience in television, however, was quite different from Tourneur's. In fact, a number of directors, including Lupino, thrived working in television, priding themselves on their ability to be creative within the strictures of tight production schedules, procedures, and style. Andrew V. McLaglen, for instance, best known for his direction of more than half the episodes of *Have Gun—Will Travel*, once boasted that he had completed shooting eleven and a half pages of a script in one day, no mean feat when we consider that those pages included his visualization of all the shots and shot compositions. Moreover, McLaglen combined creativity with efficiency, packing as many unexpected images as he could into one shot (Spencer). Lupino had always joined pragmatism with artistry, and television proved to be a medium that suited her well. She, like McLaglen, enjoyed the specific challenges of television, in which directors began working on a television project after the script had been written and finalized. The director commanded the crew during the actual filming or taping of the show and was responsible for choosing the different camera angles and shot compositions that were to be used. Some scripts contained shooting instructions, such as a required close-up. But otherwise the director was free to be creative. McLaglen managed to add creative touches in just such an instance. When required to shoot a close-up of Paladin (Richard Boone) entering a room, he shot the famous chess-piece logo on Paladin's holster rather than a close-up of his face (Spencer). McLaglen was the ideal creative partner for Boone, drawing out the effects he desired from the actor's performances (Spencer). In short, there was always room for making an individual mark on a television episode as its director.

Like Lupino, the most efficient directors immediately began meeting the actors and planning their staging, shots, and shot compositions as soon as they received the script. An episode of an anthology drama such as *Screen Directors Playhouse* took about two weeks for pre-production. A thirty-minute television episode received far less, with one day for rehearsals and three days for shooting. It may have been difficult, but was by no means impossible, to be creative on these schedules. One reason for the difficulty was that directing cinematographers and lighting designers for creative rather than merely competent results took time. Montgomery Pittman, who wrote and directed episodes of *The Twilight Zone, Sugarfoot*, and *Maverick*, was another director recognized in the industry for his efficiency and discipline. While Pittman's writing and directing largely went unnoticed by viewers of the period, today his efforts are recognized for their creative inroads, recognized on some 3,100 sites on the Internet (Desmond). As a writer, one thing Pittman was able to do was change *Sugarfoot*'s protagonist, Tom Brewster (Will Hutchins), from a dour moralist into a character with humor by featuring his light-hearted doppelgänger, also played by Hutchins, in the episodes "The Canary Kid" and "The Return of the Canary Kid." Hutchins had often written letters to the producer complaining about the "melodramatic" Tom Brewster, and Pittman offered The Canary Kid as a solution to Hutchins's unhappiness with his role, allowing him to express more of his strengths as an actor. In directing these episodes, Pittman used a split-screen technique for humor and irony (Desmond).

Like McLaglen and Pittman, Lupino was one of the exceptional directors, recognized for her ability to bring out exactly what she wanted from actors. She was also perfectly suited to working with television committees and collaborating with others. The qualities of efficiency and diplomacy that she had brought to her filmmaking were the same qualities she brought to the small screen, along with her ability to work with tiny budgets and her hands-on knowledge of all facets of production. She had liked the challenges directing for The Filmakers, and these qualities served her well in television.

Further, it must be remembered that the industry is far different today. Recollections by the television writer and producer Irma Kalish give a picture of how it was to work behind the scenes. Kalish began her long career writing an episode of *The Millionaire* in 1955, working in an environment in which most of the writers were freelance, able to adapt to different genres and pitch ideas (while today, a show has a staff of writers and no one makes a pitch), and in which there were very few entrepreneurs; the shows were generated by the studios and run by a producer, or perhaps an assistant producer, story editor, and secretary. As Kalish recalls, "There are producers who work for hire and there are line producers, who are basically production managers but have producer credit (which they are able to negotiate for). In those days, there were very small production units and very simplistic shows. The budget for shows like *Sunset Strip* was about $70,000 for black and white shows out the door. Finished. If you went over $5,000 or so, you were in deep trouble (now, of course, an episode is millions of dollars)." She also noted that television at the time was not simply the profit-driven, mechanical business that we perceive today:

> There was more of a feeling of family. People were professionals, but there was a spirit of camaraderie, fun and not taking one's self and what we were doing too seriously. I think that's probably different now. I don't know if that spirit, that family feeling or that fun still exists the way it did then. The whole industry now is corporate driven and not an industry that was designed and built by individual men. When I started, Harry Cohn was still running Columbia, Jack Warner was still running Warner Bros. The individual men who created the business, the original people who started the networks, they were still there running everything. Interestingly enough, I started at Warner Bros. They had an enormous number of shows in the 60s and they were very popular. Warner Bros. supplied the entire ABC primetime network because a couple of guys at ABC and Warner were friends. Virtually, on a handshake, ABC said, in effect, "We'll take all your programs" and Warner said, "We'll give you all our product." So the whole ABC primetime lineup, at that time for some years, was Warner Bros. shows (*Maverick* was one of the shows that was very big). They had Western and Detective shows—*77 Sunset Strip, Hawaiian Eye, Surfside 6, Cheyenne, Sugarfoot, Colt .45*, etc. It was a great time of productivity for the writers and for the studios.

Lupino's experience and sensibility were well suited to this kind of work environment, a more collegial one than we find today. Her connections throughout Hollywood were another advantage she had in negotiating the world of television. In addition, her versatility, visual acuity, and ability to work fluidly in multiple genres allowed Lupino, whether as writer, producer, or director, to make her mark as a feminist auteur and infuse her television episodes with her signature perspectives on gender.

"No. 5 Checked Out"

When she did step behind the camera again, Lupino directed the generically hybrid investigation of gender and space "No. 5 Checked Out" for

Screen Directors' Playhouse. Based on her own original story of the same title, "No. 5 Checked Out" stands alongside classic noir portrayals of men and women whose desires and actions are tested in extreme circumstances and surroundings. An active lip-reader, Mary Jarvis (Teresa Wright) is a deaf teacher who has given up on finding a husband after being abandoned by her fiancé because of her deafness. She has come to her family-owned vacation cabins two weeks before the season begins "to try to forget all over again" because she has just run into her former fiancé with his new wife. Mary's first act on a windy night is to close the windows. With this gesture, Lupino symbolically establishes the central motif of the story: how a woman might establish independence within a closed space that is also threatened from the outside.

Mary wishes her father (Ralph Moody) well as he leaves to visit an ailing uncle. While her father tries to encourage her with ameliorative speeches (including the prospect that they will one day have the money to see "that specialist in the east"), he also loses patience as he counsels Mary to look toward having a "home of your own." Mary, however, feels sorry for herself. "There's no hope for me," she says. Like most of Lupino's benevolent patriarchs, Mary's father is ineffectual as he insists that she should "quit talking like that." Mr. Jarvis then promises that neighbor "Timmy" will look after her, since Mary's father will "feel much easier if there's a man around." Lupino approaches gender with her signature irony from the beginning of the episode: it is the men around Mary who threaten her. This is seen even from her father, who shakes her in a scene emotionally accentuated by a canted, slightly low-angle shot as Lupino records Mary's reaction.

After her father leaves, two criminals, well-meaning Barney (William Talman) and vicious sociopath Willy (Peter Lorre), arrive looking for a place to hide just after having robbed a bank. In films such as *M, Stranger on the Third Floor,* and *The Maltese Falcon,* Peter Lorre played archetypal noir figures. With Barney's appearance, too, Lupino gives us an image of the quintessentially noir male protagonist, showing Barney's eyes caught within the shadow cast by the brim of his hat (see figure 35).

Indeed, much of "No. 5 Checked Out" is classic noir. Many of its scenes were shot using low-key lighting to convey the danger that surrounds isolated life at the Deep Lake Cabins resort; Lupino's chiaroscuro lighting contrasts with the natural daylight of the bucolic setting. The

FIGURE 35 *Screen Directors Playhouse*, "No. 5 Checked Out" (aired 18 January 1956): Barney (William Talman) arrives

opposition in lighting recalls the visual style of *Out of the Past*, a film with which this episode can usefully be seen in dialogue. Like the 1947 film, "No. 5 Checked Out" (as well as *Outrage*) presents a country landscape whose ostensible function as an escape from the dangerous city is challenged by the noir threats that seep into it. Shots of Mary and Barney by the lake are reminiscent of Jeff Bailey's trysts with Ann Miller in rural California in *Out of the Past*. Even the name of the resort, Deep Lake Cabins, evokes the oneiric tone of film noir—one thinks here of Betty Elms's statement in *Mulholland Drive* (2001) that she is from Deep River (Ontario), indicating director David Lynch's interest in the psychic rivers of consciousness.

Here, the deep cabins of Barney and Mary's consciousness are seen in the repeated moments in which one or the other of the characters drifts off into her/his own world. Often, when Mary has turned away from Barney so that she can no longer hear him (an act of "checking out" that Lupino represents as a positive resource for Mary), Barney speaks, knowing she can't hear him, saying words typically cast as voiceover in film noir: "See, I just can't turn it off. I gotta run. I gotta get away fast." (see figure 36).

The story's interest in the idea of belatedness also links it to film noir. Like other noir protagonists, Barney has tender feelings for Mary that come too late to be acted upon; their burgeoning romance is never consummated. Earlier, we referred to Mr. Jordan's worry that he might make the same mistake twice in *The Bigamist*. So too in *Not Wanted*

FIGURE 36 Mary (Teresa Wright) "checks out" while Barney narrates the situation in "No. 5 Checked Out"

Sally meets Drew after she has been "ruined" by drifter Steve Ryan. Lupino's noir sensibility plays heavily through Barney's fatalism. He has inadvertently become a doomed criminal (Barney thought he was simply driving the getaway car for a bank robbery, which subsequently became a murder scene) and, like Walter Neff or Jeff Markham, he is on a dead-end ride "all the way to the end of the line and it's a one-way trip and the last stop is the cemetery" (Neff's voiceover in *Double Indemnity*, 1944).

While Barney experiences his futile desire for Mary as traumatic, for Mary the relationship is emotionally fulfilling. Her deafness functions as a protective wall against loss and danger. Mary is never aware of her proximity to death and murder, and in this way Lupino establishes her as another central female consciousness struggling to reach fulfillment in an unsympathetic or dangerous environment. Mary's deafness is, for Lupino, a way to develop the idea of Mary's alienation: while she is initially isolated within a society insensitive to her disability (represented by her fiancé abandoning her and her subsequent retreat to the cabins), her isolation becomes a source of power and strength as she is able to ward off the menacing forces around her.[3]

Barney and Mary's first meeting follows an intriguing moment of home noir in which Mary's turmoil and latent power are revealed by the vital presence of a radio. Just after her father has left, Mary goes to the radio and begins to touch it lovingly. That a deaf woman turns to the radio for solace is perplexing, until we realize that this is Mary's way of tapping her imagination as she re-creates in her mind an idea

FIGURE 37 "No. 5 Checked Out": Mary and her radio

of what she wants for herself in her surroundings. Mary's sensual connection to the radio (see figure 37) revises our perception of her domestic role in the cabin and registers her mood of loss and desire. The radio may remind Mary of her loss of hearing, but it also serves for the viewer as an extratextual allusion to the radio having been superseded by television, a point particularly relevant to *Screen Directors Playhouse*, which broadcast its radio dramas, frequently featuring Lupino, from 1949 to 1951.

Mary caressing the radio foreshadows the desire that is about to be "switched on" by Barney's appearance, itself directed by Lupino as a kind of visitation for Mary. While Mary works at her desk, impervious to the blasting sound of the radio but soothed by its strangely dreamlike effects, she cannot hear Barney knocking on the office door. He enters, thinking that the loud music is what keeps her from noticing his presence. Mary eventually turns slightly and notices him but without a startle reflex, as if Barney's arrival is in natural continuity with her state of mind, an invocation or product of wish fulfillment.

Having left Mary and moments later checked in to Cabin No. 5, Barney pulls the blinds down (another act of shutting things out), and we are introduced to his sociopathic partner Willy (Lorre). Lorre's delivery of his lines and general comportment present him as a sociopath who finds humor and absurdity in the country cabin hideout and in domesticity more generally. His first comments satirize Barney's horror that a man with two children was killed in the bank robbery ("Boys or girls?" Willy asks). Willy's grim humor can also be seen when he laughs hysterically at Barney's plea for the car keys, reminding him that there is "no way out" (see figure 38).

Lupino's home noir helps to mark Willy's malevolent glee. Surrounded by ceramic canards, country-cute clocks, and crocheted throw rugs, the men's presence in these cabins brings into high relief the "unhomely" nature of domestic objects. Earlier, we saw that the radio signals Mary's desire; now, the strangeness of objects displays the sociopathic infection that has crept into the remote cabins. In one scene, Willy returns to the cabin with grocery items from the village. Through close-ups, even the food becomes estranged from sustenance and comfort: Willy, offering Barney some treats from the local store, remarks maniacally, "Nice pumpernickel, I know you like it. I got you chocolate bars. And, look! Boned turkey! And deviled ham. Pickles! I got you something to read, nice books!"

FIGURE 38 "No. 5 Checked Out": sociopath Willy (Peter Lorre) laughs at Barney's concerns

As Willy catalogues the domestic fare that has been defamiliarized in this troubled space, Lupino also extends home noir to Mary's outdoor costume, which includes a large industrial flashlight she carries with her around the grounds. While the flashlight obviously has a utilitarian function in the dark night, it also serves as one of Lupino's objects that resonates with the instability and danger of Mary's environment. Highlighting details of domestic life as props in a crime story, with this episode television literally brings noir into the space of the family home.

Related to home noir in "No. 5 Checked Out" is the transposition of a typical rural recreation, fishing, into a backdrop for murder. The finale of the episode, here again, recalls *Out of the Past*. It is worth recalling that the 1947 film noir also features a deaf character, The Kid. Like Mary, he is a tough outsider whose vulnerability is shown though his deafness. Moreover, as suggested above, both *Out of the Past* and "No. 5 Checked Out" blur the conventional distinction between urban criminality and bucolic spaces free from the taint of the city in film noir. This dichotomy was similarly broken down in another noir film that Lupino was involved with, *On Dangerous Ground* (1952), in which Lupino played not a deaf but a blind woman (also named Mary) endangered by sociopathic male behavior. As in *On Dangerous Ground* and *Out of the Past*, "No. 5 Checked Out" suggests the impossibility of separating city iniquity from rural safety. That iniquity even invades objects in the cabin interiors that then lose their stability. Unable to keep danger cordoned off in the city, noir protagonists have to confront the ubiquity of modern violence and alienation. Mary's deafness has marginalized her and sent her running into the woods. While noir escape and running away are usually revealed to be futile (as they are for Barney), for women they play out differently, since, for Lupino, most modern settings bar women from meaningful action. In this context, Mary's growth, though seeming to ratify repression (she never knows of the violence and danger that have surrounded her), is measured by her having transformed her disability into a source of strength. She has the power to "check out" of realms defined by masculine violence and predation.

And, indeed, in Mary's resilience we see Lupino's interest in deafness as a means of controlling the terms of Mary's environment. When Barney says melodramatically, "I'm no good," Mary responds, "If you're going to talk that way, I'm going to tune you out." Barney has given something to Mary that she has not received from other figures in her life. Confidence doesn't come for Mary from her work in the school where she is employed; nor does it come from her well-meaning but patriarchal father. Rather, it comes from the noir loser who has nothing more to lose. Inspired by Barney's gentle friendship, Mary responds to his compliments on her fortitude and talent. Barney says, "You get by with [being deaf] just great. I mean that. . . . It's wonderful the way you read lips." More than simple appreciation for Mary's resilience is his envy of her power to "tune out" the malevolence around her. Mary's ability to "check out" is here seen as a "gift": "Wouldn't it be something if you could teach a guy not to hear. . . . Sometimes it would be great if you could turn it all off. All *you* got to do, honey, is turn your head or close your eyes. . . . I'd trade with you anytime. . . . Sometimes I'd give anything to be able to turn it all off. You've got something very important, Mary. It's kind of a gift." In a world in which even escaping to cabins in the woods cannot ward off malevolent forces such as the amoral evil represented by Willy, Mary's power to shut off the noise becomes a powerful symbol of female fortitude, one that Lupino explored throughout the rest of her directing career, culminating ten years later in the space she imagines for women in *The Trouble with Angels*—in connection with another central character named Mary.

In the penultimate scene, Mary thanks Barney for his support: "Maybe I wasn't ready for it before," she says, "but I think you're right. I feel sure I will meet somebody, someday." When Barney says, "I know you will," Mary is already drifting off into her own world, a place where she can imagine the sounds of the radio and where she is protected from inimical forces around her. Further, Lupino's sympathy for Barney, the trapped noir protagonist whose vulnerability and kindness are clear in his feelings for Mary and the fact that he does not judge her as being "disabled," is fully in line with her cinema of empathy, in which we empathize with outsider figures.

In the final scene, Willy approaches behind Mary while she is fishing and shoots Barney, which of course Mary doesn't perceive. Just before Willy is about to shoot Mary in the back, Barney rallies, for his last redemptive act, to kill Willy. Dead bodies strewn behind her, Mary remains, even at the end of the episode, unaware of the threat that has surrounded her. She continues fishing, a pastime that Lupino has already associated with violence in *The Hitch-Hiker*.

The episode concludes, like so many of Lupino's finales, inconclusively, with Mary continuing to face the lake. What we do know, however, is that Mary has developed a unique power to cordon herself off in a world she can control and in which she can thrive. The last shot in the film is of the car keys falling out of Barney's hand as he lurches down the hill toward Mary in his final moments. With the image of the car keys, Lupino focuses the camera once again on an important object, this one seeming to rebel against a traditional "vehicle" for escape and fulfillment. Barney's mobility has run its course. Mary's, however, will take place in her mind and imagination, since conventional spaces—from the city to the lakeside—fail to sustain individuals, especially women.

"No. 5 Checked Out" is an intriguing entry into television for Lupino, and the analysis of this episode is an apt transition to our discussion of Lupino's rich and generically varied career directing television.[4] Throughout, as we will see, Lupino continued to meld a tough noir vision with an empathic passion for outsider figures and their particular troubles with gender.

Ida Lupino, Television Director

Lupino's work as writer, director, producer, and actor for television from the 1950s through the 1970s was stunning for the time, given the few women inhabiting roles behind the scenes. The television industry has traditionally been more accepting of women than the film industry because it is less hierarchically organized. Women have found positions there more easily than in mainstream Hollywood film, where the director is still seen as a masculine controlling agent. Even so, Lupino's contributions to the industry tell an important feminist story in American media history. Until 1989, Lupino held the record for having directed more episodes than any other woman working in television. Her television directing, we argue, is worth analysis—not just because of her unique status as a woman who stood behind as well as in front of the camera, but also because the episodes she directed reflect her lifelong artistic themes. Mary Celeste Kearney and James Moran's description of Lupino's "scattered work in television" (139) does not do justice to her overall output, which echoes her attraction to stories about bewildered people; her analysis of the confusion and frustration accompanying conventional gender and social roles; her critique of institutional power set against individual agency; her stylistic debt to film noir; and her sense of humor and irony often expressed through the mise-en-scène. It is worth noting that if, as Jeremy Butler suggests, "irony . . . has not found extensive application in television studies" (*Television Style* 24n53), Lupino's work may be particularly fitting for just such an analysis.

Drawing on the work of Horace Newcomb and Robert S. Alley, Kearney and Moran write that the "figure of Lupino as a 'female Hitch,' whose nomenclature suggests the freedom and status of an auteur, is misleading within the context of a television industry whose creative efforts are shaped and controlled almost exclusively by producers rather than by directors" (138). In fact, Alfred Hitchcock himself dubbed Lupino "the female Hitch" for her action and suspense episodes on television.[5] At least anecdotally, this contradicts the idea that the only auteur in television is the producer or writer. In any case, several points need to be made here concerning Lupino's influence on the television episodes she directed.

Multiple industrial practices contribute to a television program. Generally speaking, "there is no single 'authorial' identity for the television communicator" (Fiske and Hartley 62), and "TV programs are the result of behind-the-scenes negotiations in a collaborative work environment" (Butler, *Television: Critical Methods* 370). To the extent that authorial presence has been ascribed to television, this identity has always been reserved for the scriptwriter and producer (or, in today's terms, the showrunner). However, even though television has always been collaborative, there have also been directors such as Lupino who, given their influence on actors and scripts as well as their directorial choices during production, have had a decided impact on television episodes. Lupino's work with material that interested her and with actors with whom she had an affinity allowed her to establish a tone in her television episodes that is especially noteworthy because producers recognized that tone and her abilities—and hired her because of them. Her work ethic, too, complemented the rigors of television production schedules. In the discussion below of the episodes Lupino directed, we see a theme of female power and thwarted desire; how women function in male-defined spaces; and dysfunctional family relationships. Even when Lupino didn't write the scripts, she was hired to direct certain episodes because her thematic interests were well known. As Norman MacDonnell, producer of *Gunsmoke*, said, "You used Ida when you had a story about a woman with some dimension, and you really wanted it hard hitting" (qtd. in Anderson, *Beyond the Camera* 111).

Despite the commonplace that directors have minimal influence on television programs, Lupino was not just a hired hand. William Donati, for example, recounts Hitchcock asking Lupino to play the lead female character in the "Sybilla" episode (1960) of *Alfred Hitchcock Presents*. Lupino didn't want the acting part, for which she would have been paid $5,000, and instead asked if she could direct the episode, for which she was paid $1,250 (227). This choice reflects Lupino's desire to make creative contributions behind the scenes, a decision borne out in this very episode, as we discuss below. In the *Hollywood Reporter* in 1972, Lupino said that she frequently turned down "special guest star" appearances on television because in those roles "you don't create anything" ("Coast to Coast"). But Lupino did contribute substantively to many television shows. These include not just quality anthology dramas, such as *Screen Directors Playhouse* ("No. 5 Checked Out") and *General Electric Theater* ("A Very Special Girl," 1962), and telefilms such as *Thriller* (1960–1962), but also half-hour comedy, drama, action, and western series. In 1966, for example, Lupino directed an episode of *Honey West*, the first television show to feature a female detective lead, played by Anne Francis.

Even Lupino's acting became part of her authorship in television, because it was sometimes linked to scripts she herself wrote (as in "The

Stand-In," or another episode of *Four Star Playhouse* in which she plays a desperate convalescent, "The Case of Emily Cameron"), and because of her creative agency as the producer of shows in which she acted. Indeed, one context that informs our sense of Lupino's creative force in television is her presence in the making of *Mr. Adams and Eve* (1957–58), the CBS series in which she starred with then-husband Howard Duff. As co-producer and actress with power in all aspects of the film industry, Lupino commanded a respect that translated into considerable influence on and off the set. In an article in *Box Office* in 1975, Lupino recalls having had "complete autonomy" during the show's run. "It was such a lovely thing. We changed dialogue, ad-libbed lines to bridge scenes" ("As Film Star, Director, Composer" 2).

On Close Readings of 1950s and 1960s Television

Looking closely at elements of the episodes directed by Lupino provides an opportunity to analyze classic television for its depth, an underexplored area in television studies. It also highlights Lupino's versatility and vision. Given our emphasis on the visual style of these episodes, we are mindful that, especially before the 1980s, television was seen as "textually anaemic" (Jacobs 434, qtd. in Butler, *Television Style* 16),[6] offering "zero-degree style."[7] However, our focus on Lupino's stylistic and thematic orientation in television is informed by several contexts, including the links we observe between her television and film work. The bias against classic television aesthetics—its "mediocre legibility," according to André Bazin—is subject to change when scholars resituate these television programs in contexts that enrich our understanding of the episodes' "hailing."[8] No text is inherently uninteresting or unavailable for critical, including feminist, intervention; the scholar or critic will dig into this material with a sensitivity for established theoretical insights (the limits of classical notions of auteurism, for example) and the prominence of distinct industrial practices, such as television's collective authorship. Finally, as Sarah Cardwell observes, scholars, readers, and viewers might value more the *act* of engaging television and their sense that these popular objects of study—even shows considered least likely to engage critical thinking, like *Gilligan's Island* (see Metz) and *Charlie's Angels*—have merit in and of themselves in a given context.[9]

As the above analysis of "No. 5 Checked Out" suggests, we approach Lupino's television work with an assumption that close readings of these shows have much to tell us not only about Lupino's talent and art but also about the richness and relevance of television content from this era. While the conventional reading of classic television of the 1950s and 1960s eschews close reading in favor of analyzing the historical industrial contexts that informed the development of the medium, we believe that this important contextual material can be supplemented by addressing the specific content of television episodes. Several years ago, Todd VanDerWerff made the interesting point that the critical habit of reading 1960s television as a cultural wilderness is misguided: "The dirty little secret here is that essentially every decade except the 1960s has been proclaimed the 'golden age of TV' at one time or another" (qtd. in Klein and Palmer 10). VanDerWerff also maintains in this article, aptly titled "The Golden Age of TV is Dead; Long Live the Golden Age of TV," that "the '60s are often seen as a phantom zone for good TV, though this idea is inaccurate. (It's largely driven by the fact that the 'vast wasteland' quote originates in that decade, and it was the first decade [in which] the true cultural significance of television became apparent, for good and ill.)" Television from this era should be looked at not only in terms of American social history, but also for its art. Included in that art are directorial choices having to do with framing, camera angles, and collaboration with actors and actresses, but also other ways in which meaning is brought to bear on television content. Jason Mittell's comments about evaluating television more generally resonate in the context of Lupino's multiple, varied, and unique roles in the television industry in the 1950s and 1960s: "What I think evaluation does more broadly . . . is to present an argument in order to open a conversation. Making an evaluative claim is not necessarily designed to construct a canon to exclude other possibilities, but rather to posit a contingent perspective on why something matters, both to me and presumably to other viewers who similarly embrace it. It is neither a statement of fact nor a proof, but an invitation to dialogue and debate" (Jacobs and Peacock 55). For example, episodes of this period commented on earlier films, adapting their content through patterns of visual style, theme, and character. In Lupino's case, this is well illustrated by her serial appearances as a version of Norma Desmond, the role played by Gloria Swanson in *Sunset Blvd.*

(Billy Wilder, 1950), which we explore below. Similarly, closely reading classic television reveals intertextualities that illuminate the art of television. These are displayed repeatedly in Lupino's work in television, seen below in images from episodes she directed that are placed alongside shots from films, or discussed in connection with cinema.

The packaging of classic television into DVD boxed sets, as well as the massive presence of shows from this era on cable television and the web, especially on YouTube, has transformed these episodes from disposable media products into often intriguing texts in archives of cultural history. Add to this hyper-availability of classic television the technology we now have to capture images and sequences for analysis and comparison, and a relatively new field for exploration opens up for critics and scholars. Indeed, closely reading classic television series allows us to see clearly the intertextual commentary and cultural critique that formed part of the backbone, as well as delight, of these series. For instance, Lupino and Howard Duff's *Mr. Adams and Eve* was a rejoinder to *I Love Lucy*, criticizing Hollywood and satirizing the domesticity ultimately valorized in comedies such as Ball and Arnaz's show. With its playful and sometimes cutting ironies, Lupino and Duff's sitcom "was the dark side of *I Love Lucy* and at the same time, self-parody" (Rickey 45).

Textual analysis of these episodes also enhances our ability to show how Lupino's thematic preoccupations were brought from film to the small screen. In Part Two, we demonstrated the versatility and fluidity of her genre work in film; Lupino found in television another arena in which to display her formidable power working with hybrid genres, since hybridity defined (and still defines) television shows. Images from *The Untouchables* or *Thriller*, for example (see below), resonate strongly with Lupino's films. These relationships and intertextualities are found in the mise-en-scène, as well as the cultural context. Television, cultural, and media studies would benefit greatly from analyzing individual shows and episodes for their rich interrelationships.

"The Return": Norma Desmond and Ida Lupino Haunt the Small Screen

Throughout her television career, Lupino performed several versions of *Sunset Blvd.*'s Norma Desmond that explored dimensions of the aging female star. Our heading here refers, of course, to Norma's insistence on the term "return" rather than "comeback" ("I hate that word!" Norma says about the latter). The echoes of Norma Desmond in Lupino's acting roles for television constitute a fascinating exposé of the exploitative workings of Hollywood. Our analysis of "Ida and Norma" also complements the portrait of female ingenuity and industry that characterizes Lupino's career as a whole. The expressive force of her television acting was tied to one of the broad themes she explored in her Filmakers' films—the failure of social institutions to support individual happiness, this time for aging women. Many of Lupino's television episodes find Hollywood to be one of these institutions, itself "a vast wasteland," to appropriate from Newton Minow's hallmark speech about television in 1961. In many ways, however, Lupino's work in television in the 1950s and 1960s gainsays Minow's comment.

One of the most dynamic characters in film history, Norma Desmond is a ghost inhabiting Lupino's repeated television portrayals of actresses; she functions as a force to criticize institutional, cultural, and filmic conventions defining women's social constrictions. Desmond's visitations in several Lupino roles obviously remind audiences of Billy Wilder's 1950 satire of Hollywood as opportunistic and exploitative. But these connections also reveal Lupino's own role in analyzing Hollywood's industrial practices. Her gender and age may have increasingly become factors Lupino could not transcend in a hostile and always challenging professional environment. She found ways to adapt to this environment, however, without losing her integrity or her acute critical eye. This flexibility is one of her hallmarks.

We give below several examples of Lupino's self-conscious references to gender, celebrity, female role-playing, and resilience in her television work that help frame her unique contributions. In 1956 Lupino wrote a story that was adapted for the small screen—it turned out to be the last episode of *Four Star Playhouse* in which she appeared (and the penultimate episode of the series)—in an episode titled "The Stand-In" (aired 19 July 1956). Lupino plays Grace Markham, a stand-in and body double for actress Marion Clayton (Virginia Field). In its voiceover narration, "The Stand-In" introduces the idea of Hollywood objectification: "A stand-in is a human prop. To be tested and measured for light and shade. Until the star steps in and the camera turns." Grace yearns to be the star. As if Grace's existence as a "human prop" were not enough to incite her

FIGURE 39 Lupino (back row, center) among the men, screening *Hard, Fast and Beautiful* (Bettmann/Getty Images)

ire, Marion Clayton receives word that her newest role will be in a film whose title symbolically refers to Grace, "The Rage of a Woman." In the production, Marion tells her envious stand-in, she will enjoy "three leading men, twenty-two changes of wardrobe, and a chance to do some *real* acting!" Marion recognizes Grace's longing, however, and arranges a screen test for her. The test does not go well. In a scene that recalls a photo of Lupino sitting in the screening room with her *Hard, Fast and Beautiful* colleagues five years earlier, Grace sits behind the male producers, who ignore her presence in the theater as well as on the screen.

Figures 39 and 40 reflect an abiding motif in Lupino's work: rooms full of men in which a woman observes or sits among them. We see this motif, too, in *Outrage*, in the shots in which Ann has to endure sitting in front of the lineup at the police station to try to identify her rapist, or later, after she assaults Frank Marini, at her hearing, facing the judge and flanked by other men. This mise-en-scène, of course, articulates aspects of Lupino's experience as a woman working in an industry dominated by men. In "The Stand-In," if Grace silently and helplessly observes men with power judging her acting, Lupino's own observations of men working behind the scenes were active, reaping significant rewards. When she was on suspension from

Warners, for instance, she availed herself of the opportunity to learn from camera operators. She visited sets and studied directing and camera work: "I used to go and sit on the set when I was on suspension—which was a great deal of the time. . . . I used to ask if I could sit in the cutting room and I'd see how a film was put together. And by God, you learn . . . you learn why a director asked you to do such and such" ("As Film Star, Director, Composer"). As the last part of this quote suggests, she also gained a deep understanding of how directors and actors collaborate. She developed a gift for working with her actors in film and television that the actors repeatedly noted. In "The Stand-In," unlike Lupino's active observation of how she learned to direct, Grace's passivity ultimately leads her to become bitter.

FIGURE 40 *Four Star Playhouse*, "The Stand-In" (aired 19 July 1956): Grace Markham (Lupino) failing to distinguish herself in a screen test

The story shifts: Grace had desperately desired, like Norma Desmond, to be in front of the camera; now she tries to sabotage Marion's career. Marion does indeed fall from Grace, who comes to despise her. That hatred fuels her energy, and she becomes perversely active as the agent of Marion's destruction. Grace plies Marion with alcohol and preys on the actress's insecurities. Over time, Marion grows despondent, depressed about her appearance and age, as the episode evokes scenes from *Sunset Blvd.* in which Norma Desmond obsesses over her appearance and her "return" to her millions of fans. Like Norma, Marion wears dark sunglasses, although, as she says, "I don't wear these glasses against the sun. I wear them against the years."

The mirror itself becomes a character in the episode, a "stand-in" for the cinema screen, which constructs an inflexible star image as the

FIGURE 41 "We had faces [then]!": Top, aging actresses Norma Desmond (Gloria Swanson, *Sunset Blvd.*), and bottom, Marion Clayton

only identity offered Norma and Marion. Referring to the static image of the female star, Marion bemoans her fate as a failed, washed-up actress: "Nobody ever leaves this town." She describes another has-been, an actress she knows driving around to all the "old places," then returning home at 4 A M to "[run] her old pictures." In *Sunset Blvd.*, Norma shows Joe Gillis *Queen Kelly*, a 1929 silent film starring Gloria Swanson that was directed by Erich von Stroheim (who in *Sunset Blvd.* plays Norma's butler, Max von Mayerling).

At the end of "The Stand-In," after Grace tells Marion how much she hates her, Marion flees, desperate and drunk, killing herself in a car accident. Marion has just starred in a kind of comeback film, a "return," in Norma's words, and posthumously wins an award for her performance, which Grace accepts on her behalf. Like the fleeting moments of glory Norma experiences—her old colleagues gathered around her at Paramount in famed producer and director Cecil B. DeMille's studio, her final deluded speech of appreciation at the end of the film—Grace's thrilled acceptance of the award (proving, Lupino's script ironically makes clear, that she is indeed a fine actress) recalls another betrayer, Eve (Anne Baxter), in *All About Eve* (like *Sunset Blvd.*, released in 1950), whose fawning acceptance of an award consummates her triumph at disposing of the older actress Margo Channing (Bette Davis). The final scene of "The Stand-In," however, discloses that Grace's destiny is to remain the irrelevant amanuensis of a dead star. She continues to write autographs for Marion, as we see her current desolation expressed through the framed photograph of her one moment of glory, accepting Marion's award.

Lupino's story recapitulates a number of themes we find throughout her writing, producing, and directing work, as well as those stories she appeared in: cultural fixations with the image of female celebrity (a theme that preoccupied Lupino from her earliest years as a contract player in Hollywood) and a postmodern blurring of image and reality; the isolation and grief of modern American men and women trying to find happiness in claustrophobic domestic spaces or labyrinthine industrial settings; and an ironic view of the futility of individual striving in a cultural landscape constructed on the basis of a mythic American Dream.

In 1959, Lupino starred in "The Sixteen-Millimeter Shrine," an episode of the science-fiction classic series *The Twilight Zone*, as secluded former movie star Barbara Jean Trenton. Like Norma Desmond, Barbara Jean is obsessed with her former celluloid self. The dense metaphors (as well as the wonderful purple prose) in Rod Serling's opening voiceover are a fitting blend of noir and melodrama: "Picture of a woman looking at a picture. Movie great of another time. Once brilliant star in a firmament no longer a part of the sky. Eclipsed by the movement of earth and time. Barbara Jean Trenton, whose world is a projection room, whose dreams are made out of celluloid. Barbara Jean Trenton, struck down by hit-and-run years and lying on the unhappy pavement, trying desperately to get the license number of fleeting fame." Moving pictures, and Barbara Jean's expulsion from them, have forced the collapse of "moving" dynamic lives. Barbara Jean cannot comprehend change. She is surely thinking of Marlon Brando and James Dean when, later in the episode, she complains about this shifting culture, "actors in undershirts, rock and roll, juke boxes." The light of youth and projected dreams has been overtaken by shadow nightmares, and a sunny Hollywood story of a "movie great" has been "eclipsed" by her own darkening years. The voiceover ends with a reference to a "hit-and-run" wreck of a career, presented as an ironic noir mirror of the "fleeting" fame that long ago preceded it.

Like Norma's mad and wistful call to the "stars [that] are ageless," Barbara Jean's fantasy (soon to be fantastical) relation to her image on the screen is a desperate bid to resume center stage. "The Sixteen-Millimeter Shrine" is the "hideous progeny" of *Sunset Blvd.*, to borrow Julie Grossman's metaphor, deepening our perspective on the grim consequences of living within a celebrity culture.[10] Marsha Orgeron also evokes the idea of the monster, connecting Lupino's self-image to Mary Shelley by way of Emmett Myers in *The Hitch-Hiker*: "Deformed at birth and rejected by his parents, Myers—like Victor Frankenstein's creature—realizes that the only thing that he can create effectively is destruction" (202). Orgeron writes that Lupino saw her own power in the film and television industries as "monstrous." While we do not fully agree with Orgeron's statement that Lupino's work "perpetuate[s] the conflicted and self-punitive role Lupino [herself] consistently dramatized" (179), her observation about gothic horror and monstrous women is apt when considered in terms of Lupino's presence in narratives about Hollywood. She refers to *Whatever Happened to Baby Jane?* and *The Big Knife*, for which director Robert Aldrich "often cast the industry in a gothic light that seems in some ways to mirror Lupino's aversion" (176). "The Sixteen-Millimeter Shrine" once again presents a Hollywood setting as a haunted space. Its music, as in *Sunset Blvd.*, was composed by Franz Waxman. The episode adapts, for the small screen, Billy Wilder's noir perspective on the American Dream, exposing the dark side of celebrity culture.

In *Sunset Blvd.*, Norma visits the Paramount lot to try to reconnect with DeMille (playing himself), but the reunion is based on her misapprehension that he has fallen in love with a script she sent him when in fact his associates want to use her car, a relic from the past, in a new period piece. Like the car, Norma herself is an object of curiosity, a magnet for older actors on the set for a brief moment until DeMille calls to his lighting engineer, "Turn the light back where it belongs." In "The Sixteen-Millimeter Shrine," Barbara Jean's visit with studio executive Marty Saul lacks the tone of patriarchal sentimentality lent to *Sunset Blvd.*'s scenes by DeMille. Saul is a brute, a "petty little man," Barbara Jean's friend Danny (Martin Balsam) reassures her, with a "mean temper and a dirty mouth." Saul had wanted Barbara Jean to play a bit part in a new movie. When offered the role of a "fortyish," "vibrant" mother, who is "very much alive," she retorts, "As opposed to what, a corpse? I don't play mothers, Mr. Saul. I never have and I won't start now."

Barbara Jean's refusal to play a mother serves as a foil to Lupino's longtime directing persona, "Mother." In stark contrast to being cast in this episode (as Norma was in *Sunset Blvd.*) as an "aging broad with a scrapbook" ("Sixteen-Millimeter Shrine"), Lupino adopted "Mother" as a dynamic, if somewhat circumscribed, role, a creative figure in the entertainment and arts industries. The role of "Mother" was a means of translating her leadership in the industry and on the set into terms acceptable to her younger colleagues. But it was also a way of altering the terms of her presence in the industry to combat the "misogyny always at the edge of things," as director Miranda July recently described, assumptions about women and Hollywood that obviously still exist today: "It's certainly tied to how women can't get older. There's a very short time span when a woman can get into the world of power and be a delightful treat" (qtd. in Dowd).

In "The Sixteen-Millimeter Shrine," Barbara Jean (like Grace Markham in "The Stand-In") lacks Lupino's adaptability. Like Norma Desmond, she must escape into a world of illusion in which she continues to be "a delightful treat." Insisting that Max Saul and the Hollywood that had given her "the brush," as DeMille says, are irrelevant, Barbara Jean wills herself into a dream state in which "[Marty Saul] doesn't exist. That studio doesn't exist. . . . From now on I keep the drapes drawn and doors locked. I don't want any of the outside world coming in. Not the Marty Sauls and the movies without sentiment, actors in undershirts, rock and roll, juke boxes, not any of it." Rejecting the dynamic *real*, Barbara Jean wishes her self, literally, out of existence. Like Joe Gillis, who only comes to terms with the world that has rejected him when he has been transformed into a disembodied poetic voice, Barbara Jean "dies," or disappears, into the cinema. The camera tracks in to a close-up: "It doesn't have to exist if I shut my eyes. If I shut my eyes it all disappears. If I wish hard enough, I can wish it all away."

In "The Sixteen-Millimeter Shrine," Danny shouts to Barbara Jean, "You keep wishing for things that are dead!" Indeed, the *Twilight Zone* episode conceives of life after being in the Hollywood spotlight as death-in-life. In *Sunset Blvd.*, Joe is already dead when he tells us Norma's story. Norma mourns a dead chimp and the loss of an earlier life and spectacle in which she was the star. Like Norma, Barbara Jean escapes in the end into illusion. She is absorbed literally into the screen, phantasmagorically reentering one of her old movies. Mary Desjardins comments on the episode's obsession with specularity: "What is a woman identified with [such] femininity to do when the only gaze desiring her is her own?" (80). In Hollywood and a youth-oriented celebrity culture,

FIGURE 42 Another aging actress, Barbara Jean Trenton (Lupino), in "The Sixteen-Millimeter Shrine" (*The Twilight Zone*, aired 23 October 1959)

the only way to achieve agency for a woman is through gothic imagination.[11] As Desjardins notes, Barbara Jean checks out of a reality that suffocates her, which indeed constitutes a kind of fantasy power that counters her despair as a faded female star. Further, the willful rejection of the real terms of her existence echoes "No. 5 Checked Out," in which Mary's deafness similarly symbolizes a woman insisting on her own terms of existence, despite the oppressive and masculine "noise" around her. Finally, in "The Sixteen-Millimeter Shrine," the quality of Barbara Jean's seemingly self-conscious gaze from the cinematic space at her friend Danny in the real world (figure 42) is a benevolent expression of contentment, a surreal joy that contrasts with Norma's madness.

Another of Lupino's striking appearances as the faded female star occurred in 1977 during the first season of that zenith and nadir of feminist popular culture, *Charlie's Angels*.[12] In an episode called "I Will Be Remembered" (aired 9 March 1977), Lupino plays Gloria Gibson, clearly referring to Gloria Swanson as Norma Desmond. In an early scene, Jill Munroe (Farrah Fawcett), Kelly Garrett (Jaclyn Smith), and Sabrina Duncan (Kate Jackson) discuss Gibson's most famous film, *The Sodbusters*, in which "she survived everything." This wry reference to Lupino's resilience is of a piece with the episode's tone of tribute and repeated references to legacy and remembrance, as signaled in the episode's title. Like Norma Desmond, Gloria wants to return to acting, echoing Norma's penultimate lines: "You see, this is my life! It always will be! Nothing else! Just us, the cameras, and those wonderful people out there in the dark."

Amid the aging character's "return"—thwarted in the *Charlie's Angels* episode by thugs trying to gaslight her—Gloria's visit to the studio is a direct quote from the "Jonesy" scene in *Sunset Blvd.* in which Norma enters the gates of Paramount on her "return." The scene raises the idea of legacy, a theme established in Lupino's appearances in other series such as *Columbo*, in which she appears with Johnny Cash in the episode "Swan Song," and on *Batman*, in which she plays the arch-villain

FIGURE 43 Top, Norma Desmond (Gloria Swanson) and Jonesy at the gates of Paramount studios, and bottom, Gloria Gibson (Lupino) in "I Will Be Remembered" (*Charlie's Angels*, aired 9 March 1977)

Dr. Cassandra Spellcraft, with Howard Duff as her sidekick, Cabala.

In "I Will Be Remembered," the scene at the gates of the studio revises the Jonesy episode of *Sunset Blvd.* with a tone of tribute. Here, the security guard says, "Forget about [a] pass, Miss Gibson. If it weren't for you, this studio would still be a bean field. You just go right in." A pointed allusion to Norma's insistence to Jonesy in *Sunset Blvd.*—"If it weren't for me, there wouldn't be any studio"—the television episode recasts Wilder's satiric display of Norma's narcissism as a straightforward tribute. The reference to the studio emerging out of a bean field echoes Gloria's famous role in "The Sodbusters," championed earlier by the Angels. Gloria *is* a "sodbuster," in terms of having helped to create the studio.

Part of the tribute to Gloria (and Lupino), the metaphor highlights her importance and maverick qualities.

At her audition, Gloria Gibson is met by the studio executives and a recalcitrant director, known for his theater work, who wants to cast a stage actress he has worked with before for a part rather than Gloria. Gibson responds to his aloofness by claiming that film acting is a distinguished art; her speech is a corollary to Norma Desmond's own defense of the grand gestures of silent film. About stage acting, Gloria says, "[Stage actors] are playing to the balcony, with big gestures, big voice. There is no balcony in films. We play in whispers, with our eyes. Our inner selves are visible. And with them we overwhelm. We reduce you to your elements. And then we rebuild and return you to yourselves. And our audience is remade. They're exalted and loyal to the stars they love and remember." After these melodramatic lines, *Charlie's Angels'* musical theme swells, and the studio producer concludes, "Your point is well taken, Miss. Gibson." Obviously a nostalgic tribute to Gloria's—and Ida's—legacy as a film actress, her speech contains multi-layered resonance. Gloria has progressed beyond her namesake's character (Norma). "There is no balcony in films," she says, and the intimacy she attributes to film ("we play in whispers") equally applies to television, the medium in which Lupino had thrived for over two decades before her appearance on *Charlie's Angels*. More than a revision of inherited narrative and character patterns, Lupino's re-embodiment of Norma Desmond inspires a conversation about female role-playing, media, and memory. Lupino's adaptations of Norma Desmond invite analysis of the different "faces" of the American actress and how women have been pigeonholed, which Lupino exposed throughout her film and television careers. In these episodes, Lupino's reenactments of Norma Desmond highlight women like Lupino herself.

Moreover, as these episodes meditate on the image of the female actress—reenacting myths in visual culture of women aging out of the spotlight, competing for its attention, and checking out of a social world that offers little room for female agency—they urge us to change our cultural norms, artistic endeavors, and the Hollywood industry. In her acting, directing, producing, and writing, we can see Lupino's abiding belief in the power of moving images to encourage these changes.

Mr. Adams and Eve

From 1957 to 1958, Lupino and Duff starred in the CBS comedy *Mr. Adams and Eve*. The couple was drawn to the project in part because Duff was struggling to find work. After a long, successful series on the radio playing Sam Spade, Duff had limited success finding film roles in the 1950s. Moreover, suspicions regarding his political associations made him vulnerable to an investigation by HUAC. The show was a fortuitous opportunity because Lupino had the cachet to pressure CBS to employ her husband (the studio initially rejected Duff until it was clear that Lupino would only do the show if Duff were given the role).

The idea for the show came, ironically enough, from Lupino's previous husband, Collier Young, with whom she maintained a close, if unconventional, working relationship, a point underscored by her friendship with actress Joan Fontaine (at the time married to Young), who guest-starred on *Mr. Adams and Eve*. The show was produced by a new company Lupino and Duff founded called Bridget Productions, named after their young daughter, under the umbrella company of Four Star Films. Many of the episodes were written by Sol Saks, perhaps most famous in television history for his work on *Bewitched*, another television show featuring a powerful woman.

In her book *It's the Pictures That Got Small*, Christine Becker astutely observes that Lupino's work in TV "mock[ed] the shallowness and pretension of Hollywood" (178). Nowhere does her satire of cultural obsessions with the Hollywood star appear more pointedly than in *Mr. Adams and Eve*. Lupino and Duff play married couple Eve Drake and Howard Adams, extravagant movie stars whose celebrity is underscored, then undercut. The show satirizes the pretensions and hypocrisies of Hollywood actors, and even more the exploitative bottom-line thinking of industry executives. *Mr. Adams and Eve* also explores the massive presence of media in modern life, the extent to which celebrity is a façade designed by trade papers and Hollywood promotion people to cover up and, in some cases, replace a dull reality.

Another striking element of the show is the bold presence of romantic intimacy, seen, for example, in the episode "The Bachelor" (aired 14 June 1957), in which a former crooning beau of Eve's is cast to appear in one of Howard and Eve's films. While the series often features love scenes

FIGURE 44 *Mr. Adams and Eve*: the racy opening credits

between Howard and Eve filmed in close-ups, this episode, comparing Eve's lackluster feelings for her former boyfriend with her desire for Howard, includes blatant sexual metaphors in the script, such as roller coasters and fireworks. Howard and Eve's relationship is steamy (not to mention stormy, as in real life), with "rocket[s] . . . blazing," as the couple embraces. Many episodes refer to the couple's sex life. In "Taken for Granted" (aired 29 March 1957), Howard and Eve reconcile after an argument, with Eve asking seductively, "Sweetheart, I want . . ." and Howard says, "To be taken for granted?"—clearly a euphemism for sex.

The representation of sexual intimacy is seen even in the sly opening of the show, which foregrounds, in animated graphics, Howard and Eve dressing in their bedroom (see figure 44). Howard zips up Eve's dress in front of their full-size bed, an interesting contrast in mise-en-scène to the convention of twin-bed bedroom sets in classic television series. In an interview for the American Film Institute, director/producer Fred De Cordova affirms that *Mr. Adams and Eve* was "the first truly sophisticated comedy on television." One of the most compelling elements of *Mr. Adams and Eve*, however, is its mockery of film and television audiences' confusion of entertainment industry–generated images with real life, exposing the extent to which viewers are in thrall to empty spectacle. For these reasons, those who view episodes on YouTube or see them in archives will find them contemporary and topical.

One episode that exemplifies the show's postmodern stance is "Dear Variety" (aired 17 June 1958). In this episode, Eve picks up a ten-year-old issue of *Variety* that has fallen off a pile of newspapers that Elsie the housekeeper (Olive Carey) is sending to Goodwill. Not noticing the date, Eve panics as she reads the news that "Consolidated" (the studio where she and Howard are under contract) has fallen on hard times. Its head will be fired. To soften the blow for J. B. Hafter, their producer (Alan Reed), a distraught Eve takes out an ad in *Variety* thanking J. B. for his tireless work for the studio ("Goodbye and Good Luck, J. B. Hafter." "A Fine American Human Being," the ad intones, and is signed "The Gang"). Not only does J. B. think he's fired, but Consolidated's board executives in New York are swayed by Eve's ad, mainly because they are so disengaged that they don't know what's going on at the studio. "I guess we must have had a financial report at the last meeting," one board member says. "But that was the day they had the golf tournament at the country club. I played in it. Tell me, what happened at the meeting?" His colleague says, "Well, I wasn't here, you idiot. I'm the one who beat you by four strokes." Trying to cover for themselves, the board members bluster, then come to the conclusion that "Hafter's out."

As Howard, Eve, and their agent Steve (Hayden Rorke) try to imagine life after Consolidated, Steve hopes he can foster new talent. "I've got a kid coming up right now," he says, "that's gonna set this town on fire. He's twenty-three. Handsome, looks like a young Clark Gable, sings, dances, composes music, had two novels published, wrote two plays, one of which is on Broadway right now, and he's a fine actor." Steve goes on to say that this prodigy is not signed yet because he's busy taking a welding course so that he has something "to fall back on." The show's emphasis on the vagaries of Hollywood and the instability of success makes it a comic version of the stories of futility and critique of the American Dream in Lupino's Filmakers' films. When Eve realizes that the trade paper on which her actions were based is ten years old, she is filled with dread and locks herself in a closet. Eventually drawn out by Howard and Steve, she settles on a new plan: she'll place another ad to reshape the perception of Hafter and Consolidated. Her oversized ad in *Variety* reads,

Bless You, J. B. Hafter (The Man Who Saved Us All). Due to quick thinking and progressive production values, J. B. Hafter has rescued Consolidated and will continue to function at full speed, with Uncle Joe at the Helm.

Thank you Thank you Thank you Thank You Thank You Thank you.

The Gang.

Of course, when the New York executives read this ad, they reverse their earlier decision and rehire Hafter, giving him a raise. "Something must have happened with this Hafter situation," the scofflaw board member says. "I went swimming and missed this morning's meeting. Were you here?" His colleague retorts, "Of course not, you idiot. I was the one who gave you artificial respiration." Those in power are incompetent and unduly swayed by a media outlet that obviously doesn't research or verify its stories, and Eve herself, in the end, is so enamored of her own copy and her success in fixing the crisis that she forgets she orchestrated both the problem and its resolution. She warmly compliments Hafter for "pulling Consolidated out of the fire," and when Howard quietly reminds her that Consolidated and Hafter "were never in a fire," she says, "Yes, they were. Didn't you read my ad?" The episode ends with a tribute to another self-referential show of Hollywood's Golden Age, *Burns and Allen*, when Howard says to Eve, "C'mon, Gracie."

The irrelevance of the truth, now that the conflicts have been resolved in a happy ending, satirizes Hollywood's fickleness and preference for pomp over reality. The show stands alongside *Sunset Blvd.* in its critique of fools and exploiters. The New York sequence reminds us of Joe Gillis's agent in Wilder's film, who, while Gillis suffers in Hollywood, is "doing time with the golf clubs," insensitively telling his client that "hunger" is good for his career. *Mr. Adams and Eve* also summons up Preston Sturges's critique of Hollywood pretension in *Sullivan's Travels* (1941). Sturges decries high-minded "message pictures" by celebrating Sullivan's escapist comedies, "Hey, Hey, in the Hayloft" and "Ants in Your Plants of 1939," rather than "O Brother Where Art Thou," a film exposé of Depression-era poverty Sullivan misguidedly wants to make. Sturges's film pokes fun at social problem films such as *The Grapes of Wrath*, as "Dear Variety" does. The Adamses' housekeeper Elsie insists when she is threatened with unemployment as a result of the supposed crisis that she "can cope with adversity. That's a line from *The Grape Crushers*," an early film of Howard and Eve's.

Early on, *Mr. Adams and Eve* had established its intent to deconstruct pretentiousness in Hollywood, easily seen in an episode from Season 1 called "Typical" (aired 11 January 1957). This episode portrays Eve's desire to live life the way normal, average people do. The flamboyant Eve fails miserably in her efforts. The show generally capitalizes on what Becker and Desjardins have discussed as the abiding tension in 1950s television between the glamor of celebrity and the immediacy and intimacy of characters' domestic lives with which

FIGURE 45 Lucy (Lucille Ball) and Ida Lupino playing herself in Lupino and Howard Duff's special appearance on "Lucy's Summer Vacation" (*The Lucy/Desi Comedy Hour*, aired 8 June 1959) (courtesy of the Estate of Ida Lupino)

viewers could identify. In "Typical," the show introduces what will be its predominant preoccupations: first, a satiric exposure of hypocrisy in the film and entertainment industries, a theme that some have argued caused the show to be canceled, despite its excellent reception and reviews; second, a more particular consideration of the idea of authenticity and the instability of "the real." As invested as The Filmakers was in depicting "real" stories about ordinary people, Lupino was also profoundly interested in the themes of performance and role-playing, as her role as the glamorous Eve Drake in *Mr. Adams and Eve* displays.

The episode "Typical" is concerned with who the "real" Adamses are, as Eve and Howard try to affect more "typical" personas than their reputation as glamorous movie stars allows. Howard recalls "the time I mowed the lawn," and Eve tries to bond with a neighbor, complimenting her on her laundry, "And you have such lovely laundry too. Mine is just something I sort of threw together." At the same time, the episode mocks Eve's posturing and the "authentic" suburban community often idealized in domestic comedy, which can be seen in the show's contrast with *I Love Lucy*, whose run ended the year *Mr. Adams and Eve*'s began (though in 1957 it would become *The Lucy/Desi Comedy Hour*, on which Lupino and Duff appeared as guests).[13]

Comparing her show to Ball's, Lupino said, "*Mr. Adams and Eve* was not a domestic comedy like *I Love Lucy*. . . . We had neighbors in our show but we hated them!" (qtd. in Anderson, *Mr. Adams and Eve* 67). In "Typical," just as doing laundry is like an outfit she's "trying on," Eve's very identity is seen as ephemeral. "Is there such a person as Eve Adams?" she asks, looking into the mirror. "Who is that staring at me? Is that a real person, a human being flesh and blood?" The show plays with the idea that television is both real and fictional, an allusion to the attempt of early television to distinguish itself as more real—more typical, more intimate—than its glamorous media relative, film (see Becker and Desjardins). At the same time, *Mr. Adams and Eve* continues a trend Lynn Spigel identifies in early television sitcoms to represent domesticity as theatrical: "Early sitcoms typically depicted the family as a theater troupe rather than as a 'real' family. These situation comedies often reflected back on their own theatricality, self-consciously suggesting that family life itself was nothing but a middle-class social convention in which people acted out certain roles for each other" (10). Some have suggested that the show's satire of the industry was the cause of its demise. In the episode "Suspension" (aired 25 October 1957), the show parodies producers' control over the actors. Lambasting Hollywood's objectification of talent, the show presents J. B. Hafter bragging to Eve and Howard about the new "mechanical brain" he has licensed, which aggregates all of the elements fans believe should be in a script for "a sure-fire box-office hit." Hafter continues, excitedly: "Then, I got my wife's nephew, a clever boy [who] got straight A's in English composition in college, got him to put all the elements together and out came 'The Princess and the Tramp.'" Adam and Eve object to being cast in a film with such a "horrible script," but Hafter maintains that industry concerns calculated "mechanically" rather than according to individuals' artistic judgment should rule: "You got talent," he exhorts Eve and Howard, "and you're both very handsome and pretty, now isn't that enough for you? Why don't you leave the thinking to me and the mechanical brain?" The satire rests in large part on the hypocrisy of Hafter's feigned paternalism, as he cajoles the couple: "I'm like a father to you." Based on examination of the script, Howard Duff calling Hafter "Dad" is ad-libbed: "Dad, go ahead and put us on suspension. Who cares?" ("Suspension").

The reference in the episode to nepotism is meaningful, too. Mary Ann Anderson writes that William Paley, then head of CBS, objected to the show's send-up of Hollywood, his wife Virginia (known as Babe) taking particular offense at the satiric portrayal of J. B. Hafter's wife "Birdie" (*Mr. Adams and Eve* 63). Lupino remembered being called into Paley's office (along with Sol Saks, the show's head writer). Paley demanded that the satire be softened. Lupino believed that Paley sabotaged the show because of his resentment.[14]

Mr. Adams and Eve also exemplifies Spigel's point that household rituals and domestic life are often parodied in 1950s television. Lupino was no beginner at criticizing social norms. To return to "Typical," Howard and Eve understand "typicality" in terms of the domestic (lawn-mowing, laundry, cooking), a realm in which television would play an increasingly large role for the show's audience. But Steve tells her and Howard that there's "nothing average, normal or typical about either of you. You're not even real. Outside of getting out of bed and dressing, there's not another thing you can do for yourselves." Equating the typical with the real, Steve highlights the show's play with the very form of television. As Howard says at the end of the episode, "You know what a great idea is: a television series with you and me playing ourselves. The way we really are." He then dismisses the notion: "Nobody'd ever believe it." In its postmodern insistence on blurring the real and the fictional, the show was far ahead of its time.

Another episode of *Mr. Adams and Eve* centers on Eve, who has been chosen as the subject of an episode of a fictional TV show, "This Is Your Past," a parody of *This Is Your Life*. Howard attempts to keep this a secret from the suspicious Eve, who believes Howard's secret is about his infidelity.[15] The pilot episode for the series, "Academy Award," focuses on Howard's jealousy of Eve after she wins an Academy Award, when they were both nominated. Rubbing salt in Howard's wound, a boy wins the Oscar for which Howard was nominated. The Awards announcer says, "At twelve years of age, Master Gerard is the youngest actor ever to receive this high honor." Eve's award is presented by an offscreen voice that is obviously meant to mimic that of Bette Davis. This play with industry comparisons of Davis with Lupino, "the poor man's Bette Davis," was not in the original shooting script ("Academy Award").

The episode, however, goes beyond in-jokes, setting the show's agenda to satirize marriage and celebrity culture. "Academy Award" pits domestic strife against the glamorous setting of the Oscars. It raises the specter of the successful and independent working woman (Lupino/ Eve). It also introduces the intent of the series to mock Hollywood pretension, as Eve's win goes to her head and she brags about the importance of "her public" and begins to "direct" Howard in every one of his actions, on and off the set. Howard retaliates by inviting a bus-load of tourists on a "Tour of the Stars' Homes" into the Adamses' domicile to greet a disheveled Eve, who quickly pretends to be the maid. One tourist asks permission to witness Howard eating his lunch: "Do you mind if we watch? We've never seen a movie star eat before. We're from Duluth."

The show's play with fiction and reality includes, in this episode, Hollywood columnist Sheilah Graham appearing as herself. Graham senses trouble between Howard and Eve after the awards ceremony, announcing that "an actor's disease called Oscar poisoning is about to set in." The episode also features a television interview with a news commentator modeled on Edward R. Murrow. Amidst fighting, Eve and Howard have to pretend to be "one of Hollywood's happiest married couples," as Ned Darrow (Joseph Kearns) introduces them on his television show. In a jab at the peace and happiness ostensibly offered by marriage and the false view of celebrity private life promulgated by the media, including Murrow's interview show *Person to Person* (1953–1961), Darrow says of Howard and Eve that "these two talented and glamorous people are proof indeed that marriage is here to stay in the fickle film capital." After the couple's barely veiled verbal sparring, the broadcast concludes with a reference to both Murrow's customary sign-off and Howard and Eve's marriage when Darrow says, "Good night [pause] and good luck!"

Eve surpasses her husband's success in "Academy Award," which also refers to female overreaching and presumption introduced in the show's title. Eve resembles Lucy, in sunglasses and scarf (figure 46), which contrasts Eve's success in show business with Lucy's repeated failed attempts to succeed, only to be admonished (even spanked) by Ricky for her misbehavior.

On a serious note, the show uncovers the trap in which Lupino herself was caught. As a woman with a long and successful career in an objectifying celebrity culture, who had tried to conform to prevailing gender standards in her personal life, she attempted to assuage Duff's anxiety about being cast as "Mr. Lupino." At the same time, in her art, Lupino actively exposes the hollowness of those standards.[16] This dynamic helps to explain the sexist posturing she undertook at times. Partly parodic, that performance is part of a powerful strain in the history of women in media, in which female pioneers feign submissiveness so as not to threaten the men they live and work with. Women have had difficulty in high-profile leadership positions because their professional and personal well-being depends on complicated psychosocial nego-

tiations with gender roles. As an example of the gender pretense in which women of classic television engaged, Christine Becker quotes variety show "femcee" Dinah Shore, who said in 1957, the year *Mr. Adams and Eve* premiered, "I select guest stars for my show who are so strongly masculine that I can't possibly overshadow them" (Becker 76). This calls to mind Lupino's comment in 1966 about her experience directing: "At times, I pretended to a cameraman to know less than I do. That way I got more cooperation." In 1958, during *Mr. Adams and Eve*'s run, *Family Circle* ran a sentimental story about Lupino-Duff's "domestic Garden of Eden," in which we again see her playing the role of the submissive, happy wife. Later, Lupino claimed

FIGURE 46 *Mr. Adams and Eve*: shots from the pilot, "Academy Award" (aired 22 March 1957)

to have stayed in her difficult marriage with Duff because the couple was "Mr. Adams and Eve," and the public wanted it that way.[17]

The most remarkable episode of *Mr. Adams and Eve* illuminates Lupino's persona as a highly competent and talented working woman in the media. The uncanny episode "Howard and Eve and Ida" (aired 22 April 1958) makes use of split-screen editing to question the relationships between performance and female identity. Lupino guest-stars as herself, a director whose no-nonsense style irks actress Eve, who is also perturbed that Howard used to date "that awful woman," as Eve calls Ida. Eve's anxiety about Lupino stems not only from jealousy regarding Lupino's relationship with Howard, but a history of having been mistaken for her when she first arrived in Hollywood: "It took me two and a half years to get a halfway decent role just because everybody said I looked like her. And you know how difficult it is to get a start in this business without having people accusing you of imitating somebody else. Do you know what they used to call me? The road company Ida Lupino!" Clearly, Lupino refers here to the absurdity of Hollywood's female image-cloning. But Eve is also incensed by the label, just as Lupino herself bristled at being called "the poor man's Bette Davis," a victim of Hollywood's machinery of female star objectification.[18] "The road-company Ida Lupino" is even lower on the hierarchy of female stardom. This scene in *Mr. Adams and Eve* offers a postmodern reflection on and critique of the idea of women as reproducible, and images of woman as simulacra to be passively consumed. Lupino's radical agency and energy contrasts with Hollywood's consumption of the female image. Lupino the director in this episode is characterized as a superbly competent artist and filmmaker, full of integrity. J. B. Hafter is happy with Lupino's choice to slim down production costs by editing out a bubble bath scene she sees as superfluous, even though glamorous Eve exclaims that this is "her best scene." The portrait of Lupino reveals Hafter's hypocrisy, but also refers to Lupino's *actual* reputation in Hollywood as a working professional artist. Hafter is seen as a Hollywood opportunist, sycophantically complimenting Lupino on her practicality and efficiency (as long as it saves him money): "That's what I like about you, Ida. You always take the practical approach. You're a very smart girl, you're artistic, but by gosh you've got a business head on your shoulders." When Hafter discovers that he can borrow a set without paying for it, he insists that the bubble bath scene be restored, but Lupino contends that a bubble bath scene makes no sense in a "hard-hitting story about the waterfront." Her comment obviously links Lupino with realist Elia Kazan, who directed the "hard-hitting" *On the Waterfront* in 1954. Lupino's persona also contrasts with Lucy Ricardo as she continually interferes in Ricky's work life in *I Love Lucy*. While Lucy's slapstick high-jinx may disrupt the status quo temporarily in carnivalesque fashion, Lupino's competence disrupts the status quo without sending her back to the kitchen.[19] It is worth adding, as another instance of how Lupino went against the grain, that *Mr. Adams and Eve* began its run in 1957, the year in which, as Christine Becker recounts, "most of the 'unruly women' were off the air" (166)—referring to shows featuring strong women such as Ann Sothern, Eve Arden, Loretta Young, and especially Faye Emerson, whose case study in Becker's book is especially intriguing. Becker also observes that this is the year Lucy Ricardo moved to the suburbs.

"Howard and Eve and Ida" includes a framing device in which Howard says at the beginning, "I've got a little problem. You see, there are two women in my life. A little problem!" Howard points to Eve and Ida, saying, "Confusing, isn't it? Stick around and see how it comes out. Personally, I'm scared stiff." Casting Lupino's doubled "face" as frightening, the episode speaks to Lupino's power as a multifaceted artist. But the episode also satirizes Lupino's positive star persona, as Eve worries throughout about Lupino's power and authenticity and admits to having "an inferiority complex about that woman ever since I first came to Hollywood." Eve complains to her agent Steve, "Why shouldn't [Howard] be in love with her?" and "Why should he be in love with me when he can have the real thing? I'm just a carbon copy, you know." Keying Lupino's power to her authenticity, the episode makes fun of the fetishization of "the real Lupino"—acutely aware of the hollowness and yet the necessity of role-playing in Hollywood—while at the same time celebrating her material accomplishments, as well as "the credibility of television as a place that *did* make room for the maverick spirit of Ida Lupino" (Becker 183). At the beginning of the episode, Howard and Eve wrack their brains trying to remember the name of someone they could hire to replace their director, Max. This person's film, they recall, was "suspenseful, fast-moving, and the direction was terrific. . . . [The name of the film] is on the tip of my tongue," Howard continues. "I can't remember

FIGURE 47 *Mr. Adams and Eve*: Eve (Lupino) and Joan Fontaine, playing herself in "The Joan Fontaine Story" (aired 18 October 1957) (Courtesy of the Estate of Ida Lupino)

who directed. It's someone we all know!" Eve eventually blurts out *"The Hitch-Hiker!* That's the name of it! And it was directed by Ida Lupino!" Later in the episode, as Lupino demonstrates her skill on the set, asking technicians to take her up on the crane for filming, Eve lashes out, "Is it a bird? Is it a plane? It's superwoman!" If Lupino had been a little older in 1925, she surely would have seen an issue of *Motion Picture Magazine* with an article called, "Why Are There No Women Directors?"[20] The piece concludes, "The strain of picture production usually wears out the strongest man in a few years. . . . It would have to be a superwoman to stand up under the strain" (qtd. in Orgeron 172–73). In the episode "Howard and Eve and Ida," Lupino's double role pits glamor against efficiency and industriousness, dismantling the stereotypical binary opposition of female histrionics and masculine professionalism and showing that glamor and professionalism are qualities that belong to one woman.[21] "Howard and Eve and Ida" gives us again the hallmark of Lupino's persona: the flexibility and adaptability she valued as part of her work ethic and a theme she continually pursued in the films and television work she produced, wrote, and directed.

In another episode of *Mr. Adams and Eve*, "The Joan Fontaine Story," actress Joan Fontaine plays herself, inciting Eve's jealousy and insecurities when her mother, Connie—also Lupino's mother's name—admits that Fontaine is her favorite actress, hurting Eve's feelings and insulting her pride (see figure 47). The fact that Joan Fontaine was at the time married to Collier Young adds to the irony here.

In the "Howard and Eve and Ida" episode, Fontaine's photo appears in the studio head's office, a sly reference to her marriage to Young, who created the series. Young married Fontaine while he and Lupino maintained their business partnership in The Filmakers, and Fontaine appeared with Lupino as Harry Graham's first wife in *The Bigamist* in 1953. In directing and co-starring in the film, Lupino undermined the "normal" configuration of social roles. In *The Bigamist*, Harry's desire for two women violates social codes; his desire is also the direct result of his gender confusion, married to a successful businesswoman (who, we must note, is also named Eve). This autobiographically intertextual hall of mirrors represents Lupino's insight that the idea of the couple married for life is nothing more than an inflexible convention forced upon a real set of complex relationships. But *Mr. Adams and Eve* turned the straightforward serious drama of *The Bigamist* into a satiric sitcom.

Throughout her career, Lupino's performance of images of the female star is a critique of the objectification of the Hollywood actress, continually evoking the inflexibility of those images—in the view of the movie industry, the star system, and the public. This rigidity, internalized by the tragic Norma Desmond, is what traps and later destroys her.

Directed Episodes, 1956–1968

In television as in film, Lupino's directing was exceptional for its use of camerawork and mise-en-scène to mix genre traits and tell stories about gender and modern society. As Lupino made her transition to television, she brought a critique of gender and social roles into her work for the small screen with a sharply honed technical acumen developed during her years as a filmmaker. Known in television as a "creative tactician on the set" (*Making Waves* 166), Lupino applied her virtuosity with the camera, as well as with lighting, shot composition, and scene transitions, in much of her television work, which, like her films, often concerned outsiders facing the trauma of their marginal status. Lupino's mise-en-scène reflects the gendered nature of such alienation and exclusion.

While Lupino did not write the scripts for most of the episodes she directed, her transgressive creative spirit can be seen throughout this work. In a general sense, it is evident how Lupino used genre, extending its conventional borders, to tell stories about gender, society, and a changing modern world. If Lupino mocks Hollywood, she also stretches the genres established by Hollywood in her television work. Her comedy episodes deal with gender and marriage, and while their stories drop the traumas found in Lupino's social problem films, they give an unsentimental view of the prospects of happiness for men and women at the margins—this tone exemplifies Lupino's "bitter wisdom," to quote Carrie Rickey (43), concerning modern America and failed social institutions.

The oppressiveness of gender roles can more easily be seen in the drama, action, and thriller episodes Lupino directed (in *Mr. Novak, Alfred Hitchcock Presents, The Untouchables*, and *Thriller*, for example), and in her work with the television western, which becomes, in Lupino's hands, about women's stories, just as her noir films told stories about female experience. Revising the standard reading of film noir and the western as masculine genres, Lupino drew out the women's stories in the television shows she directed, even while acceding to industrial demands controlled by men.

Before moving on to Lupino's distinctive genre work in television, we discuss some of the dramatic work Lupino did for the small screen, which, like "No. 5 Checked Out," bridges Lupino's film work behind the scenes with her TV directing. After directing *Screen Directors Playhouse* in 1956, Lupino directed an episode of Joseph Cotten's anthology drama *On Trial* (produced by Collier Young). "The Trial of Mary Surratt" aired on 2 November 1956 and featured Virginia Gregg as Surratt, one of the alleged conspirators in the assassination of Abraham Lincoln. The script concerns issues of justice and victimization, centering on the rush to judge Surratt guilty. While the question of Surratt's role in the assassination continues to be debated by historians, the fact that she was the first woman ever to be executed by the United States must have interested Lupino, whose direction focuses on Surratt as doubly an outsider—an accused traitorous assassin and a woman.

Lupino describes her experience on this episode as a kind of trial by fire at the beginning of her television directing career: "It was shot in three days, with three or four days to prepare. I sat up day and night doing all the research I could on the assassination of Lincoln. Television—there's nothing rougher, nothing rougher. And from then on it became like a snowball. They'd book me in advance because they had to have answers in advance and I couldn't direct movies again until 1966, with *The Trouble with Angels*" (McGilligan and Weiner 227). Particularly striking in "The Trial of Mary Surratt" is a scene in which

Senator Corbett (Ray Collins) and Capt. Robert Westwood (Joseph Cotten), her attorney, interrogate Surratt in her cell. Surratt's house was purportedly used as a headquarters for the gang of assassins that included Surratt's son John. Surratt claims not to have known about the plan and, in the dramatized episode, is challenged by Senator Corbett: "How can I believe you?" As she replies, Virginia Gregg is shot in medium close-up, her face the only thing illuminated in her dreary cell. Traumatized, angered, and frustrated, Surratt responds, "You can't. You're a man." She continues, her eyes looking away, as she recalls, "I fetched their meals, made their beds. Took messages for them." Gregg draws out the word "man" in her speech: "They didn't bother to tell me anything. They didn't trouble to say, 'We're thinking of killing the president.' Didn't make any difference what I might think. What m-a-a-a-n tells a woman what he's plannin' till it's all done?" Surratt then turns back to the senator, challenging him: "Does your wife know that you're here in the jail tonight? Did you ask her what she thought about your coming here?" Stunned into silence, the senator shakes his head no. Whether or not Mary Surratt was involved in the plan to assassinate Lincoln in real life, this portrait presents Lupino and Gregg countering Surratt's guilt with an impassioned feminist defense of a woman's plight and invisibility in a male-defined world in which, her defense notwithstanding, she is scapegoated and executed. As in "No. 5 Checked Out," we see in another example of Lupino's early television work her gift for creating atmosphere and how she coaxed actors to give passionate and charismatic performances that interrogate social issues and gender roles.

In the early sixties, Lupino directed a number of dramatic episodes, including for the shows *Dr. Kildare* (1961–1966), *Sam Benedict* (1962–1963), and *Mr. Novak* (1963–1965). The episode of *Dr. Kildare* that Lupino directed in its third season, "To Walk in Grace" (aired 13 February 1964), bears a distinct connection to the motifs that preoccupied Lupino in her Filmakers work. The female-authored story (written by Joy Dexter) involves a writer, Helen Scott (Gena Rowlands), who visits Blair Hospital to research a new book she wants to write about dedicated doctors. Jim Kildare (Richard Chamberlain) initially assumes the worst of the novelist, dismissing her and mocking her writing, which he thinks is sentimental melodrama:

This imaginary doctor of yours, this likable young internist, what does he do? Does he perchance fall in love with a beautiful young patient, who just happens to be suffering from a rare, hopeless disease? And of course you'll have her die because that makes for a heart-rending ending. Oh, no, I know how it will end. The doctor has to give up being an internist and as the sun sinks slowly in the west, we find our hero all alone in his tiny ill-equipped laboratory searching for a cure for the mysterious malady that struck down his beloved.

The story begins by addressing a theme that would have attracted Lupino, romantic idealism and disillusionment. As the episode progresses, however, it focuses on another signature motif for Lupino, empathy for lost and vulnerable individuals. Viewers (and eventually Kildare) learn that Helen herself has a fatal illness.

As Kildare is followed in his rounds by Helen, he comes to understand that her interest in patients and doctors is neither exploitative nor sentimental, but empathic, leading him to change his perspective and feel empathy for her too. She nurtures a young boy who has just lost his parents in a car crash. "People do suffer in this world a lot—from love, from hate, from loss," she tells the despondent boy, "but the thing to remember is that it can be borne." She also helps an angry suicidal young woman (who has been left by her married lover) cherish her days when others (like Helen herself) have little agency to determine if they live or die. The dominant themes of this episode, resilience and empathy, are trademark motifs in Lupino's films, as they were to be in much of her television work. "To Walk in Grace" also features a moving portrayal of Helen Scott by Gena Rowlands, one of many sensitive and charismatic female performances created under Lupino's direction.

Sam Benedict was based on the real-life San Francisco attorney Jake Ehrlich. The show reunited Lupino with Edmond O'Brien, whom she directed in *The Bigamist* and *The Hitch-Hiker*. Lupino's two directed episodes, "Everybody's Playing Solo" (aired 1 December 1962) and "Sugar, Spice and Everything . . ." (aired 6 February 1963) featured a young Yvonne Craig (who would later be best known as Batgirl in the television series *Batman*). In *Sam Benedict*, Craig plays innocent young girls yearning for excitement and expression, linking these stories to Sally Forrest's roles in *Not Wanted* and *Hard, Fast and Beautiful*.

In "Everybody's Playing Solo," Craig plays Angela Larkin, who accuses Nicholas Coria (Joby Baker) of raping her. An intriguing reversal of *Outrage* in one sense, the episode is at the same time consonant with Lupino's earlier film, since Angela's accusation is the result of youthful fear and desire, signature Lupino themes. Fifteen-year-old Angela lives with her grandparents. "Bored watching television," she dresses provocatively and goes to the bar, leaving with jazz pianist Nicholas, who strongly echoes Steve Ryan (Leo Penn) in *Not Wanted*. Son of an immigrant, Nick is, like Steve, a musician preoccupied with his cultural marginality: "All jazz musicians are kooks. . . . A lot of people think jazz musicians are the lowest, anyway." As in the film, Lupino taps into a frustrated youth culture and artist figures aware of themselves as devalued and irrelevant to the workings of mainstream society.

In "Sugar, Spice and Everything . . . ," Craig plays amnesiac Amy Vickers, accused of killing her husband. The vulnerable Amy, like the young characters in the previous episode of *Sam Benedict* Lupino directed, is lost, marginalized, misunderstood, and notably exploited by her husband when he was alive, and by the townspeople, who see her as a fallen woman instead of the innocent child she is. In both episodes of *Sam Benedict* and, indeed, in much of her drama and action directing, Lupino emphasized the isolation of her protagonists by composing intimate two-shots that encourage us to empathize with a character seen in profile, while her or his interlocutor faces the camera.

In "Sugar, Spice, and Everything . . . ," Amy introduces herself naively as a "premiere danseuse." In her jail cell, child-like and impervious to her incarceration, she dances a ballet to music played on a transistor radio. Lupino begins the sequence shooting Amy's feet dancing, then, in low angles, dramatizes Amy's paradoxical state (innocent and jailed) by emphasizing the shadows of the prison bars that surround her as she dances in her cell. She is locked up, but also freed by her art.

The year after Lupino directed *Sam Benedict*, her work on *Mr. Novak* extended her deep interest in alienated youth and the social problems facing young people in modern America. The series starred James Franciscus (best known for his later role as a blind investigator in *Longstreet*) as a teacher at a Los Angeles public high school. Franciscus once observed that he wanted to do *Mr. Novak* because he was tired of the stereotype of the bumbling absent-minded teacher. Defying stereotypes may also have attracted Lupino. Two of the episodes she directed, "Love in the Wrong Season" (aired 3 December 1963) and "May Day, May Day" (aired 2 March 1965) deal with desire between students and teachers. The episodes once again lead us to empathize with all of the characters. For instance, the repressed remedial instructor Ariel Wilder (Patricia Crowley) converts her fear of men into a nonthreatening but inappropriate relationship with a seventeen-year-old boy who has a crush on her. In one scene, the two recite love poetry to each other in her apartment. A mirror in Ariel's living room reflects the emotional distortion in the two sharing an intimate moment, yet the scene also emphasizes the young boy and frightened woman's mutual loneliness and isolation: their bond as outsider figures is made visible through Lupino's mise-en-scène.

Another episode, "A Day in the Year" (aired 24 March 1964), is about the topical issue of drugs. Martha, one of Mr. Novak's students, overdoses while in class. Subsequently, Mr. Novak patrols the halls, suspiciously watching all of the students at Jefferson High, wondering which ones are using or dealing drugs. This sequence is shot from Mr. Novak's POV as he walks down the hall, intercut with his reaction shots. Because Lupino frames Mr. Novak in medium close-up, however, he seems to float down the halls surreally as he observes the students. First, Novak sees a kid taking pills, then Lupino cuts and zooms in to reveal that the pills are Vitamin C. The camera pans across a wall behind which a student is seen rolling up his sleeve. Instead of track marks, the camera, after moving behind the wall, reveals a girl goading the boy to show his muscles. The camera then lights on three boys in a group—a drug deal? Lupino moves in to show them harmlessly sharing phone numbers from an address book. Finally, the camera dollies in on three girls holding a box one of them is opening, after which the camera reveals the box's contents to be a bracelet, not pills, as Mr. Novak had suspected. The camerawork suggests that surveillance is not the answer to the problem of teenagers and drugs for Mr. Novak or viewers, particularly as it becomes paranoid (Novak's suspicion in a world of harmless realities) and hallucinatory itself (Novak floating down the halls). Another striking scene in "A Day in the Year" includes an extended shot from inside a boy's locker, associating the school environment with claustrophobia, as we watch the investigators search for evidence from that perspective, through the open locker door.

Comedies

Often, critics have commented that Lupino found her niche in television action shows, westerns, and thrillers. Lupino's noir sensibility and
style indeed translated well in these genres. But her versatility and ability
enabled her to make all her work for television resonate with themes and
aesthetic approaches found in her film directing. Looking at the comedy
episodes Lupino directed allows us to think critically about the motifs
of shows such as *The Donna Reed Show, Bewitched, Gilligan's Island*, and
The Ghost and Mrs. Muir, all of whose themes were aligned with Lupino's interests. The "directorial sensibility" Wheeler Winston Dixon finds
in Lupino's action and western shows can also be found in this supposedly lighter fare. With their domestic and gender concerns, for example,
The Donna Reed Show, Bewitched, and *The Ghost and Mrs. Muir* were
perfect vehicles for Lupino. With their overarching themes of frustrated
desire, *The Ghost and Mrs. Muir* and *Gilligan's Island* aptly correspond
with Lupino's philosophical orientation. Lupino acknowledged in 1972
that after the work on action shows, she "had a terrible time getting anyone to let me direct a love story" ("Coast to Coast"). If there were few
obvious or conventional love stories in the episodes Lupino directed,
the comment does not take into account the characters' passions Lupino
was able to draw from her actors and the striking treatment of gender
in her television work, whether focused on men or women. Thus, for
example, in her episodes for *The Untouchables*, Lupino brought to bear
her sensitivity to oppressive gender roles, as can easily be seen in the
last episode she directed for the series, "The Torpedo," discussed below.
Similarly, her work in comedies tapped their subversive elements, often
from the strong female leads rather than their personas. Even though
these shows seem to endorse happy domesticity, under Lupino's direction the episodes at times exhibit the perspective of home noir. Again,
the critical commonplace that Lupino was far from being a television
auteur simply does not hold.[22] Closer attention to these episodes productively complicates Lupino's role in media history.

It seems as if *Mr. Adams and Eve* would have been the perfect vehicle
for Lupino's directing talent; however, Lupino shied away from directing Howard Duff.[23] Apart from one episode of the show she directed,
"Teen-Age Idol," her earliest work in television comedy was in 1959, for

season 2 of *The Donna Reed Show.* "A Difference of Opinion" (aired 10 December 1959) certainly belongs on Lupino's turf, since the episode is about marital arguments and their effect on the family. Donna Stone accepts a dinner invitation from a couple neither she nor husband Alex (Carl Betz) likes, and the two fight about whether or not he or they will attend. Donna plays a conventionally feminine role maintaining appearances, wanting to keep the peace with their acquaintances by going to dinner at their house and, as the episode evolves, in their own house, as they try to hide their argument from son Jeff (Paul Peterson) and daughter Mary (Shelley Fabares). Under the guise of the actors' star texts and comedic charm, the episode delivers familiar Lupino themes: diverging desires based on gender roles and the repression of emotion into patterns of domesticity not easily disrupted.[24] A comic home noir functions in the Stones' household, in shots like those below. In a sense, the effects of home noir in classic television are particularly resonant, as they make creative use of television's "small-screen" aesthetics touted by Horace Newcomb (*TV: The Most Popular Art* 248–50). Such intimacy, exploited by television's historical role as part of the fabric of viewers' domestic lives (a dynamic part of the living room), emphasizes the suppressed anxieties and potential feminist disruptions and rebellions in the happy households of *The Donna Reed Show*, *Bewitched* (starring Elizabeth Montgomery as Samantha Stevens), and *The Ghost and Mrs. Muir* (starring Hope Lange as Carolyn Muir).

Donna's forced optimism, for example, suggests a darker side of the domestic space she inhabits. In the second image of figure 48, Jeff's crossed arms serve to acknowledge his and Mary's awareness that things are awry, which we see more clearly in the third image, in which the Stones argue, and the last shot, showing Jeff and Mary eavesdropping. The scenes of dissension take place in prominent domestic spaces—the kitchen and bedroom—allowing an ironic counterpoint to the setting in the actors' expressions and blocking.

In the 1960s, Lupino worked more on comedy series: she directed three episodes (and co-directed a fourth) of *Gilligan's Island*, and the last clearly documented television episode she directed was on *The Ghost and Mrs. Muir* in 1968. She would surely have connected with the ensemble cast and also the conceit of *Gilligan's Island*, a theme of frustrated desire and futility, apparent in the first episode she directed for

FIGURE 48 *The Donna Reed Show*: "A Difference of Opinion" (aired 17 December 1959)

the series, "Wrongway Feldman" (aired 24 October 1964).[25] Try as they might and as close to success as they repeatedly get, the castaways cannot be rescued. Also, the show's lead character is innocent and hapless in a way that would have appealed to Lupino; Bob Denver, the actor playing Gilligan, was reportedly Lupino's favorite among the cast (Anderson, interview).

The last of Lupino's contributions to *Gilligan's Island* was a co-directed episode, "The Producer" (aired 3 October 1966), in which Harold Hecuba, a powerful, egotistical Hollywood auteur played by famed comic actor Phil Silvers, crash-lands on the island for a short stay. Lupino brought her sense of irony and her experience with Hollywood male egos to this assignment: Hecuba shares his initials with Howard Hughes, whom Lupino knew well from Hollywood and didn't respect much because of his extortionist tactics with The Filmakers. The episode parodies Hollywood producers' narcissism and their absurdly controlling influence and authority. Gilligan has the idea to produce a musical adaptation of *Hamlet* on the island, and Hecuba attempts to school the islanders in acting, showing them how to play every single role. Direction of this scene includes shaking the camera, not indicated in the shooting script ("The Producer"), to bridge Hecuba's frenzied vignettes. The destabilized camera movement creates a disorienting experience for the viewer, who is now in sync with the solo *artiste* Hecuba as he performs each role in quick succession. After this scene, Hecuba flees the island without the castaways, who later hear on the radio that he has announced his new inspiration, a blockbuster film he has named *Hamlet, The Musical*. Having stolen Gilligan and his friends' idea, Hecuba is merely another in a long line of hypocritical Hollywood exploiters that Lupino would satirize in her career.

Some of the challenges Lupino faced in directing for television were to be found on the set of *Gilligan's Island*. While in public comments Lupino generally spoke optimistically about the camaraderie she experienced working in television, she did reveal the difficulties of her own isolation as often the only woman on the set. In the *Hollywood Reporter* in 1972, Lupino commented, "In the beginning the producers didn't think I could bring in a show on schedule and, of course, I did. I really just thought that a woman directing was an oddity, but I never felt like I was on a crusade for a cause. I've walked on sets and felt resentment from actors and crew members because I was a woman. Once I walked on a TV stage after directing a picture and I was greeted with 'Slumming, darling?' from a stagehand" ("Coast to Coast"). The comment clearly refers to Lupino's move from film to television—in 1966, Lupino had returned to direct another episode of *Gilligan's Island* after directing *The Trouble with Angels*; however, it's unlikely that any male director arriving on set would have been addressed this way. (According to Mary Ann Anderson, the comment was, in fact, uttered by Natalie Schafer, the actress who played Mrs. Howell on *Gilligan's Island* [interview].) The anecdote pokes a hole in the façade of the "Mother of Us All" (the inscription on Lupino's television directing chair). A conciliatory and non-threatening role that men and women alike on the set would attach to Lupino, as we have seen, "Mother" gave Lupino the means to take control of the set without alienating her co-workers. In an interview with Graham Fuller in 1990, Lupino on one hand assented to the role: asked if she had troubles getting taken seriously, she said, "No, because I was used to being with men. I always felt like I was one of the crew. When I came on the set in the mornings, everyone would say, 'Good morning, Mother.' And I used to say, 'Morning, boys.'" On the other hand, Lupino knew very well that many men felt ambivalent about her as their leader. She tried to overcome their ambivalence by assuming the role of a mother. As she said, "While I have encountered some resentment from the male species for intruding into their world, I give them no opportunity to think I've strayed where I don't belong" (qtd. in Anderson, *Beyond the Camera* 115). Moreover, as the Schafer anecdote indicates, women, too, resented her power as director. As the "Howard and Eve and Ida" episode of *Mr. Adams and Eve* demonstrated, Lupino was very much aware of how she was perceived as director, particularly by women, anatomizing and making fun of it.

Directing film and television gave Lupino a creative opportunity to criticize the gender roles she negotiated so carefully in her professional life. Many episodes Lupino directed featured women in the lead roles and addressed issues of gender and role-playing that Lupino had dealt with extensively in her film directing, producing, and writing. For example, the final episode on record that Lupino directed was for *The Ghost and Mrs. Muir*, which was adapted from a 1947 film starring Gene Tierney and Rex Harrison. In "Madeira, My Dear" (aired 14 December 1968), Carolyn (Hope Lange) faces multiple obstacles in her attempts to meet Captain Gregg (Edward Mulhare), the handsome ghost only she can see, for a romantic date. Carolyn is beset by domestic annoyances (she's carrying too many groceries; the kids unexpectedly need to be picked up at school; the washing machine overflows; Scruffy the dog is barking and nipping at everyone's heels). The Captain is irked by her unavailability. Of course, the larger source of melancholy—that Carolyn is in love with a ghost—underlies these missed opportunities. Lupino's motifs from the films she wrote, directed, and produced appear here, a woman beset by domestic responsibilities and also a sense of belatedness and thwarted desire.

But perhaps the most intriguing comedy episode Lupino directed was during the first season of ABC's *Bewitched*, in which Samantha is a witch married to mortal Darrin Stevens (Dick York). As viewers of the sitcom are well aware, Darrin prohibits Sam's use of witchcraft in order to live in a "normal" household so that he can wield power as "man of the house." Lupino directed an episode called "A Is for Aardvark" (aired 14 January 1965), in which not only the themes but the aesthetics demonstrate her hand at work. Norman MacDonnell said that television producers asked

FIGURE 49 *Bewitched*: Darrin rings his bell in "A Is for Aardvark" (aired 14 January 1965)

Lupino to direct "[stories] about a woman with some dimension." In these comedies about women, Lupino expressed her sense of irony in shot composition and scene construction.

The title "A Is for Aardvark" is a reference to Darrin's crossword puzzle, with which he occupies himself as he recovers from a fall incurred while groping in the dark to lock the back door. The logic of this episode, which recurs in the series, is that Darrin's prohibition on witchcraft is more disruptive than the magic itself. If Darrin had allowed Samantha to use her powers to lock the door in the first place, he wouldn't have fallen down the stairs and hurt himself.

Darrin's bed rest is played for comedy as he orders Samantha around and summons her to bring him trivial items, such as a pencil to do his crossword puzzles. He has a bell beside him (see figure 49) to command Samantha's appearance, and his first gesture as a convalescent is to make a paper airplane, which he sends down the stairs to bid Samantha to bring him a banana. Eventually, Samantha is exhausted and resorts to witchcraft to administer to Darrin's needs and desires.

Like most episodes of *Bewitched*, "A Is for Aardvark" depicts Sam subverting Darrin's rules, using witchcraft in this episode to "solve the servant problem" that results from Darrin's bedridden neediness. Samantha refers to herself as a servant here, but doing Darrin's bidding is only an exaggerated version of what Darrin desires from Samantha in the first place, which is to follow his commands (the main one being that she shouldn't use witchcraft). In this episode, Samantha floats a pencil to him to spare herself. "Too tired," she admits, "to dash up the stairs again," Samantha's fatigue is a metaphor for her general role as a subservient wife, a position only witchcraft can remedy.

In this episode, which the show's producer William Asher tellingly said "represented the message of the entire series" (Pilato 187), Samantha and Darrin arrive at a compromise. Sam casts a spell on the house so that it—rather than Samantha—delivers whatever Darrin requires. *Dispelling* the idea that women hold the power, the magic agency is redirected onto the domestic space itself, in effect allowing Darrin to control that space too, now that he is confined in it during his convalescence. Darrin increasingly relies on his power to conjure up the objects of his desire, as the episode parodies the masculine wish to remain in con-

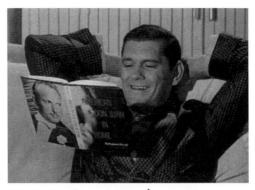

FIGURE 50 *Bewitched*: "A Is for Aardvark": Darrin reads *American Don Juan in Rome*

trol. Darrin's magic enhances his manly powers, which can be seen when Samantha first grants Darrin command of the house. When he practices by saying, "Banana! Come! Darrin!" in a low declarative monotone, Sam replies, "You don't have to sound like Tarzan," casting Darrin as a Neanderthal and further showing that her own witchcraft transgresses Darrin's patriarchal power. Indeed, the episode is about Darrin's discovery of how appealing Sam's power is. He is seduced by the advantages of witchcraft: ease and comfort; immediate gratification; and rapid consumption. (Such luxury is underscored in the title of the book Darrin reads with his hands tucked behind his head, *American Don Juan in Rome* [see figure 50].) "You've given him a taste of power," Endora (Agnes Moorehead), Samantha's mother, warns, to which Sam insists, "Not Darrin. He won't succumb." Endora's reply, "If he's mortal, he's greedy," underscores the witches' moral superiority and, ironically, their restraint in using their magical powers.

In one scene (see figure 51), Darrin's arms are crossed self-indulgently behind his head as he conjures up the perfect sandwich. The episode cuts from his comfort to a shot of Sam ironing clothes in another room. This parallel editing compares a masculine appropriation of power with the domestic condition of women from which Sam's own powers—when allowed or expressed—would release her. Betty Friedan's *The Feminine Mystique* was published in 1963, a year before *Bewitched* premiered. That same year, however, as Walter Metz observes, Friedan wrote an essay that extended her analysis of "the problem that has no name" to

FIGURE 51 *Bewitched*: Darrin relaxes while Samantha irons in "A Is for Aardvark"

television representations of domesticity. Metz argues that Samantha Stevens is a rejoinder to Friedan's sense of the television wife as a "stupid, unattractive, insecure little household drudge" (qtd. in Metz 18)—in fact, Metz points out that Endora's language to describe Samantha's life with Darrin replicates Friedan's: Life with "Derwood" (Endora's name for Darrin) is "boring" "drudge[ry]."[26]

Action, Thrillers, Mysteries

In Lupino's thrillers and mysteries, notes Wheeler Winston Dixon, her style "is often adventurous and individualistic." Indeed, it may be easier to see Lupino's mark on action series, thrillers, and mysteries than on other genres because many were telefilms, and the longer format allowed her an opportunity to display her agility with camerawork, the composition of space, and pacing. As a matter of genre convention, the action and thriller telefilms she directed also more readily invited and employed the noir style at which, as we have seen, Lupino was adept. *Thriller* (hosted by Boris Karloff), for example, was mainly scored by Jerry Goldsmith, whose plangent violins remind viewers of the composer's best-known score, for the noir masterpiece *Chinatown* (1974). (Goldsmith also scored Lupino's last directed film, *The Trouble with Angels*.)

In an early episode from *Thriller*'s two-year run, Lupino shows her virtuosity behind the camera—and she further connects with material that resonates with her abiding empathy with marginalized and innocent victims. In "Mr. George" (aired 9 May 1961), Lupino uses unique visual tricks to characterize those who victimize the innocent as grotesque. Young Priscilla is a Wordsworthian child, visiting the cemetery to plead with her deceased guardian Mr. George: "Please come back. I want you to live with me again." Meanwhile, Priscilla's cousins are plotting to kill her to steal her inheritance. Mr. George remains in the house as a ghost to protect her from her greedy, murderous relatives. In one scene, one of these relatives, Adelaide, tells Priscilla that a treasure chest in the attic is a good place to hide. George's voice tells her to leave the attic and go to her room, and as Adelaide leans into the chest, it shuts on her head, though Lupino pans away just before the lid closes to a singing toy bird and then back to show Adelaide dead.

The wonderful Hitchcockian macabre in Lupino's camerawork is seen again later in the episode, when cousin Jared tries to kill Priscilla by whacking her on the head with a swing on a playground pulled back behind her. Priscilla heeds George's call to run away from the swing set to the playhouse, and the swing is magically suspended high in the air for a moment while she does so. It then whips back down to hit Jared in the head, killing him. The camera takes the place of the swing, falling down to the grass over Jared's dead body and past it, linking child's play and murder in an expressive camera sequence.

Like many of Lupino's stories, *Thriller*'s "The Last of the Sommervilles" (aired 6 November 1961) addresses the venal desires of greedy family members. In this regard it is similar to "The Masks," the celebrated episode of *The Twilight Zone* (aired 20 March 1964) Lupino later directed (she was the only woman ever to direct the show), in which a greedy, hypocritical family descends on the wealthy patriarch Jason Foster (Robert Keith). Under Lupino's direction, the actors give bravura performances as false, conceited, and selfish offspring. Purportedly to celebrate Mardi Gras, Jason stages a ritual in which he makes everyone don grotesque and animalistic masks for the evening, as the family snipe narcissistically at one another. When the clock strikes midnight, Foster dies, and his heirs discover that their faces have become the masks they have been wearing. Justice has thus been meted out to them for their mercenary behavior. Lupino wrote the script for "The Last of the Sommervilles" (with her cousin Richard Lupino), exhibiting her reprised themes. She took to the director's chair nine times for *Thriller,* giving her the opportunity to establish a consistent visual style.

In the episode, Rutherford Sommerville comes to see his aunt Celia to pay respects (but really to milk her for money). His father, Celia's brother, has died, and thus Rutherford is the "last Sommerville." Ursula, a cousin ("fourth time removed by marriage"), has been taking care of "Aunt Celia" for ten years and is scheming to inherit her fortune. She has already killed Sophie, Celia's sister. Rutherford and Ursula now team up to kill Celia, which occurs in a macabre sequence, here described by Barbara Scharres: "In one continuous close-up shot [Celia] reaches for the sponge, her hand hovers over it in a moment of indecision, she reaches instead for the chocolates, just when you think she's safe, her hand darts back to the sponge, grasps it, and she is electrocuted. Comedy, suspense, and a tour-de-force display of Lupino's wittiness come together in one shot. In contrast to the often static camera work of fifties and sixties television, Lupino made extensive use of the moving camera" (qtd. in O'Dell 174). Meticulously wrought scenes such as this one may explain the Film Forum's screening of "The Last of the Sommervilles" (as well as "The Lethal Ladies," discussed below) in a program called "Genre Is a Woman" in New York City in June 2016.

In the end, Ursula turns on Rutherford, leading the hapless man into a bog where he drowns. In a series of twists, Ursula marries her lover, but is then killed with him when they drive their car into the bog (now heavily populated with dead Sommervilles). We don't see Ursula meet her fate. However, in an understated and ironic conclusion typical of Lupino's work, we are told of Ursula's death in an epilogue narrated by Dr. Farnam, Celia's friend (played by Boris Karloff).

The episode is noteworthy for its strong women. But Celia (Martita Hunt) does not see this trait in Ursula (Phyllis Thaxter), despite the latter's evil glee, belittling her niece as "really very dull, you know, but so dependable," but then adding, "After all, I'm quite fond of you, Ursula. You're so useful." The younger woman plans her revenge and a way to gain access to Celia's money, using the dull-witted Rutherford as her pawn. Though she relies on Ursula, Celia flings insults at her, suggesting that at some level she knows the younger woman is untrustworthy, even villainous. Celia may seem doddering, but she is one of Lupino's underestimated women who has more strength of mind and insight than is initially apparent. When Rutherford first asks, then demands, money from her for a new business scheme in Paris, Aunt Celia changes the subject

FIGURE 52 *Thriller*: "The Last of the Sommervilles" (aired 6 November 1961)

repeatedly, though later admits to Ursula, "It's not that I mind lending him a thousand dollars. But I want to know he's doing the right thing." When Celia is murdered, just past the episode's halfway mark, the effect is disorienting given the viewer's empathy with the character (not unlike with the death of Marion Crane the year before in Hitchcock's *Psycho*). That empathy is enhanced by the fact that Martita Hunt also played Miss Havisham in David Lean's *Great Expectations* fifteen years earlier. Another isolated woman in a gothic mansion, Miss Havisham hovers over Celia as a ghost. Lupino coaxes Hunt to draw from that earlier role to enrich her interpretation in this episode. Lupino keeps the visual interest high, depicting, for example, Dr. Farnam taunting the guilty Rutherford in a canted angle that once again uses Lupino's signature two-shot with one actor's face in profile and another's straight on (see figure 52).

In an episode of *Thriller* that aired later that month, "The Closed Cabinet," Lupino uses mise-en-scène to establish women as confined and struggling to break free of the frames that contain them. The episode begins in 1580, at Mervyn Castle, when Beatrice kills her abusive husband, then herself. Mervyn's mother, Dame Alice, curses the family for generations to come with a spell that is "beyond the wisdom of man to fix or the wit of men to discover." Says Alice, "Who fathoms the riddle lifts the curse." Three hundred years pass, and young Eve comes to the Mervyn estate to visit her cousin Lucy, who has married one of the two remaining Mervyn men. In love with the Mervyn brother Alan, Eve is nearly seduced by the ghost of Beatrice into repeating the murder-suicide. Resisting the curse—refusing to kill a phantom Mervyn

FIGURE 53 *Thriller*: "The Closed Cabinet" (aired 27 November 1961)

patriarch after bravely inhabiting a haunted room and eventually confronting the ghost of Beatrice—Eve solves the riddle: it is apparently "woman" whose wisdom is beyond that of men.

The episode features many visual images of note. We see repeated shots of Eve through the grates and bars of the dungeon, the slats of the stairwell in low-angle shots, and portals in the walls, and Lupino supplements this visual representation of trapped women in a stunning sequence in which Eve's gaze meets that of the ghost Beatrice (see figure 53). These "impossibly long charged moments [during which] they stand and stare at each other" (Scheib, in Kuhn 54) are interrupted by Eve's love interest, Alan Mervyn, symbolically demonstrating female empathy and bonds threatened by male intervention. In the end, Eve has the power to resist the curse's demand that she kill a man and then herself, breaking the chain of violence and solving the mystery of "The Closed Cabinet" (in which resides the deadly weapon, a knife). Eve's strength resisting the curse is cast in terms of her independent mind. Eve combats the voice in her head of Beatrice urging her to commit murder and suicide: "But I don't know what those words mean! Why should I kill him?" This episode rehearses a story often seen in Lupino's work about gender trauma and violence. Although the genre is horror, Lupino's signature can still be seen thematically, a mise-en-scène focused on enclosed spaces, and in the use of a female gaze (a motif, as we have seen, central to Lupino's last directed film, *The Trouble with Angels*).

In *Thriller*, Lupino repeatedly brought her penchant for a noir atmosphere and story that interrogates or explores the power of singular women. One such example is "La Strega" (aired 15 January 1962), in which "La Strega," "the witch," migrates between the beautiful Luana (Ursula Andress), the damsel in distress, and the grotesque old "strega" (Jeanette Nolan), driving the artist Tonio (Alejandro Rey) mad. Tonio fails to save Luana from her grandmother, the witch. Tonio kills the witch and is later told by the local priest of a conversation he has just had with the grandmother. Panic stricken and traumatized, Tonio runs to where he buried the witch, exhumes the body, and finds Luana there instead. The authorities take him away, thus fulfilling La Strega's curse that Tonio will go mad and die in his cell. This episode was noted in a recent *Sight and Sound* issue for Lupino's "beautifully atmospheric" treatment in the horror genre (Sélavy 28).

One of the last episodes Lupino directed for *Thriller* is called "The Lethal Ladies" (aired 16 April 1962), in which the actors play in two different stories about women's vengeance on men who exploit or try to dominate or eliminate them. The women in "The Lethal Ladies" are Lavinia Sills, a rich woman whose husband squanders her money and cheats on her, and, in the second installment, Miss Quimby, a mousy but devoted librarian who is passed over for the job of head librarian because of gender bias, replaced by the horrible Dr. Bliss. The episode is memorable, as many of Lupino's directed stories are, because of its references to female power and how it is underestimated. Boris Karloff introduced each episode of *Thriller* with a frame narrative, much as Rod Serling did on *The Twilight Zone*. At the beginning of "The Lethal Ladies," Karloff's frame narrative involves him directing a short scene in which a nurse murders a doctor, at which point Karloff turns to the camera to say, "Well, my friends, you've just seen a startling example of, uh, the weaker sex in action. . . . For though man may have more muscle than woman, there can never be any defense against the unexpected. And we all know that the ladies are, uh, well, shall we say, full of surprises." Karloff's words refer as much to the characters in these tales as they do to Lupino as the woman directing the episode. Clearly the dual stories in this episode attracted Lupino because they are centrally concerned with women and the issue of control. The women are played excellently by Rosemary Murphy, whose characters take their revenge. The women die, too, but not before they punish the men for their "delusions of male superiority," as Karloff narrates. Moreover, the episode includes Lupino's compelling camerawork, as in the scene in which Dr.

Bliss discovers that he is trapped in the book vault and will die there. Lupino films the trapped man from above, underscoring his inescapable enclosure and terror.

These episodes of *Thriller* explore female power and curiosity. They show women in trouble because of their ambition, triumphant because of their independence and bravery, or angrily insistent that they not be exploited or taken for granted.

Earning her reputation as "the female Hitch," Lupino shared the elder director's perverse sense of humor and love of irony. In the sixth season of *Alfred Hitchcock Presents* (1960–61), Lupino directed two episodes, "Sybilla" and "A Crime for Mothers." Lupino loved working on this show because Hitchcock gave her much creative control (Anderson, interview). Just as Hitchcock brought his macabre sense of humor and irony to his filmmaking, Lupino connected with these modes of storytelling in her television directing. She was also adept in using cut-ins and cutaways to spark viewers' curiosity and imagination; focusing on objects (such as mirrors and walking sticks) or two- and three-shots to represent claustrophobic spaces or unholy alliances; and using pans and close-ups to enhance suspense. *Alfred Hitchcock Presents* is also notable for its women in control—it was produced by Hitchcock's longtime collaborator Joan Harrison. Harrison's work parallels Lupino's in some important ways, both women having an unusual presence behind the scenes in film and television (Harrison was one of three female producers of the period, along with Virginia Van Upp and Harriet Parsons). She was Hitchcock's secretary and assistant, and then his scriptwriter beginning in the 1930s. In the 1940s, Harrison forged a successful career as an independent film producer, making "feminist-inspired noir" (Lane 98), including *Phantom Lady* and *The Strange Affair of Uncle Harry* in 1944, then *Nocturne* (1946), *They Won't Believe Me* (1947), and *Ride the Pink Horse* (1947). Like Lupino, Harrison navigated the gender politics of her position with savvy (see Snelson), and, like Lupino, she made the transition from film to television in the 1950s.

"A Crime for Mothers" (aired 24 January 1961) features a bravura performance by Claire Trevor (who had played Millie Farley ten years earlier in Lupino's *Hard, Fast and Beautiful*). Trevor appears as Lottie Meade, an alcoholic trying to extort money from Mr. and Mrs. Birdwell, who adopted Meade's child years earlier but without legally completing the adoption. Mrs. Meade enlists help from a sleazy private detective, Phil Ames (Biff Elliot), who persuades her to abduct the child for ransom. During the kidnapping, Lupino employs close-ups, stunning shots of Trevor's beaming bewildered face, followed immediately by one in which she takes a large swig from her bottle. Not having seen the child since she was a baby, Meade relies on the investigator to identify the child. The conclusion of the epi-

FIGURE 54 *Alfred Hitchcock Presents*: "A Crime for Mothers" (aired 24 January 1961): young Eileen jumping with a bottle of bourbon on Meade's couch

sode exposes her accomplice to be a friend of the Birdwells, who has led Mrs. Meade to kidnap his own daughter and not the Birdwell child. Ames threatens to expose a now-desperate Mrs. Meade to the police, and order is restored.

Trevor's performance recalls her role as Millie, here playing another desperate mother figure. Mrs. Meade, however, is presented more stereotypically as a drunk—as even her surname indicates—not as the complicated controlling figure discussed in Part Two. Trevor's virtuoso performance as Mrs. Meade is enhanced by Lupino's ironic mise-en-scène, when, for example, "Eileen" (really "Margaret," Ames's child) first arrives at Meade's apartment, having just been kidnapped. She jumps up and down on the couch, revealing a bottle of liquor that Lottie has hidden between the cushions.

This absurd portrait of domesticity has a subversive edge, as does the last shot of the child's doll that ends the episode, as if the trappings of childhood are as much home noir figures of threat as they are of sustenance and consolation. Indeed, the episode begins with Mr. and Mrs. Birdwell excitedly playing with an oversized doll they plan to surprise Eileen with for her seventh birthday, which is the occasion of Mrs. Meade's appearance. Visually representing the disruption of the birthday celebration, Lupino has the bizarrely life-sized doll positioned between Mrs. Meade and Mrs. Birdwell, signifying Eileen as an object under dispute, as well as a lifeless substitute for the child. Later in the episode, when Mrs. Meade

FIGURE 55 *Alfred Hitchcock Presents*: "A Crime for Mothers": Top to bottom, Mr. and Mrs. Birdwell with the life-size doll; the Birdwells; and Mrs. Meade (Claire Trevor)

first sees the child she thinks is Eileen just before kidnapping her, Lupino cuts to a close-up of Mrs. Meade as she exclaims, "She's a doll." Lupino's visual strategy often seems designed to indicate the artificiality of people's roles in social settings. Even in the context of mystery and thriller stories, she repeatedly exposes the grotesquerie of social roles, especially in domestic situations.

The artifice of social roles is also the theme of the earlier episode Lupino directed for *Alfred Hitchcock Presents*, "Sybilla" (aired December 6, 1960). A female creative team was responsible for this episode: the teleplay was written by popular mystery novelist Charlotte Armstrong, based on a story by Margaret Manners. As noted, Hitchcock originally asked Lupino to play Sybilla, but Lupino countered that she would rather direct for a far lower fee than she would have earned acting in the episode.

"Sybilla" is a perverse portrait of marriage, a perfect subject for Lupino. The episode features Alexander Scourby, perhaps best known for his portrayal of mob boss Lagana in Fritz Lang's classic film noir *The Big Heat* (1953). Here, he plays fastidious and solipsistic writer Horace Meade, who has just married Sybilla, portrayed eerily by Barbara Bel Geddes. The story is told by Horace in flashback, as he recalls the beginning of his marriage, which he considers "as incredible as finding [himself] on the moon."

From the outset, Sybilla's affect is strange. She is an "angel in the house," expressing no desire but to be a perfect wife: "I don't want to make any mistakes, never. You must always tell me just how you prefer everything. I only want to please you," Sybilla says to Horace. Her even-tempered acquiescence to Horace begins to provoke him, and he feels increasingly trapped by her control over his environment. He expresses his feelings in his diary, which he locks inside the desk given to him by Sybilla as a wedding gift: "I could find absolutely nothing to complain about. At first, I was ready to defend myself against all rearranging and habit-breaking, but Sybilla was too clever for that. I began to feel like a man beating against air, imprisoned by invisible walls." Horace's claus-trophobia continues to mount. His voiceover narrates, "It is unbearable. She's holding me with cobwebs. She studies my tastes. And there's no civilized way out . . . I cannot bear it much longer." Horace decides to poison Sybilla, but she has exchanged liquids in his medicine cabinet without his knowledge, so the plan fails. At this point, Sybilla is reading a book of horror stories, and she explains to Horace that one of these is an especially "psychologically interesting" tale of a man who makes a copy of a diary in which a murder plan is revealed; the diary is placed with his lawyer in case he dies mysteriously. A very Hitchcockian cut-in shot of an extra key in a drawer reveals suddenly to Horace that Sybilla has a key to his desk and has, presumably, read his diary. He determines that Sybilla must live, lest his murder plan be revealed. With Horace now resigned to remaining married to Sybilla, their roles reverse, as he is now her protector: "In the years that followed it became second nature for me to look after Sybilla and watch over her." After Sybilla dies, Horace fully expects the copy of his diary to come to light, but no copy of his diary is in her lawyer's safe. It seems that Sybilla's unacknowledged machinations have saved Horace's life, a recognition that leads him to say, at the end of the episode, that Sybilla has been "a perfect wife." He is grief-stricken, realizing after she dies that he loves her. Echoing the prophetess she is named for, the Sybil, Sybilla's certainty that one day Horace will love her is ironically confirmed only after her death.

The episode is a parody of marriage roles, in keeping with Lupino's penchant for dissecting matrimony. The six images in figure 56 demon-strate Lupino's visual critique. In the first, we see a reaction shot, part of a shot-reverse-shot sequence in which Sybilla presents Horace with her wedding gift, a large desk wrapped in a huge bow. Sybilla's gift of the desk symbolizes that she has taken over his work life, and Horace's distress is palpable. Though Sybilla's affect never changes throughout the episode, it is clear in Lupino's mise-en-scène that this is a story about female subversion. Lupino has Bel Geddes hold her wedding bouquet to her chest throughout the initial sequence (seen in the first two shots); the forced stance establishes that Sybilla's purpose here is to be nothing more than a "bride," soon to become a "wife." At breakfast, Sybilla spoons sugar onto her plate, as Horace's voiceover says, "She was always so gentle, so agreeable." This figuration is enhanced by Bel Geddes's disarming smile, in which her lips cover her teeth, defining her acquiescence. The smile, however, seen in several of the images, is subversive. It is of a piece with a number of details signaling Sybilla's power over Horace, despite her ostensible role as angel in the house. Behind Sybilla and Horace (the second image in figure 56) sits a Bacchanalian statue, providing a counterpoint to the stable domestic space Sybilla is now disrupting. Sybilla needlepoints as Horace grows annoyed at her presence; her pricking of the stitches symbolizes an aggressive affront to him. As she stabs the canvas in the fourth image, she describes the mystery story she has read that provokes Horace's suspicion that she is aware he has tried to kill her. In the third image, Sybilla passively drinks the liquid meant to poison her. Her hair is down to signal a Victorian-inspired femininity that is complicated, once again, by the smile playing on her face. In the sixth image, even as she dies, she smiles once more. The fifth image shows one of Bel Geddes's costumes, featuring a collar that looks like a doiley, thus portraying Sybilla as continuous with the domestic objects featured in the house. The painting behind her, however, is of Horace's mother, signifying the presence of female control that Sybilla has come to embody. This is confirmed in the dialogue later in the episode when Sybilla asks Horace, "What was your mother like?" He answers, "She was a fine woman, a wonderful person. I was devoted to her but she managed me." Sybilla's responds, "Ah, but I don't, you know," signaling her awareness of Horace's anxiety that he is being controlled. Like the painting of Annie in the episode of *Have Gun—Will Travel* discussed below, Sybilla is a provocative figure who sets off men's insecurity and projection. Like a literal painting, Sybilla seems to be a flat surface. With her crystallized smile and opaque character, she is similar to a film noir femme fatale like Laura in Otto Preminger's film of the same name or even Evelyn Mulwray in *Chinatown*, characters who force Mark McPherson and Jake Gittes, respectively, to reveal their own neuroses.

"Sybilla" not only shows the subversiveness of female power, even as it seems to be constrained by a narrowly defined social role, but also functions as a critique of the repeated cultural habit of projecting male fantasies and anxieties about gender onto the image of women. Given Lupino's onscreen charisma and penchant for playing knowing and cynical characters, it isn't surprising that she turned down the role of the impassive Sybilla. But it also isn't surprising that Lupino would have been attracted to a story that ex-

FIGURE 56 *Alfred Hitchcock Presents*: Sybilla (Barbara Bel Geddes) and Horace (Alexander Scourby) in "Sybilla" (aired 6 December 1960)

amines marriage and male anxiety about female betrayal. Two years earlier, Hitchcock had directed what is perhaps in the history of American film the most powerful and acute analysis of male projection of desire onto the figure of the woman, *Vertigo*. Lupino seems to have been thinking about *Vertigo* when she shot the first and second images shown in figure 56, since there Sybilla strongly resembles the portrait of Carlotta Valdez holding a bouquet of flowers, a painting important in the earlier film. The comparison is more striking when we consider that in *Vertigo* Barbara Bel Geddes played Midge, the practical but lovelorn friend of retired detective Scottie Ferguson. An artist and designer, Midge, having seen the portrait, parodies Scottie's obsessional love for a dead woman by painting herself in Carlotta's place (see figure 57). Instead of shifting Scottie's interest to Midge—her intent—the prank backfires because

FIGURE 57 The image of Barbara Bel Geddes painted in place of Carlotta Valdez in Hitchcock's *Vertigo*

of Scottie's inability to see women as active subjects, only as desired objects, emblematized by the portrait of Carlotta. In "Sybilla," Bel Geddes's character prods the male protagonist to project onto her his desire for a woman figured as object—idyll, angel in the house, portrait. Horace's temporarily heightened sense of power is doomed because he is using this fantasy of woman to strengthen his male ego. Horace, like Scottie (and Jake Gittes in *Chinatown* and Devlin in Hitchcock's *Notorious* [1946]) is skeptical about women, his very mistrust the source of the trauma that besets him.

The Untouchables was another series that gave Lupino an opportunity to work creatively within the constraints of a brisk television shooting schedule. It also allowed Lupino to explore the theme of criminality, as she did in *The Hitch-Hiker*. One of the most striking elements of *The Untouchables* is its interest in multiple storylines and how it generated viewer interest in the criminals, often presented as bewildered individuals, themes that attracted Lupino. For example, in "A Fist of Five" (aired 4 December 1962), Lee Marvin plays a cop who is fired because of his violent tendencies. The episode evokes not only Robert Ryan's untethered Jim Wilson in *On Dangerous Ground* (1951), in which Lupino co-starred, but also *The Big Heat*, Fritz Lang's 1953 film in which Marvin appeared as Vince Stone, criminal sidekick to the mob boss. In *The Big Heat*, Glenn Ford's Dave Bannion attacks his boss for being a "scared rabbit," afraid to tackle city corruption, just as Mike Brannon (whose name is quite similar) in "A Fist of Five" lambastes his boss, calling him a "fat politician cop." With nothing to lose, Brannon breaks bad, enlisting his brothers to help him steal $150,000 from Anthony "Tough Tony" Lamberto (Frank DeKova). Lupino advances the narrative using a montage to introduce Brannon's brothers, beginning with close-ups, then moving the camera to reveal context and each character, while Walter Winchell narrates in voiceover. As we see in a distinctive four-shot (not designated in the shooting script) that reveals the brothers' community and perhaps their entrapment in Mike's scheme, one of the brothers (Keir) is played by James Caan ("Fist of Five"; see figure 58).

FIGURE 58 *The Untouchables*: "A Fist of Five" (aired 4 December 1962): four of the brothers, including Keir Brannon (James Caan)

An Irish version of the short-tempered Sonny Corleone, Keir Brannon anticipates Caan's role in *The Godfather* that would make him famous ten years later. In "A Fist of Five," the portrait of a loyal Irish family (including a loving matriarch and the guilty and recalcitrant son Denny [Roy Thinnes]) adds another storyline to the main one in which Eliot Ness pursues Tony. A further storyline gives us Tony's own background; he married a woman named Angie who is crippled by a bomb that was meant for Tony. In one composition (again, a recurring shot of Lupino's that includes a profile and character facing the camera), Ness tries to draw Angie out. Her mistrust of Ness is apparent in the shot, as park gates behind them suggest another trap, or cage (see figure 59).

Rather than noir, *The Untouchables* has been categorized as "police drama," presented in a "more naturalistic, socially realistic mode ... more concerned with the everyday lives of cops and the mechanics of crime-solving" (Ursini 277). However, the series episodes that Lupino directed offered her opportunities to work in an Expressionist style. "The Man in The Cooler" (aired 5 March 1963) has been noted for its "Murnau-ish touches" (Nolan 62). Here, Lupino again establishes thematic resonance in her mise-en-scène, which depicts the villain "Fat Augie" in a meat-packing

FIGURE 59 *The Untouchables*: "A Fist of Five": Ness (Robert Stack) and Angela Lamberto (Phyllis Coates)

FIGURE 60 *The Untouchables*: "Fat" Augie and the mirror in "The Man in the Cooler" (aired 5 March 1963)

warehouse, the only place, we are told, that is cool enough to accommodate the large man. With the use of mirrors, Lupino accentuates Augie's grotesqueness, as well as the irony of his "office" setting with hunks of meat in the background (see figure 60). Lupino approached one violent scene in the cooler with her typical "feminine" coaxing: "Peter, darling, hold the knife this way. And make sure we see that sweet meathook" (qtd. in O'Dell 173).

Peter Bart quotes one actor she worked with in *The Untouchables* recalling her "bending over him and cooing, '[Lovey] bird, remember you've been shot in the belly. You must suffer, darling.'"

In the third-to-last episode aired in the series (7 May 1963), Lupino directed "The Torpedo," about a hit man "gone yellow." Rehearsing the themes of *The Hitch-Hiker*, the story features Charles McGraw as Holly Kester, whose feminized name undermines his masculinity as emblematized in his role as the "torpedo" for a bootleg kingpin called Kurtz. This episode explores Holly's failure in a masculine role (loyal thug) and links gender anxiety to genre when his fellow gangster Burt Engle casts Holly's "troubles" as melodrama. "Aw, c'mon," says Burt. "Don't play Stella Dallas for me." Lupino uses shot-reverse-shot sequences and close-ups throughout the episode to show Holly's unease. In one scene, we see Holly grab the place where his gun should be but isn't, a gesture not in the shooting script ("Torpedo"); as he reaches toward his chest, the shot doubles its significance: Lupino's mise-en-scène emphasizes Holly's lost "heart," the missing "torpedo" generating his fear and anxiety. His entrapment and gender crisis are also clear in shots of a wounded Holly shut out of the apartment of his now-disgusted girlfriend Rita (Gail Kobe), after he has confided in her about his lost nerve.

Like *The Hitch-Hiker*, "The Torpedo" explores the high stakes not only of violent encounters but also of gender confusion, a sense of failed masculinity that causes Lupino's male characters, like Roy Collins and

Gil Bowen—and Harry Graham in *The Bigamist*—to feel alienated and bewildered. In this sense, the action/adventure niche of many of the stories Lupino directed are a MacGuffin. They function as a distraction from what really interests "the female Hitch": characters lost in a maze of social roles incommensurate with their psychological and emotional states. Lupino's television work consistently dramatizes these preoccupations.

In 1963–64, Lupino directed episodes of *The Fugitive*. Many will remember the show's conceit: Dr. Richard Kimball (David Janssen) chases the one-armed man he believes murdered his wife, the crime for which Kimball was wrongly convicted. In a noir twist of fate, Kimball narrowly escapes execution because the train tak-

FIGURE 61 *The Untouchables*: Holly Kester (Charles McGraw) in "The Torpedo" (aired 7 May 1963)

ing him to death row crashes, and he is able to flee the scene and his pursuer, Lt. Philip Gerard (Barry Morse). With its "mood of alienation and fatalism," the action thriller was a good match for Lupino. In "Fatso" (aired November 19, 1963), Lupino once again demonstrates a virtuosity with scene construction and with leading her actors to turn in compelling performances.[27] Jack Weston's portrayal of Davy Lambert is unusually poignant for a guest appearance in a weekly television show. Weston was best known for his comic performances (*Cactus Flower* [1969], *Same Time Next Year* [1978]), but he was also a stage, film, and television actor whose variety and depth can be seen in his malevolent appearance in the thriller *Wait until Dark* (1967) and in his sensitive portrayal in this episode of *The Fugitive*. The shooting script describes Davy as an outsider, in terms that we might say elicited Lupino's cinema of empathy:

"Davy is below average mentally. Not an extreme case, he is one of the many thousands of people in our society who don't quite measure up to the norm in intelligence but who can fit in quite well when given encouragement and understanding. Davy, who is starving for this sort of reassurance, has responded with pathetic eagerness to Carter's [Kimball, incognito] friendly attitude" ("Fatso").

Davy is in jail sleeping off a drunk and befriends the fugitive in their cell. Kimball's arrest for a minor traffic accident puts him in danger of being discovered by Gerard. Kimball's own sense of alienation is triggered by Davy's feelings of loss and aloneness. Estranged from his family, who blame him for a fire that burned the family farm years earlier, Davy has the affect and self-doubt, but also the warmth and friendliness, of a child. Like Kimball, he has been wrongly blamed, since his cruel brother Frank, jealous of their mother's attention to Davy, in fact started the fire (adding fuel to the psychological fire by calling him "Fatso," a name and identity Davy has internalized). As he grows to care for Davy, Kimball is able to express more of himself, since his medical training allows him to share expertise and help to treat Davy's psychological wounds.

Davy's gentleness is evoked by Weston's sensitive performance and enhanced by Lupino's mise-en-scène. Davy reminisces with Kimball about his early years on the farm before he was cast out by his family, turning to food and alcohol to assuage his pain. In the first image in figure 62, Lupino captures Davy's angst and loneliness, as the noir shadow of his abject body and of the prison bars are seen alongside scrawled writing, including "mother," scratched into the wall. Davy was close to his mother, which aggravated his brother's ire, leading the brutish Frank to frame Davy for the arson. In the second image, Davy recalls the early bucolic pleasures of the farm and nearby stream with its "itsy bitsy fish, but boy do they taste good. You fry 'em plain with just a dab of butter." Davy's childlike affect disarms Kimball, who quietly observes him, as this shot makes clear in an interesting use of depth of field. Alongside the bottom image in figure 62, Lupino inserts a close-up of the men's hands as they shake, underscoring their bond. In this image, we see Davy's openness to Kimball, a charm contrapuntal to the fatalistic tone more generally characterizing the show. In scenes such as this one in the cell where Kimball and Davy meet, Lupino makes the most of space, blocking, and montage, none of these visual details appearing in the shooting script. Her juxtaposition of Davy's naïve and self-lacerating personality ("Why would anyone buddy up with a big fat stupid slob like me?" he says later on the train) with Kimball's caring yet careful or diffident engagement enhances the actors' chemistry, as well as the story's drama.

Westerns

Early in her career in television, Lupino directed the most literary of television westerns, *Have Gun—Will Travel* (1957–1963). The show, featuring Richard Boone as Paladin, the paradoxically cultured western hero, was unique, according to Gaylyn Studlar, because of "its dandy's more subversive implications" (7). Boone was instrumental in reinforcing Lupino's entry into television directing; he had, according to Kearney and Moran, "admired her hardboiled style" (138). Indeed, in the work Lupino did for *Have Gun—Will Travel*, she brought her noir vision to the small-screen western. In one episode in particular, Lupino introduces two of the themes central to her films—cornered women and homosocial communities.

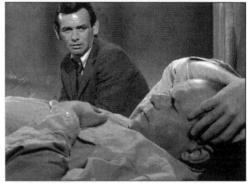

FIGURE 62 *The Fugitive*: Davey Lambert (Jack Weston) and Richard Kimball (David Janssen) in "Fatso" (aired 19 November 1963)

Lupino directed several episodes of *Have Gun—Will Travel* during the run of the show, but one of the most interesting of these is "Lady on the

Wall" (aired 20 February 1960), set in an old ghost town named Bonanza, "the biggest little town in the world." In Bonanza, four men sit at the bar and stare at a portrait, toasting to "Annie," the subject of the painting. The episode's repeated four-shots of these men visually underscores the town's identity as barren, save for this community of has-been miners, whose only hope resides in their obsessive viewing of Annie's portrait. "You think we'd stay in this town full of empty houses," one of the men intones, "if it weren't for Annie?" Lupino's camera work as the men are introduced dynamically integrates close-ups of the men's faces into pans, as she did in the scene discussed above from "A Fist of Five" in *The Untouchables*. Visually constructing a community of men opposed to outsiders such as Paladin, Lupino gives viewers an intimate look into the lives of these men, who are noir figures of loss in a dead town: "Now Bonanza's a ghost town and we're almost ghosts," one of the men, Elmer, says.

The plot of "Lady on the Wall" is constructed around the disappearing portrait, but the episode's fascination is in Lupino's mise-en-scène, which makes use of the portrait's thematic resonance and the men's fixation on the idea of Annie as a lost virtuous angel in the house that nevertheless presides over them in the form of the painting. The men cling to a fantasy of youth and desire that Annie represents. In fact, the episode strongly echoes noir classic *Laura* in its exploration of the notion of woman as image, "derealized," in Mary Ann Doane's terms, into the object-fantasy of, in this case, the homosocial gaze of men in a defunct western town. In *Laura*, Detective McPherson falls in love with the portrait of Laura, and the film concerns itself with male cognitive dissonance once the real woman Laura appears and cannot live up to the perfection McPherson has projected onto her image (for Laura *may* be involved in the murder of Diane Redfern, and McPherson must suspend his desire for Laura until she is proved innocent). As in *Laura*, "Lady on the Wall" depicts male desire for female perfection as a salve for men's own mortality. In fact "Annie" has a counterpart in reality, Genevieve, "Miss Felton," who works at the bar and secretly observes the men's fetishized objectification of her younger self. Miss Felton is elderly now, and is trapped in an image of herself "to be looked at." When she reveals her true identity as "Annie," the men's disillusionment is captured by Lupino, whose camera pans the four men in close-up, doubling the initial introduction of the men in the episode. Each exclaims, "Annie.

Oh no—can't be. Not Annie. Ugh, no." Affirming Miss Felton's saddened acquiescence, Lupino's close-up of the woman lends her a subjectivity otherwise denied her. As Miss Felton says, "These gentlemen don't even know I'm alive anymore."

In keeping with his gallant character, Paladin is the only one who recognizes Genevieve's worth and beauty as her older self. Comfortable in a "feminized civilization," as Gaylyn Studlar has observed about Paladin (7), he merges masculine prowess with compassion for women, corresponding to Lupino's vision of empathy and gender equality. Just as Boone helped Lupino cross into television directing, in this episode Paladin helps Genevieve break free of her "framed" status in the portrait. Lupino represents the bond between Paladin and Genevieve in an intimate shot-reverse-shot sequence, including stunning close-ups, while the men behind them continue to stare at the painting.

The depth of the episode is a consequence of Lupino's directing. She communicates the themes of shattered youth and ideals, belatedness, and marginalized women through shot composition, mobile framing, and

FIGURE 63 *Have Gun—Will Travel*: The old men of Bonanza and Miss Fenton (Lillian Bronson) with Paladin (Richard Boone) in "The Lady on the Wall" (aired 20 February 1960)

mise-en-scène. In its noir depiction of thwarted desire, the episode is a hybrid of melodrama, film noir, and the western. It further exemplifies Lupino's creative merging of genres, while Lupino maintained a unique visual style that echoes patterns throughout her film and television careers.

The year after this episode, Lupino took on *The Rifleman*, directing a story about an assault on a woman that again brings *Outrage* to mind. The episode, "The Assault" (aired 21 March 1961), begins with harmonious music and an establishing shot of a bucolic ranch house. The episode cuts to a love scene shot in close-up between wrangler Cade Conway (Paul Mantee) and Vashti Croxton (Linda Lawson). The scene quickly becomes violent, as the couple begins to argue about where they will marry. Calling Vashti "the orneriest pig-headed woman," Conway inadvertently tears her "Sunday dress," insisting nonetheless that she "deserved it." Filmed in claustrophobic shots of the room, Vashti begins to whip Conway with a belt she has grabbed from the mantelpiece. In a scene that could well have inspired Samuel Fuller to open *The Naked Kiss* in the way he did three years later, Vashti whips her beau, insisting that they will marry where she wants. Resembling the baroque sequence in which Kelly (Constance Towers) beats her pimp with a shoe in Fuller's film, Vashti's assault on Conway ends with him hitting her across the face, at which point she falls, unconscious, to the ground. Lupino excelled in guiding actors to express emotional bewilderment, which Conway does at this point, as he moans to the unconscious woman, "Oh, Vashti. Don't leave me!" He panics, takes her money, and runs.

After this bizarre prologue of domestic abuse, the story shifts to a comic mode when harmless scammer Speed Sullivan (Bob Sweeney) comes upon the stricken Vashti and tries to revive her. He is, however, later framed for the assault by Vashti herself, who wants to protect Conway from the violent wrath of her brother and father, King Croxton (King Calder) and Thess (Meb Florey). Lupino films the two scenes with the latter characters as they corner the hapless Sullivan in canted low-angle close ups and threaten that they will "make him hurt a little."

Lupino's contribution to the episode can clearly be seen in one of the last scenes, after Luke, the Rifleman (Chuck Connors), senses that Vashti has lied to protect her lover Conway and has performed his duty as the "good guy" by coaxing Vashti to admit that she couldn't live with herself if she persisted in framing Speed. When Vashti 'fesses up, the men in her family turn on her: "I ought to put the whip to you," says her father. This scene functions effectively to provide a context for Vashti's desperate (and "ornery") rebellion throughout the episode: she battles Conway and then lies to protect him because he is her vehicle for escaping an even more oppressive masculine world, that of her home.

In defending herself to Luke, King, and Thess, Vashti claims that she has the "worst part of being a wife," taking care of her brother and father, even as the two "lock me up." In a landscape in which Conway's assault seems the lesser of two evils, Vashti's entrapment evokes a familiar home noir, this time set on a western ranch. About Conway, Vashti says to her father, "He can't hit near as hard as you can." Meeting her victimization with an equal measure of rebellion, she insists to her father and brother that she will go off looking for Conway: "And you come looking for him and the first piece of lead you catch is gonna be from me." When they ask Vashti if they should help pack her things, she fires back "What things?!" figuring home as privation, isolating and claustrophobic, and more dangerous than the outside world.

As we have seen, Lupino brought her versatile camerawork and directing skills—her penchant for a crowded mise-en-scène and montage often signifying irony, for example—to the small screen across genres, contributing to some of the most provocative television episodes aired during the 1950s and 1960s. Popular writing about Lupino's directing work during this time fetishized the unique gender arrangements on the set. Writers noted the velvet pants and lipstick she wore, and they reveled in Lupino's assumption of the "Mother" role. But Lupino's manipulation of gender roles went well beyond her persona on the set. Her interventions across genres in television reiterate the narrative preoccupations and rich mise-en-scène we see in her films, while maintaining a focus on issues of gender.

Particularly interesting in this regard is the theme of failed idealism, a noir trope demonstrated in all of Lupino's films for The Filmakers. We see this motif of disillusionment visually represented in two episodes from western series she directed in the 1960s: one, the episode discussed above from Have Gun—Will Travel, "Lady on the Wall," the other, from The Virginian, "Deadeye Dick." While thoroughly engaged with the western landscape, in the process earning Lupino a reputation for "action" directing, both episodes explore gender trauma and the theme of thwarted desires. Thus, her television genre work, perhaps most strikingly in "Lady on the Wall," is linked to Lupino's noir analysis of modern social relations in all of her film work.

The Virginian's "Deadeye Dick" (aired 9 November 1966) also explores gender relations, beginning with a scene on the train by which young Marjorie travels from the east with her mother to visit Aunt Livvy in Medicine Bow, Wyoming. "Deadeye Dick" parodies Edward Wheeler's serial dime novels about Deadwood Dick, which appeared in the 1870s and 1880s and inaugurated the fictional western genre.

Having spent much of her ride reading *Deadeye Dick's Last Shot; or, All for the Love of Bessie Burton*, Marjorie is enamored of the dime-novel's romantic view of the West, reading aloud to her mother, "Bessie Burton's eyelids fluttered open, and her lovely clear blue eyes gazed up at the handsome countenance of Deadeye Dick." While her mother advises that she exchange the fictional for a real view of the western landscape, Marjorie prefers to allow her imagination to run free, seeing in "The Virginian" (James Drury), after her arrival, a version of Deadeye Dick when he kicks some tumbleweed away from "Old Percy," the horse leading Marjorie's buggy. Just as in the episode Marjorie reads from *Deadeye Dick*, the manly hero (The Virginian) saves the heroine (now, Marjorie) from a startled horse; the episode introduces these scenes in a humorously romanticized landscape, in which Marjorie repeatedly interprets The Virginian through the lens of *Deadeye Dick*.

Although The Virginian tries to redirect young Marjorie's attention to young Bob Foley, an aspiring attorney who has taken a fancy to Marjorie, the would-be lawyer has none of the western hero's masculine prowess. We see him falling off a horse, for example, as Marjorie looks on. The episode recalls John Ford's *The Man Who Shot Liberty Valance* (1962), which, like "Deadeye Dick," begins and ends with the arrival and departure of a train, marking a tension between modernity and the mythic West. Both stories pit a feminized eastern lawyer (Ranse Stoddard and Bob Foley) against a masculine western cowboy (Tom Donaphin and The Virginian). In the film, Tom Donaphin (John Wayne) is, finally, overshadowed by the more modern figure of civilization, Stoddard (James Stewart), though not without an accompanying tone of trauma, as Donaphin's exit from the western scene is overlaid with a powerful

FIGURE 64 *The Virginian*: "Deadeye Dick" (aired 9 November 1966)

sense of mourning. The television episode is more comic but displays a similar pattern of the modern eastern figure of civilization competing with the laconic tough-guy western cowboy. The Virginian's anonymity gives him an air of mystery (he is never named), allying him with the classic western male hero and with film noir protagonists. Film noir shares with westerns such as *The Man Who Shot Liberty Valance* an ironized view of legendary American heroes, such as the western cowboy and the hardboiled detective or urban *flaneur*. Like these figures, the characters that appear in Lupino's film and television work often twist ideas of heroic idealism, reflecting Lupino's vision that in American Dreaming lie the seeds of disappointment.

"Deadeye Dick" reveals Marjorie's adolescent fantasies to be misguided, even absurd, and the episode is comically resolved when Bob Foley assumes the role of western hero by inadvertently saving Marjorie from outlaw kidnappers. He admits to The Virginian at the end that he had closed his eyes when firing at the villain. Figure 64 shows Marjorie's diary entry and her goggle-eyed view of the western hero as a romantic icon, and Lupino's sense of irony as she dissolves from a high-angle shot of Marjorie's dreamy expectations of dancing with The Virginian to one of her disappointing date with Bob Foley.

While much of the episode exploits Lupino's talent for mixing location action shots (of Bob's bumbling attempts to learn to be a "real" cowboy so that he can impress Marjorie, then of her actual kidnapping by outlaws) with close-ups and shot-reverse-shot sequences that enhance the episode's psychological drama, it culminates in a resonant four-shot of Bob and Marjorie riding back to Medicine Bow, Bob having captured the outlaws singlehandedly, thus winning Marjorie's admiration.

In 1967, Lupino directed one of her last television episodes, "My Brother's Keeper" (aired 22 November 1967) from *Dundee and the Culhane*, a western featuring British actor John Mills as lawyer Dundee on the frontier. His legal assistant and foil, Culhane (Sean Garrison), is the western hero who teaches Dundee how to survive in the frontier. Lupino's empathy for the outsider lends Mill's Dundee complexity and humor. In the episode, Dundee awkwardly rides a horse across the landscape to save a young boy who has been abducted and whose father has been killed. An earlier scene in which the grandfatherly Mills sings "The Bonny Bonny Banks of Loch Lomond" to the boy as a bedtime lullaby interrupts the normal action of the western genre in an extended and poignant interlude. This reveals Lupino's ability to work fluidly with genres, including shifts in tone.

One year earlier, in 1966, *TV Guide* covered Lupino's directing of *The Virginian*. In the article, Lupino says she is called upon not for love stories but action, "a runaway horse, two shootouts, and a cattle stampede" (qtd. in Anderson, *Beyond the Camera* 114). Lupino made similar comments over the years, but we note that, in fact, she did direct many love stories in television: between Dundee and the boy; a teenager and his teacher; a woman and a female ghost; and a host of other offbeat tales of attraction, desire, and characters drawn to each another based on mutual experiences of loss and alienation. Despite the arch tone of many references to Lupino as "Mother" over the years, the label also captures her empathy with actors on the set, particularly with their vulnerability. O'Dell quotes one of Lupino's comments about empathizing with actors: "I don't ever say 'Do this. I want you to stand here. I want you to do that.' Having been an actress, I know what it is like to be put into an uncomfortable position" (173). Lupino's remarks call to mind Murray Pomerance's recent description of "the director's manner" in working with actors: "The message 'I am here with you; I am helping you; you can count on me for support' is the content of the directorial gesture at its strongest" (59). Lupino's television directing displays her empathy with actors. This empathic style is a facet of the sensibility found in the films she directed. The strength of her "directorial gesture" moves her well beyond the implications of the sometimes limiting maternal metaphor. In addition to her directorial leadership, Lupino brought to her television work a special attention to space and place as crucial to narrative—at times functioning as active characters themselves. Thus, despite Lupino's allusion to the narrative patterns and classic elements of the western quoted just above, her directing work in the television western was anything but conventional.

Men and women now in their fifties and sixties may be unaware of how present Ida Lupino was in their childhood. Those of us who watched classic television when we were young, many of its shows and episodes directed by Lupino, may wonder what this creative and courageous woman would do with characters like Walter White (Bryan Cranston) from *Breaking Bad* and Sansa Stark (Sophie Turner) from *Game of Thrones*: the former having twisted the "father knows best" ideal; the latter buffeted from one trauma to another. Building on the legacy of Lupino and other path-breaking women in film and television, Michelle McLaran has distinguished herself directing these shows, which are dramas full of action, special effects, and violence. We can only further imagine how Lupino might have directed Peggy Blumquist (Kirsten Dunst) from the second season of the FX show *Fargo*, as this wanna-be feminist character embarks on her confused path and for whom empowerment never arrives, or the equally bewildered Carol and Therese in the film *Carol* (adapted from Patricia Highsmith's *The Price of Salt*), provocatively directed by another independent-minded creative filmmaker, Todd Haynes.

We wonder what "Declarations" Ida Lupino would make in today's world, how she would have negotiated the barriers that still stand in the way of talented women eager for opportunities in film and television. Would she have continued to embrace the nickname of "Mother," not only an identity on set that helped her to nurture colleagues, but also a managerial style and political strategy? Lupino's role on the set as "Mother," wearing velvet pants and lipstick, certainly prefigured many women television directors working today, such as Lesli Linka Glatter, whom Maureen Dowd observed filming the Showtime political thriller series *Homeland*: "I watched the director Lesli Linka Glatter on the 'Homeland' set in Berlin, charging up and down the street getting ready to blow stuff up while she reapplied her Cranberry Cream lipstick." *Transparent* creator and director Jill Soloway seems to have inherited some qualities from "Mother":

> On set, Soloway thinks of her job as akin to being a good mom: "Kids come home from school, want to put on a play in the back yard. You help them build a stage; you make sure they take breaks, have a snack." (Soloway has two sons, Isaac, nineteen, and Felix, seven.) Jeffrey Tambor told me, "I have never experienced such freedom as an actor before in my life. Often, an actor will walk on a set and do the correct take, the expected take. Then sometimes the director will say, O.K., do one for yourself. That last take, that's our starting point." (Levy)

"Women are naturally suited to being directors," insists Soloway. "It's *dolls*," she continues. "How did men make us think we weren't good at this? It's *dolls* and *feelings*." Soloway's insight reminds us of Lupino's sensitivity to actors and actresses and her unique melding of empathy and toughness.

In the 1960s and 1970s, second-wave feminists made us alert to the language and dangers of "othering" people. No one remained "other" for Lupino; instead, she imagined making art and being in relationships in terms of dialogue and community. In her films and television work, Lupino highlighted strong women, such as those in *The Trouble with Angels*, who assert leadership characterized by empathy and self-confidence. In fact, in 2003, *People* magazine reported that the first thing Elizabeth Smart did when she returned home after her kidnapping was to watch *The Trouble with Angels*. Certainly this choice must be read first within the wholly private lexicon of this girl's trauma. However, it may also participate in a cultural landscape that Lupino would have recognized, where female rebellion was often cloaked in a "safe" disguise and fraught with paradoxical desires. It's possible that Elizabeth Smart found—as did so many girls and women—both solace and empowerment in the imaginary spaces that Lupino built.

Lupino has served—we might say she productively haunts—the careers of women in the media who assume a feminist leadership style more freely, as they make art and media across diverse genres. Yet, even as strong women artists and professionals make their mark in the media, the practice of stereotyping in the film industry persists. We can see this in press coverage of McLaran's short-lived position at the helm of the forthcoming Warner Bros.' blockbuster *Wonder Woman;* the job has since been given to Patty Jenkins, best known for directing the remarkable 2003 film about serial killer Aileen Wuornos, *Monster* (2003). Recent press releases also tout the fact that Marvel hired Nicole Perlman and Meg LeFauve to write the screenplay for Disney's forthcoming *Captain Marvel,* while at this writing Angelina Jolie is reportedly a top choice for directing the film (Child). As has been observed, "The so-called glass ceiling for female directors helming major studio pictures is thick enough that an exception to the rule qualifies as news whenever it occurs" (Mendelson). In 2015, writer and director Leslye Headland said, paraphrasing Samuel Johnson, that in the minds of the men who maintain control in Hollywood, "a woman directing is like a dog playing the piano: at best, a novelty or fad; at worst, an aberration" (qtd. in Dowd).

Writer Shonda Rhimes, creator and producer of *Grey's Anatomy,* among many other shows, has said about women behind the scenes in Hollywood, "Truly creative things happen when one thinks differently, yet nobody wants to think differently" (Swartz). Rhimes's comment serves to underscore Lupino's remarkable courage and accomplishments in an earlier, tougher era for women, in which her drive to think and act differently set her apart.

Most agree that television has been more open than film production to women working behind the scenes. Sarah Treem, showrunner for Showtime's *The Affair,* noted recently that the industry has been "a little bit of an oasis" for women (Dowd). In the 1970s through the 1990s, Kim Friedman, Debbie Allen, Gail Mancuso, Betty Thomas, Pamela Fryman, and others made landmark contributions to television directing, some, like Lupino, having the good fortune to use their acting careers to jump into directing.

The inroads women have made in television as compared with the film industry surely can be attributed to the perceived riskiness of big-budget film productions and the concomitant sense of television as a less valued cultural space. Traditionally, television has been seen as a domestic sphere, lending itself to "the feminine touch"; however, these assumptions now seem obsolete in a diverse network, cable, and web-based television landscape in which shows have far surpassed even the "Quality TV" of the 1980s and 1990s (recall HBO's marketing blitz in the middle 1990s, "It's Not TV. It's HBO"). And yet, these examples of women directing diverse genres, including those traditionally deemed "masculine," point to the power and ability of women to achieve significant success directing, producing, and writing across media. As is true for all accomplishments by women through the centuries, there are long and rich histories that frame and help us understand and appreciate these achievements.

ACKNOWLEDGMENTS

We would like to thank Christine Becker, Gwendolyn Audrey Foster, Sarah Kozloff, Barton Palmer, and Nancy West for reading and commenting on parts of our manuscript. All gave us support and encouragement. Our appreciation goes to Marilyn Campbell and Anne Hegeman at Rutgers University Press and especially to our superb copyeditor, Eric Schramm. We would also like to express our heartfelt gratitude to Leslie Mitchner, editor in chief at Rutgers, for her support, wisdom, and belief in this project.

Julie Grossman: I would like to thank Jill Beifuss, Tom Boland, M. J. Devaney, Patrick Keane, Julie Olin-Ammentorp, Ann Ryan, and Kim Waale for reading early pieces and versions of this project. Additional thanks go to Tom Bower, Amy Breiger, Jeremy Butler, Helen Hanson, Tom Leitch, and the staffs at the British Film Institute, the Library of Congress, the Margaret Herrick Library of the Academy of Motion Picture Arts and Sciences, the Paley Museum of Television in New York, and the UCLA Film and Television Archives; the 2015 "Thinking Serially" conference at the CUNY Graduate Center (especially Michael Healy); and, at Le Moyne College, Linda LeMura, Tom Brockelman, Kate Costello-Sullivan, the Research and Development Committee, the Joseph C. Georg Endowed Professorship, and my exceptional department chairs, Jim Hannan and Dan Roche. Huge thanks to Steve Wilson at the Harry Ransom Center at the University of Texas, and also to Michael Gilmore. Many thanks to Fuller French for introducing me to his jaw-dropping collection of television scripts in Fort Worth. And a warm and very special thanks to Mary Ann Anderson, who gave us significant material help and whose deep affection for "Ida" and fabulous storytelling were an inspiration in writing this book. My deepest thanks, as always, go to Phillip Novak for his patience and unfailing support.

Therese Grisham: I would like to thank Hillary Plemons, who attended my classes on "home noir" and Ida Lupino at Facets Multimedia in Chicago, for noticing the similarity between *Outrage* and *M* that got the project rolling. I would also like to thank Susan Doll, who wrote wonderfully about home noir on *Movie Morlocks*, the official TCM blog, which encouraged me to carry on with it. Additional thanks go to Charles Coleman, film programmer at Facets Multimedia, for all of his support and recommendations; Milos Stehlik, director of Facets, for inviting me early on in this project to talk about Lupino on "Worldview" on WBEZ, where he is film contributor; Liz Howard, for her friendship and her unflagging support; Owen Field for his vast knowledge of film noir and for his continuing inspiration; Gertrude and William Grisham for believing in my abilities; and Esther Grisham Grimm for taking my abilities as a given. My deepest gratitude goes to Max and Bruno for their loving, and essential, companionship.

NOTES

Part One. Introducing Ida Lupino

1 An earlier version of the company was called Emerald Pictures (named after Lupino's mother, Connie Emerald), a collaboration between Young and Lupino and
Anson Bond, with whom the two parted ways after the completion of *Not Wanted*
(1949).

2 Lupino's public statements about Hopper's warm support contrast with more
familiar portraits of the famed columnist, notably that of Jennifer Frost in *Hedda
Hopper's Hollywood: Celebrity Gossip and American Conservatism*, which show
Hopper's sometimes vicious endorsement of conservative values. Frost recounts,
for example, Hopper's aggressive promotion of domestic household values, even
as she reported on strong independent actresses she admired. This contradiction
indicates the overall inconsistencies within Hollywood communities, characterized by strong personal or professional bonds and competing ideologies, as well as
gender expectations alternately affirmed and rejected.

3 In a stunning report published in the summer of 2015, the University of Southern
California's Annenberg's School for Communication and Journalism revealed
that out of 107 filmmakers directing the top-grossing films of 2014, only two
were female, or 1.9 percent. Another key element of the study is that only 30.2
percent of the 30,835 speaking characters evaluated were female across the 700
top-grossing films from 2007 to 2014. This calculates to a gender ratio of 2.3 to 1.
Only 11 percent of 700 films had gender-balanced casts or featured girls/women
in roughly half (45–54.9 percent) of the speaking roles. A total of 21 of the 100 top
films of 2014 featured a female lead or roughly equal co-lead. This is similar to the
percentage in 2007 (20 percent), but a 7 percent decrease from the 2013 sample
(28 percent). In 2014, no female actors over forty-five years of age performed a
lead or co-lead role.

These findings, which can be found at http://annenberg.usc.edu/pages/~/
media/MDSCI/Inequality%20in%20700%20Popular%20Films%2081415.ashx,
were also reviewed by Manohla Dargis in the *New York Times* (August 5, 2015,
http://www.nytimes.com/2015/08/06/movies/report-finds-wide-diversity-

gap-among-2014s-top-grossing-films.html?_r=0). Maureen Dowd's exposé in the *New York Times* on November 20, 2015, includes many declarations from prominent women behind the scenes testifying to the gender inequalities in Hollywood.

4 Stout worked on *Fort Apache* (1948), *She Wore a Yellow Ribbon* (1949), and *The Quiet Man* (1952). He became the only second-unit photographer to receive an Academy Award for cinematography, shared in 1952 with cinematographer Winton Hoch for his work on Ford's *The Quiet Man*.

5 Tischler is probably best known as a producer. He went on to co-produce 130 episodes of the television series *M*A*S*H*, for which he won an Emmy Award in 1976.

6 Foster goes further: "If there are any true heroes in *The Hitch-Hiker*, it is the Mexicans who value human life enough to save these two men, and thwart Myers' reign of terror" (53).

7 See, for example, Osteen's analysis; Rabinovitz in Kuhn; Foster; and David Greven's essay in *Bright Lights Film Journal*.

8 We are grateful to Sarah Kozloff for her comments on this point.

9 For an excellent discussion of the orginal script, "Bad Company," and the details of *Not Wanted*'s history in connection with the PCA, see Waldman.

10 At the home for unwed mothers later in the film, Sally tells Mrs. Stone that she is nineteen.

11 A color scene of an actual cesarean section performed during birth, including every bloody detail, is often included on DVDs today of *Not Wanted*. However, Lupino and The Filmakers had nothing to do with the inclusion of this scene. Jack Lake, a roadshow promoter, is responsible for re-releasing the film into an exploitation movie, changing the title to *The Wrong Rut*. It played in drive-ins from 1962 to 1972 (editorial review from Image Entertainment's DVD release of *The Wrong Rut/Birthright*, May 16, 2006).

12 Hopper continues in her *Los Angeles Times* column, "Her company, Filmakers, plans to do a picture based on the harrowing experiences of the two captives with Ida directing. That should be right down her alley. She says that the true horror and suspense of the story, as detailed by Damron, have not yet been revealed by the press" (2 February 1951).

13 Richard Koszarski observes that Lupino "display[s] the obsessions and consistencies of a true auteur. . . . In her films *The Bigamist* and *The Hitch-Hiker*, Lupino was able to reduce the male to the same sort of dangerous, irrational force that women represented in most male-directed examples of Hollywood film noir" (371).

14 See *Time* magazine's "'I'm Gonna Live by the Gun and Roam': Portrait of an American Spree Killer" in April 2014 and Mary Ann Anderson's *The Making of "The Hitch-Hiker."*

15 As it was, the film ignited letters of protest about its representation of road culture, many rejecting Lupino's dark revelation of the dangers of hitch-hiking (see "RKO Refuses to Blunt Its 'Hitch-Hiker' Blurbs Tho Ride-Thumbers Beef").

16 See Maureen Dowd's "The Women of Hollywood Speak Out": "And there is still such an atmosphere of fear that many female directors told me they hide their pregnancies until the last possible minute. One director confessed that she actually hides her child, refusing to put a photo of her son on Facebook, fearing 'it could end my career.'"

17 Sarah Kozloff writes,

> Orchestral performances, however, prioritise the score/screenplay. Another possibility might be to think of filmmakers as jazz musicians, sometimes playing notes as written, sometimes improvising together according to the (shared) music in their heads. The Duke Ellington Orchestra comes closest to providing an apt analogy because of the blurring of roles and collaboration. Ellington, an accomplished pianist, led his ensemble in playing the compositions of other composers (including some written by his band members), but he also wrote or co-wrote 1,000 pieces, some of which highlighted the talents of particular instrumentalists and many of which were arranged by his long-time composing partner Billy Strayhorn. (*Life of the Author*)

18 For a rejoinder to a dismissive view of melodrama, see Sarah Kozloff's essay in *An Introduction to Film Genres*: "Melodramas . . . depict the world as sharply divided into good and evil, with the suffering virtuous people deserving of pathos and admiration" (82). Kozloff emphasizes the values of melodrama, often "stories that genuinely touch us through their unabashed courage in facing emotional currents generally kept hidden or unspoken. In a paradoxical way, melodramas do focus on the 'one true thing': how we feel" (108).

19 Other critics take their lead from Lupino's personal comments, using Lupino's biography and offscreen comments about feminism and gender to lambaste her films. They confuse Lupino's filmmaking with her avoidance of feminist platforms—"I never thought of myself as a crusader," she repeatedly claimed—as can be seen in comments by Redding and Brownworth in their 1997 *Film Fatales: Independent Women Directors*, in which they call *Hard, Fast and Beautiful*, "indisputably a melodrama with an ending that will disappoint feminists (which Lupino claimed not to be)" (37).

While a smattering of scholars before the 1990s and a larger number since then have come to recognize Lupino's stylistic sophistication and the poignancy of her dark meditations on postwar struggles, still others continue to mistake Lupino's realist depiction of female trauma for an endorsement of her women characters' failure. In other cases, a tendency to judge Lupino's representations of gender leads to outright misreadings of her characters. The latter can be seen in Marsha Orgeron's 2008 analysis of *The Bigamist*, which focuses on the guilt of Harry's wife, Eve. Orgeron sees the film as punishing Eve's ambition: "Eve's ruthless independence and self-sufficiency are the real crime here." It is exceedingly difficult to imagine anyone watching this film seeing Eve as "ruthless." The film presents a crisis in gender roles without judging the main characters, which some of Lupino's critics fail to do. This brings to mind Carrie Rickey's comment about claims that Lupino's films are antifeminist: "That's an epithet, not a description of Lupino's considerable directorial skills." In *The Bigamist*, Lupino shows Eve's fervent desire to succeed in business *and* her love of Harry. Only Harry cannot rejoice in Eve's ambition. Harry is envious of her, and he interprets her talent for business as an assault on his masculinity. He also feels that Eve has abandoned him, projecting onto her a sexual "frigidity," as she excels in selling deep-freezers for their joint company. But for Orgeron, seeing Harry as a character for whom we feel empathy necessarily means that Eve is presented as victimizer, which is simply not in keeping with the spirit of the film ("Depicting [Harry] in this sympathetic fashion makes Eve's trespasses all the more reprehensible" [Orgeron 186]).

If "feminist criticism has found it hard to look at Ida Lupino's work on its own terms" (Kuhn 5), a corollary to this statement is an assumption about Lupino's desire to submit to conventional roles in her life so as not to call attention to her gender transgressions in her filmmaking: "Lupino made films about punishable, hyperbolic ambition in part to contrast with her own relatively modest participation in a male profession, while she further modeled her publicity to ensure that her reputation did not transgress too greatly a woman's role in 1950s Hollywood and, more generally, in America" (Orgeron 203).

20 Quart and Orgeron find Lupino's representation of Millie Farley's exploitation of her daughter reprehensible: "Far more viciously than in *Mildred Pierce*, the ambitious mother here, associated with career, must be denounced as a selfish schemer from start to finish" (Quart 27). Orgeron similarly finds the role problematic. While she is absolutely right that Millie's desolate end is the "price to pay for making one's way in a man's world," she confuses once again a portrait of gender trauma for an evaluation of behavior and then its punishment: "While I am tempted to consider the female roles in *The Bigamist* and *Hard, Fast and Beautiful* as Lupino's attempts to critique instead of replicate negative representations of ambitious women, the films themselves work against such an interpretation. One does not walk away from either film with the sense that Eve's or Milly's [*sic*] fates were unjustified; rather both women appear to 'get what they deserve'" (Orgeron 194–95).

This seems to us patently wrong. Rather, the Farleys in *Hard, Fast and Beautiful* represent the postwar family under seige in its confusion about gender and social roles. Marriage is a trap, female ambition causes suffering, for mother and daughter, and the world of American capitalism "gone noir" transforms individual talent and drive into a snakepit of competition and consumption. The villain in this story is the manipulative representative of commercial sports, Fletcher Locke, not these two women or their father, who are, in different ways, desperate for a life different from the one they are leading. Lupino herself said of Millie that she is a woman with ambition, not that she is wrong to be ambitious. What other way was open to her, in her striving to be upwardly mobile as part of the promise of the American Dream? Certainly, Will, her husband, won't help her; he wants no part of it.

Mandy Merck discusses Wendy Dozoretz's attribution of the negative portrait of Millie Farley to "the ideological imperatives of postwar familialism." As we discuss in Part II, Merck distinguishes her own reading of Millie by noting the important fact that "the film's denouement is hardly the 'happy ending' that the RKO executives prescribed" (in Kuhn 83).

21　This quote is from Dowd's interview with actor Alec Baldwin: "'They call it shooting,' he says. 'Its groupings are called units. They communicate on walkie-talkies. The director is the general. There is still the presumption that men are better designed for the ferocity and meanness that the job often requires. I've worked with so many [expletive] male directors. They should open a window and let more women in.' (Jill Soloway prefers not to yell 'Action!' because it sounds too much like 'Attack!')"

22　A good example of this is Osteen's apt description of *Outrage* in which "rape merely exaggerates the oppressive sexism that underwrites [Ann Walton's] world" (204).

23　In the late 1990s Scheib became curator at Kino International to remaster several of Lupino's films. At that time, she again wrote about Lupino's "bewildered lost people" and the "shallowness of the mainstream and the void it projects around it—the essential passivity of ready-made lives" (MoMA).

24　These include a book-length application of the tenets of the *politiques des auteurs* to Lupino's work by Lucy Stewart (1980); a monograph for BFI on *The Bigamist* (2009) by Amelie Hastie; and, most notably, Annette Kuhn's 1995 edited collection *Queen of the B's: Ida Lupino Behind the Camera*. This last volume presents a significant body of scholarly work on Lupino's career, including essays on all of her films, as well as a chapter on her television directing, and useful appendices and filmographies. In 2017, as part of a book series at the University of Edinburgh Press intended to foreground underappreciated filmmakers (called *Re-Focus*), *The Films of Ida Lupino* appeared, which will help to secure a greater place for Lupino in film history.

25　In 1993, while Lupino was still alive (she died in 1995 at the age of seventy-seven), Louis Antonelli undertook a restoration of *The Hitch-Hiker*. Lupino's assistant and conservator Mary Ann Anderson has published several trade books with compelling photographs to celebrate Lupino's accomplishments: *Mr. Adams and Eve* (2010); *Ida Lupino: Beyond the Camera* (written with Lupino and published in 2011); and *The Making of The Hitch-Hiker* (2013). Throughout the last two decades, film festivals have regularly paid tribute to Lupino, including the Melbourne Film Festival in 1996 and the Lumière Festival in Lyon, France in 2014. UCLA and The Museum of Modern Art have featured Lupino's work many times. Curator Anne Morra at MoMA champions Lupino's films, as does Barbara Scharres at the Gene Siskel Film Center at the Art Institute of Chicago. See David

Everitt's 1997 piece in the *New York Times*, in which he quotes Scharres, "I should say that any woman director who manages to make her career in Hollywood, especially at that time, is by virtue of that a feminist." In the MoMA Blog *Inside/Out*, Department of Film Curator Charles Silver quotes *Modern Women: Women Artists at The Museum of Modern Art*, in which his colleague Anne Morra says that Lupino's work "remains singular, a vital contribution to the evolution of women in cinema and of American independent film production in general." In 2015, the Seoul International Women's Film Festival not only showcased Lupino's directing work but also published a significant program book titled *Ida Lupino: Noir Queen Crosses Taboos in Hollywood* (2015). This volume reproduces essays that have appeared in print and in online journals, adding original scholarship. Printed both in Korean and English, *Ida Lupino: Noir Queen* further attests to the international appeal and appreciation of Lupino's work.

26 The critical habit of damning Lupino with faint praise has slighted her astonishing role in film history. With the resources available at her independent production company, she wasn't going to make sleek Hollywood films, as did others from the period: *Samson and Delilah* (1949), with a budget of $3 million, or *The Three Muskateers* (1948), which had a whopping budget of $4.47 million (IMDb). Two of the postwar period's social problem films—*The Best Years of Our Lives* (1946) and *Gentleman's Agreement* (1947), were budgeted at $2 million and $2.1 million, respectively. In stark contrast, *Not Wanted* had a budget of $150,000. Because it made $1 million, however, Lupino and Young had funding to continue the company, later changing its name from Emerald to The Filmakers, as Malvin Wald took the place of Anson Bond in the company.

In 1954, ironically just before the company would fold after an unwise venture into distributing its own films, a venture Lupino resisted, The Filmakers was lauded by the *Motion Picture Exhibitor* "as an infant company whose open secret was that it was light on financing and heavy on courage" ("Filmakers Proves"). The Filmakers moved into distribution because Howard Hughes as the head of RKO, their distributor, had given them a raw deal by charging the company with all advertising costs. As Sarah Kozloff writes, "The fact that the serious, black and white, low-budget, Academy ratio films that Lupino favored didn't offer enough potential profit also played a role in the company's demise" ("On Dangerous Ground").

27 The Court's decision was based on the Sherman Antitrust Act of 1890, which states in Sections 1 and 2, "Every contract, combination in the form of trust or otherwise, or conspiracy, in restraint of trade or commerce among the several States, or with foreign nations, is declared to be illegal," and "Every person who shall monopolize, or attempt to monopolize, or combine or conspire with any other person or persons, to monopolize any part of the trade or commerce among the several States, or with foreign nations, shall be deemed guilty of a felony" (Title 15 of the United States Code, Chapters 1 and 2, Monopolies and Combinations in Restraint of Trade; Federal Trade). Meant to foster competition, these sec-

tions of the Code were used in the suit filed by independent exhibitors against the eight major and minor Hollywood studios in 1938. Because the exhibitors won the case in 1942, but the studios did not comply with the ruling, the Supreme Court, according to a clause of its ruling, revisited the case three years later, in 1945. However, it must be said that the Federal Trade Commission had been investigating the monopolistic practices of the studios since the silent era, so questionable industrial practices were nothing new. The outcome of the 1948 decision was that if the studios did not divest themselves of the exhibition venues they owned, they could be charged with felonies. The Paramount consent decrees forced the studios to dismantle their vertical integration by 1953. Still, Hollywood was slow to comply and continued to divest itself throughout the 1950s.

28 After World War II, most films were being made by independent film companies, which resulted in the package-unit system of production. As Janet Staiger writes, the system of production before the war was the producer-unit system based on the strategy of "an individual company containing the source of the labor and materials" (Bordwell et al.). However, the package-unit system was based on the concept that a producer organized a film project, secured the financing, and arranged for the laborers as well as the equipment and sites for the production through a leasing arrangement with the major studio and other support firms. "Costumes, cameras, special effects technology, lighting and recording equipment were specialties of various support companies available for component packaging" (Bordwell et al.).

29 Frequently, the experts (and other cultural authorities such as novelists) strongly implied that the dread of the breadwinner role was evidence of homosexual tendencies, which were signs of arrested adolescence. Psychoanalyst Lionel Ovesey, for example, wrote a case study about a twenty-three-year-old homosexual: "He lived alone and his social existence was a chaotic one, characterized by impulsive midnight swims and hitchhiking." This young man, Ovesey continued, was uninterested in having a career (Ehrenreich 25).

30 For an extensive discussion of postwar American realism, including analysis of the relationship between American film and neorealism, see Palmer, esp. chapter 4 (e.g., "The American postwar cinema manifests its own burgeoning realist traditions," and "The American filmmaking establishment did not take up the challenge to imitate or appropriate the neorealist style" [114]).

31 Sklar continues: "These expansive claims for neorealism's importance to postwar Hollywood rank among the mysteries of historiographer fashion. No doubt systematic research may yet produce intriguing and perhaps significant modes of specific affinities and practical interactions. For the present, however, most such theoretical assertions remain unexamined, undocumented, and generally improbable" (72). Our research on Lupino uncovers the affinities and practical interactions of Lupino's films with those of neorealism.

32 Italian neorealism has attained almost mythical status as a source for diverse American realisms, which, for the most part, retain their commitment to individualism, unlike neorealist films. Moreover, as Peter Bondanella writes in "Italy,"

Outside of Italy, little was known of Italian cinema during the fascist period (1922–43), and this ignorance created the erroneous idea abroad that the postwar Italian cinema had arisen miraculously from the ashes of the war. In retrospect, it is clear that many important contributions laying the groundwork for the creative explosion we know today as Italian neorealism must be credited to the prewar period, and the fascist regime played a major role in these contributions. The regime built one of the world's great film complexes, Cinecittà (inaugurated by Mussolini in 1937), and founded a major film school, the Centro Sperimentale Cinematografico (1935). Both of these institutions are still in operation and constitute the backbone of the present industry. Several film journals—*Bianco e nero*, the official organ of the Centro, and *Cinema* (edited at one time by Mussolini's son Vittorio)—helped to spread information about foreign theories and techniques through translations and reviews. Most of the great directors, actors, technicians, and scriptwriters of the neorealist period received their training in the fascist period, and some directors, such as Roberto Rossellini, made their first important films in the service of the fascist government. The most significant influence upon Italian cinema during the fascist era came not from Hollywood but from the French cinema of the same period. The term "neorealism" was in fact first used in an essay by Umberto Barbaro to describe the cinematic style of French directors such as Carné and Renoir. (347)

33 R. Barton Palmer writes of *Marty*, which was originally a teleplay written by Paddy Chayefsky (also directed by Mann and first broadcast in 1953 on *The Philco-Goodyear Television Playhouse*), that the film was "resolutely unglamorous" (61). In addition, "Unlike the stage-bound teleplay, the film records the actions of the socially typical characters in an environment whose complexities, if not all made the subject of dialogue, emerge clearly with extended cinematic *ekphrasis*, with pictures that are literally worth thousands of words. The film's street scenes are filmed in a carefully calculated, unprepared fashion that looks backward to neorealist works such as *Bicycle Thieves* and forward to New Wave productions like François Truffaut's *The 400 Blows*" (63).

34 Generally, *Outrage* and *M* are not visually or narratively commensurate; nor is *M* simply an Expressionist film. However, here we concentrate on what Harry Horner drew from a powerful Expressionist scene from *M* to employ in similar terms in *Outrage*. It should be noted that in most of *M*'s narrative, nothing "happens." The film is an analytical montage of signs, as Nicole Brenez writes. Further,

In *M*, there are no events because there is only information. The film's fictional material is not made up of people who confront or love each other but of the reading and interpretation of different signs. In the images, this takes the form of the extraordinary multiplicity of shots of posters, newspapers, books, documents, maps—a key stylistic trait in silent film that is paradoxically taken to its height in his first sound film. The film progresses by passing us from one type of writing to another, and reaches a climax when the police start encircling

Beckert. This sequence constitutes an inversion of the normal scalar system: The human populace appears as an insert shot in relation to the shots of graphics succeeding one another without interruption. (Brenez 71–72)

Part Two. Lupino's Ingenious Genres

1 See also Gaines's discussion of Gledhill, who "has conceived melodrama as a virtual 'genre producing machine,' a machine that generates further genres (Gledhill, 2000, 227, 229). Pair this with Richard Dyer's recent work on pastiche (2007)," continues Gaines, "and we have a marked shift in genre theory" (*Gender Meets Genre* 19).

2 Kozloff takes the idea of Lupino's low budgets further: "We will never know what [Lupino] could have been capable of had she been allotted the ample resources or supported by powerful male backers of directors such as Kazan, Hughes, and Houseman" ("On Dangerous Ground").

3 Jeanine Basinger, "Giving Credit," in *Directors Guild of America Quarterly*. Guy-Blaché was the very first female director, in fact, moving from France to Hollywood, where she was known, as Basinger notes, for her innovative work with the new medium, using special effects, double exposing the film, running film backward and in reverse, and color tinting.

4 Mahar's book and others recount the historical inclusion of women behind the scenes in Hollywood's early years only to be pushed out of the industry after World War I when filmmakers sought financial backing from Wall Street, whose masculinist business model precluded the contributions of women.

5 See the *Women's Film Pioneers Project*, https://wfpp.cdrs.columbia.edu/pioneer/ccp-dorothy-arzner/, as well as Mayne, Johnston, and Geller.

6 See, for example, Cowie, "Film Noir and Women"; Gates, *Detecting Women*; Grossman, *Rethinking the Femme Fatale in Film Noir*; Hanson, *Hollywood Heroines*; Kaplan, *Women in Film Noir*; and Wager, *Dames in the Driver's Seat*.

7 See also Johnston, who observes that Sally "finds a substitute for the child in the person of a crippled young man" (216).

8 As Mandy Merck astutely notes, "It is not surprising that a film as interested in performance as this one, a film which is set next door to Hollywood and whose central character is clearly modeled on the pushy 'stage mother,' should foreground the performative aspects of femininity. What *is* remarkable is the connection it draws between the playing of this role, the playing of competitive sport, and work" (81).

9 See, in particular, Barbara Koenig Quart's harsh judgment of Lupino's representation of women: "Far more viciously than in *Mildred Pierce*, the ambitious mother here, associated with career, must be denounced as a selfish schemer from start to finish" (27).

10 In Tunis's story, Fletcher is described as a "suave young mucker." Tunis attacks the appropriation of sports by modern capitalism in his portrait of Fletcher, whose "one ambition in school and college had been to become a champion; early in

his career it became evident that he had neither the persistence nor the patience" (278). Lupino grafts this critique of American capitalism to a portrait of failed gender and family roles.

11 We note here that Elisabeth Bronfen and others, including Collins and Jervis and Royle, have explored the unconscious forces that animate modern social space. Like Bronfen (especially in her *Home in Hollywood: The Imaginary Geography of Cinema*), we read against the grain of conventional domestic fantasies of home. However, while Bronfen's work is aimed at revealing psychoanalytical fault lines within the home, our interest in home noir, which we see as a distinct construction of film noir, corresponds not to a psychoanalytic presence of the uncanny but to sociohistorical structures revealed by film noir's engagement with modernity.

12 Starting in the 1990s, a number of interesting books have been published that deal with film and the architecture of space. These works, including Merrill Schleier's *Skyscraper Cinema*, Pamela Robertson Wocjik's *The Apartment Plot*, and Edward Dimendberg's *Film Noir and the Spaces of Modernity*, provide an important critical backdrop for our understanding of representations of space in the modern landscape, though they aren't of particular relevance to home noir (in this context, see also Vivian Sobchack's influential essay "'Lounge Time': Post-War Crises and the Chronotope of Film Noir").

13 Among the many studies that have been useful to us in detailing the shift from the Victorian to the modern in home architecture is Foy and Schlereth, *American Home Life, 1880–1930*.

14 See Amelie Hastie's comparison of the arrangement of beds in *The Bigamist* with Lupino's "poetic rendering" of failed marriage in the representation of beds in *Hard, Fast and Beautiful* (55–56).

15 This section takes its title from the website *A Mighty Girl*, http://www.amightygirl. com, which calls itself "the world's largest collection of books, toys, movies, and music for parents, teachers, and others dedicated to raising smart, confident, and courageous girls." *A Mighty Girl* also features a blog about women in history who have made contributions to changing the world. Co-founders Carolyn Danckaert and Aaron Smith write:

> After years of seeking out empowering and inspirational books for our four young nieces, we decided to create *A Mighty Girl* as a resource site to help others equally interested in supporting and celebrating girls. The site was founded on the belief that all children should have the opportunity to read books, play with toys, listen to music, and watch movies that offer positive messages about girls and honor their diverse capabilities.
>
> Girls do not have to be relegated to the role of sidekick or damsel in distress; they can be the leaders, the heroes, the champions that save the day, find the cure, and go on the adventure. It is our hope that these high-quality children's products will help a new generation of girls to grow and pursue whatever dreams they choose—to truly be Mighty Girls!

We find the name and contents of the site perfect to describe the spirit of *The Trouble with Angels*—and Ida Lupino.

16 We are indebted to Ken Anderson's delightful and informative blog post on "fun nun" movies, "*The Trouble with Angels* (1966)."

17 Gypsy Rose Lee's mother was famously portrayed by Rosalind Russell in the 1962 musical *Gypsy*.

Part Three. Lupino Moves to Television

1 For an excellent discussion of film stars' transition to television, including a case study on *Four Star Playhouse*, see Becker. She debunks the myth that film stars "were deserting to the enemy" (63), showing the richness of their experience and opportunities in television.

2 This story and transition are also recounted in "Coast to Coast" and in Graham Fuller's 1990 interview with Lupino.

3 In his essay "Femininity and Language in Ida Lupino's 'Checked Out,'" Ehsan Khoshbakht argues that the story reveals a break between sound and image, which disrupts the male gaze.

4 Celebrating the excellence of Lupino's work in this episode, the Melbourne International Film Festival screened "No. 5 Checked Out" in 1996, with the idea that the episode represents "a compelling case for the viability of the short form in film." See the Festival's Archive, http://miff.com.au/festival-archive/film/21528.

5 It is widely known that Lupino was called "the female Hitch." It was Lupino, talking with Mary Ann Anderson, who stated that Hitchcock himself was the source of the nickname (M. A. Anderson, interview).

6 Butler "reject[s] the definition of style as the mark of the individual genius on a text (though certainly geniuses create elements of television) or as a flourish somehow layered on top of the narrative (although some style is decorative). A program does not need geniuses or flourishes to possess style" (*Television Style* 15). See also Jaramillo 74.

7 Borrowing from Roland Barthes's "zero-degree style of writing," John Thornton Caldwell describes the "zero-degree style," "effaced style," or "antistyle" present in pre-1980s sitcoms, a view that, until recently, scholars have generally acceded to. The rise of "quality television" and subsequent explosion of epic-televisual shows such as *The Sopranos* and *The Wire*, then *Breaking Bad* and *Mad Men*, have given rise to expanded discussion of television aesthetics and "second-degree style," or "maximum-degree style" (see Barrette and Picard, for an example). Jeremy Butler, Christine Geraghty, Sarah Cardwell, Jason Mittell, and Jason Jacobs have, among others, challenged the notion that aesthetics and style have little place in the field—see, for instance, Butler's *Television Style*, and Jacobs and Peacock. Lupino's television directing of 1950s and 1960s invites a close look at style, an area little regarded generally because of production practices as well as the fact that "these productions were typically made very cheaply with limited sets" (Jaramillo 73).

8 Bazin is quoted by Butler in *Television Style* (2). Butler discusses the powers of
   television style in terms of Althusser's notion of "hailing," describing "the process
   by which a society's ideology calls out, 'Hey, you!' and encourages you to become
   one of its subjects" (14; see also 116).

9 One example of this potential richness can be seen in the source for the name of
   Gilligan's Island's S.S. *Minnow*. Wishing to mock Newton Minow's famous "vast
   wasteland" speech in 1961, producer Sherwood Schwartz named the boat after the
   FCC chair. Schwartz believed that Minow had "shipwrecked" television by giving
   too much creative power to the networks (Johnson 90–91).

10 See Grossman, *Literature, Film, and Their Hideous Progeny*.

11 See Desjardins: "The social and personal problems of women are worked through
   fantasy, specifically through the generic conventions of domestic melodrama, in
   which the wife or mother and home are idealized, or through the gothic, in which
   women's place is rendered as 'nowhere,' or an 'elsewhere' and the dread of annihi-
   lation threatens stability" (83–84).

12 See, for example, Levine, who discusses the "contradictions" that "permeated the
   programme—the Angels transcended conventional gender roles by working in a
   typically male occupation but at the same time were represented as quintessentially and fundamentally female" (93).

13 In 1959, Lupino and Duff appeared in an episode of *The Lucille Ball/Desi Arnaz
   Show* together, "Lucy's Summer Vacation" (8 June 1959), in which Howard and
   Ida (the actors playing themselves) have been invited to the same cabin at which
   Lucy and Ricky are vacationing. At the beginning of their stay, high-jinx ensue
   when neither couple knows the other is there. The episode plays on Lupino/Duff's
   star text drawn from *Mr. Adams and Eve*, canceled the year before—when, for
   example, the cosmopolitan Ida mistakes the lake for a swimming pool ("Must cost
   a fortune to keep it heated"). Her glamor is parodied after Ida claims she wants
   to go fishing with Howard and Ricky early the next morning: "Are you kidding?"
   Howard responds. "You never got up before noon in your life unless you got paid
   for it." In *The Lucy Book*, Geoffrey Mark Fidelman rather bracingly claims that
   this episode is "the *only* episode of the entire *I Love Lucy* format that is actually
   bad" (131). He argues that the episode is missing producer Jess Oppenheimer and
   cinematographer Karl Freund and that it is the first one filmed without a live
   audience. Fidelman quotes producer Bert Granet, who says that the "comedy was
   forced" (132) and that "Lupino and Duff were no longer major stars. . . . [They
   were] second-rate guest stars" (132). The story within the episode hinges on Lucy
   and Ida's frustration with "the boys," who pay little attention to them because all
   Ricky and Howard want to do is fish. Plotting to land a night with their husbands,
   Lucy and Ida drill holes in the fishing boat, but the scheme backfires when Ricky
   and Howard decide to take their wives on a romantic boat ride after all on what
   Ida now calls "The S.S. Swiss Cheese." The climax of the episode belies the critics'
   lambasting, as Lucy and Ida's desperate attempts to patch up holes in the boat
   with chewing gum and their feet are quite funny. The women pretend to romance

Ricky and Howard to distract them from the gum popping up to reveal water spraying through the holes. Ricky serenades with his guitar, until Lucy grabs it to use as an oar, paddling in vain as the boat sinks. According to Anderson, filming the episode was difficult. The lake and the mood were "cold"; neither couple was getting along at the time (65).

14 There is further conjecture about missing episodes of *Mr. Adams and Eve*, which at present is only available for viewing at several television archives (The Paley, in New York City and Los Angeles ["Typical" and "Howard and Eve and Ida"]; the UCLA Film Archive ["Dear Variety," "Come On to Mars' House," "The Bachelor," and "Typical"]; the Harry Ransom Center at the University of Texas, Austin ["Active Duty," "The Fighter," "The Flack," "Magazine Story," "Suspension," "The Bachelor," and "The Mothers"]; and the Library of Congress ["Taken for Granted"]). There are twelve separate episodes held in total at the archives, while sixty-six episodes were produced altogether. One episode, "Howard Goes to Jail," was sold on eBay some years back (see Anderson, *Mr. Adams and Eve* 63), as was "The Producers," and three others are in circulation on the web (YouTube), "Academy Award," "The Mothers" (also at the Harry Ransom), and the spoof of *This Is Your Life*, "This Is Your Past." Scripts for many of the episodes are held at the Harry Ransom Center; some are also in Fuller French's collection at the Arts Library in Fort Worth, Texas.

15 In one instance of life following fiction, the year after this episode aired, Lupino herself was featured on *This Is Your Life*, an experience she apparently hated. While the episode features staged appearances of family relations she had long distanced herself from, it also introduced audiences to Lupino's real-life "discoveries," Mala Powers, Sally Forrest, and Keefe Brasselle. In the one affecting moment of tribute to Lupino, Powers turns to her and says, "You not only gave me the greatest chance of my life, but you gave me something more, the greatest gift that an actor can have. You believed in me. And I just had to succeed for you."

16 The parody of Howard Adams's jealousy in "Academy Award" surely functioned in part to sublimate Howard Duff's longtime resistance to being "Mr. Lupino." If *Mr. Adams and Eve* was about the absurd predominance of celebrity in a modern image culture, such critique wouldn't save Lupino herself from a marriage torn apart by power struggles, the demand for role-playing within Hollywood, and conflicting attitudes toward gender and marriage. A survey of clippings from the several years before *Mr. Adams and Eve* reveals repeated episodes of Lupino/Duff arguments (including violent public ones, such as the "brawl" on Sunset Strip reported in the *Los Angeles Examiner* in March 1953 [see Ludlow]), separations, and reconciliations, a cycle that had the couple negotiating among paparazzi, entertainment reporters, and women's magazines to whitewash their tumultuous relationship.

17 The comment about the cameramen is quoted in Anderson, *Beyond the Camera* (115). Concern about her marriage unfortunately kept Lupino from working at times: in interviews, she repeatedly mentions the opportunities to direct in

Europe she refused—see, for example, the *Los Angeles Herald Examiner*, which quotes Lupino in November 1972: "'It would have meant staying away for perhaps a year,' she said. 'It's tougher for a woman than a man, if she's married. You know, I'm not a fella'" (Moss). In an interview with Patrick McGilligan and Debra Weiner in 1974, she said, "I've had offers to direct but they would have taken me out of the country, which would have meant leaving my home, my daughter, being away from here months and months on end. It's a rough setup." She continued, "That's where being a man makes a great deal of difference. I don't suppose the men particularly care about leaving their wives and children. During the vacation period the wife can always fly over and be with him. It's difficult for a wife to say to her husband, 'Come sit on the set and watch'" (229)..

In later years, Lupino would share her resentment toward Duff (who decidedly did not want to "sit on the set and watch"), particularly after he left her a final time in 1972: "My personal life knocked me for a loop. . . . Twenty-four years with one person and then suddenly nothing—and just a week before our anniversary. . . . It's a rotten feeling. He's with his young lady in Malibu . . . and my life is different" (Loynd); "There comes a time in a man's life when he's gotta get a new pair of shoes" ("As Film Star, Director, Composer"). Before Duff, Lupino's first marriage to actor Louis Hayward ended after he came back from World War II with post-traumatic stress disorder. In the late forties, Lupino married Collier Young, the only husband with whom she could work and be with as an equal. The stress of The Filmakers and the appearance onto the scene of Howard Duff and Joan Fontaine (who married Young) precipitated the end to their marriage, though Lupino and Young remained friends and working partners for many years. Lupino certainly earned her cynicism about marriage. But, as she said in a *New York Times* interview in 1969, "You weather the storms" (Stone).

18 Years later, after *The Hitch-Hiker* and her success on television directing action and suspense series, Lupino joked, "I used to be the poor man's Bette Davis. Now, I'm the poor man's Don Siegel" (qtd. in Huber).

19 Desjardins nicely recounts the critical debate about whether Lucy Ricardo represents submission or subversion: "Lori Landay points out that Lucy's ineptness mitigates her subversiveness of Ricky's rules. Alexander Doty argues that the program conflates 'the infantile and the female through its characterization of Lucy through her various lacks' (lack of control over language, music, and her own body). Patricia Mellencamp sees Lucy as a 'rebellious child whom the husband/father Ricky endured, understood, loved, and even punished, as for example, when he spanked her for her continual disobedience'" (147–48).

20 Of course the time during which this article appeared marks, as Karen Mahar has observed, the beginning of Hollywood's systematic exclusion of women as filmmakers: "By the mid-1920s, female directors and producers, many of whom were critically and commercially successful, found themselves defined as unfit" (2).

21 Such deconstruction continues to resonate as subversive, if, as Dowd reports, Hollywood studio heads assume, "Even if she doesn't cry . . . what if the woman in charge turns out to be some dizzy dame who is indecisive?"

22 See Hastie (13). Keogh also comments on her being a "hired hand." It is worth noting here the probability that Lupino directed many more episodes than are documented: she refers in an article for the *New York Times* in 1969, for example, to an episode of *The Bill Cosby Show* she directed (see Stone), and Mary Ann Anderson reports that Lupino remembered being called frequently to direct episodes at the last minute (interview). Sometimes the result of directors being too hungover to show up at work, these contributions would not be publicized. Looking at the list of *The Bill Cosby Show* episodes, a likely episode to which she may be referring is "Home Remedy" (aired 28 December 1969), officially attributed to Richard Kinon, with whom Lupino worked on *Mr. Adams and Eve* and for whom she may have subbed.

23 As in the whitewashed account of their marriage discussed in note 16, Lupino spoke with Louella Parsons in 1957: "When I directed Howard, it wasn't good. Now we have another director and we are getting along so well it's almost boring" ("Ida's Is a Working Marriage"). It is also worth noting that Lupino was originally set to direct *Private Hell 36* (1954), one of the last films distributed by The Filmakers. The decision to replace Lupino with Don Siegel owed to her realization that directing Duff wouldn't work.

24 For a reading of the show's "protofeminist sensibility," see Morreale.

25 This episode is notable, as Metz reports, because it was the first of the series to feature a guest star, which subsequently became a signature format of the show. "Wrongway Feldman" starred Hans Conried as the hopelessly discombobulated pilot and proved so popular that Lupino was brought back later that season to direct a sequel, "The Return of Wrongway Feldman" (aired 13 March 1965).

26 Julie O'Reilly discusses the domestic persona of Elizabeth Montgomery, who seemed to revel in a conventional marriage to the show's producer William Asher during the run of *Bewitched*. Montgomery's public comments on "the joys of marriage and family [, including] recognition of Asher as patriarch" (O'Reilly 27) bear resemblance to conformist remarks Lupino intermittently made that were also a complex negotiation with public expectations. O'Reilly goes on to concur with other critics that despite its seeming acquiescence to gender norms, *Bewitched* was also quite subversive.

27 The quote is from Ursini, who called *The Fugitive* "the most self-conscious *noir* series and undoubtedly the most successful one" (284). However, Jeremy Butler sees "its visual style [as] actually less noir than previous programs" (*Television Style* 100). Both Ursini and Butler point to *Peter Gunn* (and Ursini, to *Johnny Staccato*) as more fully employing a noir visual style in the period. Despite *The Fugitive's* use of high-key lighting (see Butler, *Television Style* 101), Lupino's mise-en-scène in the episode "Fatso" is striking, including the use of shadows in the prison scene, as discussed here.

WORKS CITED

"Academy Award." *Mr Adams and Eve* (pilot). Story and screenplay by Charles Lederer and Collier Young. 17 Aug. 1955 (aired 22 Mar. 1957). Four Star Films. Archived at the Harry Ransom Center, the University of Texas, Austin. Accessed 12 May 2016.

Adams, James Truslow. *The Epic of America*. Boston: Little, Brown, 1931.

Agee, James. *Agee on Film*. New York: Random House Modern Library, 2000.

Altman, Rick. *Film/Genre*. London: BFI, 1999.

Anderson, Ken. "The Trouble with Angels (1966)." Blog post. *Dreams Are What Le Cinema Is For . . .* http://lecinemadreams.blogspot.com/2014/10/the-trouble-with-angels-1966.html?m=1. Accessed 24 Dec. 2015.

Anderson, Mary Ann. Interview with the author. 6 Aug. 2015.

———. *The Making of The Hitch-Hiker, Illustrated*. Albany, GA: Bear Manor Media, 2013.

———. *Mr. Adams and Eve, Illustrated*. Albany, GA: Bear Manor Media, 2011.

Anderson, Mary Ann, and Ida Lupino. *Ida Lupino: Beyond the Camera*. Albany, GA: Bear Manor, 2011.

"As Film Star, Director, Composer, Ida Lupino Excels in Entertainment." *Box Office*, 29 Sept. 1975. Margaret Herrick Library, Academy of Motion Picture Arts and Sciences, Beverly Hills, CA.

Balio, Tino. *Grand Design: Hollywood as a Modern Business Enterprise, 1930–39*. Berkeley: U of California P, 1993.

Barrette, Pierre, and Yves Picard. "Breaking the Waves." *Breaking Bad: Critical Essays on the Contexts, Politics, Style, and Reception of the Television Series*. Ed. David P. Pierson. Lanham: Lexington Books, 2014. 121–38.

Bart, Peter. "Lupino, The Dynamo." *New York Times*, 7 Mar. 1965. Margaret Herrick Library, Academy of Motion Picture Arts and Sciences, Beverly Hills, CA.

Basinger, Jeanine. "Giving Credit." *Director's Guild Association Quarterly*, Winter 2011. http://www.dga.org/Craft/DGAQ/All-Articles/1004-Winter-2010–11/Features-Giving-Credit.aspx. Accessed 3 Dec. 2015.

Becker, Christine. *It's the Pictures That Got Small: Hollywood Film Stars on 1950s Television*. Middletown, CT: Wesleyan UP, 2008.

Belton, John. *American Cinema / American Culture*. 4th ed. New York: McGraw-Hill, 2013.

Benshoff, Harry, and Sean Griffin. *America on Film: Representing Race, Class, Gender, Sexuality at the Movies*. 2nd ed. Hoboken, NJ: Wiley-Blackwell, 2009.

Biesen, Sheri Chinen. *Music in the Shadows: Noir Musical Films*. Baltimore: Johns Hopkins UP, 2014.

Bondanella, Peter. "Italy." *World Cinema Since 1945*. Ed. William Luhr. New York: Ungar, 1987. 347–79.

Bordwell, David, Janet Staiger, and Kristin Thompson, eds. "The Classical Hollywood Style, 1917–1960." *The Classical Hollywood Cinema: Film Style and Mode of Production to 1960*. New York: Columbia UP, 1985.

Breen, Joseph. Letter to Anson Bond (14 Feb. 1949). Production Code Association File on *Not Wanted* (1949). Margaret Herrick Library, Academy of Motion Picture Arts and Sciences, Beverly Hills, CA.

———. Letter to Ida Lupino (14 Feb. 1949). Production Code Association File on *Not Wanted* (1949). Margaret Herrick Library, Academy of Motion Picture Arts and Sciences, Beverly Hills, CA.

———. Letters to William Feeder (18 Apr. and 21 May 1952). Production Code Association File on *The Hitch-Hiker* (1953). Margaret Herrick Library, Academy of Motion Picture Arts and Sciences, Beverly Hills, CA.

Brenez, Nicole. "Symptom, Exhibition, Fear: Representations of Terror in the German Work of Fritz Lang." Trans. David Phelps. *A Companion to Fritz Lang*. Ed. Joe McElahaney. Hoboken, NJ: Wiley-Blackwell, 2015. 63–75.

Bronfen, Elisabeth. *Home in Hollywood: The Imaginary Geography of Cinema*. New York: Columbia UP, 2004.

Brownlow, Kevin. *Behind the Mask of Innocence: Sex, Violence, Prejudice, Crime: Films of Social Conscience in the Silent Era*. New York: Knopf, 1990.

Bubbeo, Daniel. *The Women of Warner Brothers: The Lives and Careers of 15 Legendary Leading Ladies*. Jefferson, NC: McFarland, 2002.

Butler, Jeremy. *Television: Critical Methods and Applications*. 4th ed. New York: Routledge, 2012.

———. *Television Style*. New York: Routledge, 2010.

Byars, Jackie. *All That Hollywood Allows: Rereading Gender in 1950s Melodrama*. London: Routledge, 2003.

Caldwell, John Thornton. *Televisuality: Style, Crisis, and Authority in American Television*. New Brunswick, NJ: Rutgers UP, 1995.

Cardwell, Sarah. "Television Aesthetics: Stylistic Analysis and Beyond." Jacobs and Peacock, 23–44.

Carman, Emily. *Freelance Women in the Hollywood Studio System*. Austin: U of Texas P, 2016.

Caspary, Vera. *Laura*. New York: Dell, 1942.

Chandler, Raymond. "The Simple Art of Murder: An Essay" (1950). *The Simple Art of Murder*. New York: Vintage Books, 1988.

Child, Ben. "Angelina Jolie Tipped to Direct Captain Marvel Movie." *The Guardian*, 16 Apr. 2015. http://www.theguardian.com/film/2015/apr/16/angelina-jolie-tipped-to-direct-captain-marvel-movie. Accessed 5 Apr. 2016.

"Coast to Coast." *Hollywood Reporter*, 16 Nov. 1972. Margaret Herrick Library, Academy of Motion Picture Arts and Sciences, Beverly Hills, CA.

Coates, Tyler. "10 Essential Movies About Nuns." *Decider*, 21 Jan. 2015. http://decider.com/2015/01/21/10-essential-movies-about-nuns/. Accessed 24 Dec. 2015.

Collins, Jo, and John Jervis, eds. *Uncanny Modernity*. Basingstoke: Palgrave Macmillan, 2008.

Colton, Helen. "Ida Lupino, Filmland's Lady of Distinction." *New York Times*, 3 Apr. 1950, X5. ProQuest. Accessed 15 Oct. 2015.

Cook, Pam. "No Fixed Address: The Women's Picture from *Outrage* to *Blue Steel*." Gledhill, *Gender* 29–40.

——. "*Outrage* (1950)." Kuhn 57–72.

Coontz, Stephanie. *The Way We Never Were: American Families and the Nostalgia Trap*. New York: Basic Books, 1992.

Cowie, Elizabeth. "*Film Noir* and Women." *Shades of Noir*. Ed. Jean Copjec. London: Verso, 1993. 121–66.

De Cordova, Fred. Interview. *Archive of American Television*. http://www.emmytvlegends.org/interviews/people/fred-de-cordova. Accessed 15 June 2015.

Desjardins, Mary R. *Recycled Stars: Female Film Stardom in the Age of Television and Video*. Durham, NC: Duke UP, 2015.

Desmond, John. "A Somewhat Forgotten Figure to Some Extent Remembered: Notes on Television Director, Script Writer, and Occasional Actor Montgomery Pittman." *Bright Lights Film Journal*, 31 Oct. 2010. http://brightlightsfilm.com/notes-on-television-director-script-writer-actor-montgomery-pittman/#.VzTf-sg8KnN.

Dimendberg, Edward. *Film Noir and the Spaces of Modernity*. Cambridge, MA: Harvard UP, 2004.

Dixon, Wheeler Winston. "Ida Lupino." *Senses of Cinema* (Apr. 2009). http://sensesofcinema.com/2009/great-directors/ida-lupino/.

Doane, Mary Ann. *Femmes Fatales: Feminism, Film Theory, Psychoanalysis*. London: Routledge, 1991.

Donati, William. *Ida Lupino: A Biography*. Lexington: UP of Kentucky, 1996.

Dowd, Maureen. "The Women of Hollywood Speak Out." *New York Times Magazine*, 20 Nov. 2015. Web. Accessed 25 Nov. 2015.

Dozoretz, Wendy. "The Mother's Lost Voice in *Hard, Fast and Beautiful*." *Wide Angle* 6.3 (1984): 50–57.

Dyer, Richard. *Pastiche*. New York: Routledge, 2007.

Ehrenreich, Barbara. *The Hearts of Men: American Dreams and the Flight from Commitment*. New York: Anchor Books, 1987.

"Eleanor and Anna Roosevelt Broadcast Over KECA on February 18, 1949." Transcript. Special Collections, Margaret Herrick Library, Academy of Motion Picture Arts and Sciences, Beverly Hills, CA.

Elsaesser, Thomas. "Tales of Sound and Fury: Observations on the Family Melodrama." *Critical Visions in Film Theory.* Ed. Timothy Corrigan and Patricia White, with Meta Mazaj. Boston: Beford/St. Martin's, 2011. 496–510.

Everitt, David. "A Woman Forgotten and Scorned No More." *New York Times,* 23 Nov. 1997. Web. Accessed 13 Mar. 2014.

"Fatso." *The Fugitive.* First draft. 13 Sept. 1963. Quinn Martin Productions. Arts Library, archive of Fuller French, Fort Worth, TX. Accessed 13 May 2016.

Fidelman, Geoffrey Mark. *The Lucy Book.* Los Angeles: Renaissance Books, 1999.

The Filmakers File. Margaret Herrick Library, Academy of Motion Picture Arts and Sciences, Beverly Hills, CA.

"Filmakers Proves It's in Business to Stay." *Motion Picture Exhibitors,* 29 Sept. 1954.

Firestone, Shulamith. *The Dialectic of Sex: The Case for Feminist Revolution.* New York: Farrar, Straus and Giroux, 2003.

Fiske, John, and John Hartley. *Reading Television.* London: Routledge, 2004.

"A Fist of Five." *The Untouchables.* Rev. first draft by Herman Groves. 27 Oct. 1962, Desilu Productions. Arts Library, archive of Fuller French, Fort Worth, TX. Accessed 13 May 2016.

Foster, Gwendolyn Audrey. *Disruptive Feminisms: Race, Gendered, and Classed Bodies in Film.* London: Palgrave Macmillan, 2015.

Foy, Jessica H., and Thomas J. Schlereth, eds. *American Home Life, 1880–1930: A Social History of Spaces and Services.* Knoxville: U of Tennessee P, 1992.

Friedan, Betty. *The Feminine Mystique.* New York: W. W. Norton, 1963.

Friedman, Lester, David Desser, Sarah Kozloff, Martha P. Nochimson, and Stephen Prince, eds. *An Introduction to Film Genres.* New York: W. W. Norton, 2014.

Frost, Jennifer. *Hedda Hopper's Hollywood: Celebrity Gossip and American Conservativism.* New York: New York UP, 2011.

Fuller, Graham. *Interview* 20.10 (1990): 120–21. London: British Film Institute, Reuben Library.

Gaines, Jane M. "The Genius of Genre and the Ingenuity of Women." Gledhill, *Gender* 15–28.

———. "Of Cabbages and Authors." *A Feminist Reader in Early Cinema.* Ed. Jennifer M. Bean and Diane Negra. Durham, NC: Duke UP, 2002. 88–118.

Galligan, David. "Interview with Ida Lupino." *Interview* 6:2 (Feb. 1976): 10–12. London: British Film Institute, Reuben Library.

Gates, Philippa. *Detecting Women: Gender and the Hollywood Detective Film.* Albany: State U of New York P, 2011.

Geller, Theresa L. "Dorothy Arzner." http://sensesofcinema.com/2003/great-directors/arzner/. Accessed 1 Sept. 2015.

Georgakas, Dan. "Ida Lupino: Doing It Her Way." *Cineaste* 25.3 (June 2005): 32–36.

Gledhill, Christine, ed. *Gender Meets Genre in Postwar Cinemas.* Urbana: U of Illinois P, 2012.

———, ed. *Home Is Where the Heart Is: Studies in Melodrama and the Woman's Film.* London: BFI, 1987.

Gonzalez, Ed. "B Noir: *The Dark Past* and *My Name Is Julia Ross.*" *Slant*, 15 May 2006. http://www.slantmagazine.com/house/2006/05/b-noir-the-dark-past-and-my-name-is-julia-ross/. Accessed 1 Dec. 2015.

Grant, Barry Keith, ed. *Auteurs and Authorship: A Film Reader.* Malden, MA: Blackwell, 2008.

Grant, Catherine. "Secret Agents: Feminist Theories of Women's Film Authorship." *Feminist Theory* 2.1 (Apr. 2001): 113–30.

Greven, David. "Ida Lupino's American Psycho: *The Hitch-Hiker* (1953)." *Bright Lights Film Journal*, 27 Feb. 2014. http://brightlightsfilm.com/ida-lupinos-american-psycho-hitch-hiker-1953/#.VnoLJZMrKCQ. Accessed 1 Mar. 2014.

Grossman, Julie. *Literature, Film, and Their Hideous Progeny: Adaptation and ElasTEXTity.* Basingstoke: Palgrave Macmillan, 2015.

———. *Rethinking the Femme Fatale in Film Noir: Ready for Her Close-Up.* Basingstoke: Palgrave Macmillan, 2012.

Guinle, Pierre, and Simon Mizrahi. "Biofilmographie commentée de Jacques Tourneur." *Présence du cinéma*, nos. 22–23 (Fall 1966): 56–83.

Halper, Donna. *Invisible Stars: A Social History of Women in American Broadcasting.* Armonk, NY: M. E. Sharpe, 2001.

Hanson, Helen. *Hollywood Heroines: Women in Film Noir and the Female Gothic Film.* London: I. B. Taurus, 2007.

Haralovich, Mary Beth, Janet Jakobsen, and Susan White. "*The Trouble with Angels* (1966)." Kuhn 118–36.

Harvard Film Archive. *Kathryn Bigelow: Filmmaking at the Dark Edge of Exhilaration.* Film series, 1–13 July 2009. http://hcl.harvard.edu/hfa/films/2009julsep/bigelow.html.

Haskell, Molly. *From Reverence to Rape: The Treatment of Women in the Movies.* 2nd ed. Chicago: U of Chicago P, 1987.

Hastie, Amelie. *The Bigamist.* London: BFI, 2009.

Heck-Rabi, Louise. *Women's Filmmakers: A Critical Reception.* Metuchen, NJ: Scarecrow Press, 1984.

Herman, Judith. *Trauma and Recovery: The Aftermath of Violence—from Domestic Abuse to Political Terror.* New York: Basic Books, 1992.

Hinkson, Jake. "Ida Lupino: Noir's Indispensable Dame." *CriminalElement.com*, 3 July 2011. http://www.criminalelement.com/blogs/2011/07/ida-lupino-noirs-indispensable-dame. Accessed 1 Dec. 2015.

Hodges, Daniel. *The Film Noir File: A Dossier of Challenges to the Film Noir Hardboiled Paradigm.* 1 June 2013. http://www.filmnoirfile.com. Accessed 15 June 2014.

Holliday, Kate. "Her Thinking Bothers Ida Lupino." Unsourced, ca. June 1945. Margaret Herrick Library, Academy of Motion Picture Arts and Sciences, Beverly Hills, CA.

Hopper, Hedda. "Ida's Ideals." *Chicago Sunday Tribune*, 4 Sept. 1949. Margaret Herrick Library, Academy of Motion Picture Arts and Sciences, Beverly Hills, CA.

———. "The Leap of Lupino." *Chicago Sunday Tribune*, 21 Mar. 1943. Margaret Herrick Library, Academy of Motion Picture Arts and Sciences, Beverly Hills, CA.

Horner, Harry. "Designing *The Heiress.*" *Hollywood Quarterly: Film Culture in Postwar America, 1945–1957.* Ed. Eric Loren Smoodin and Ann Martin. Berkeley: U of California P, 2002. 180–85.

Huber, Christopher. "Mother of Us All: Ida Lupino, The Filmaker [*sic*]." *Cinema Scope* 65. http://cinema-scope.com/features/mother-of-all-of-us-ida-lupino-the-filmaker/. Accessed 24 Dec. 2015.

Hurd, Mary. *Women Directors and Their Films* Westport, CT: Praeger, 2007.

"Ida Lupino: Through the Lens." *Biography.* Dir. Torrie Rosenzweig. A&E. 1998. Television documentary.

"Ida Wants to Be Herself." Warner Bros. Studio Publicity Materials, ca. 1942. Margaret Herrick Library, Academy of Motion Picture Arts and Sciences, Beverly Hills, CA.

Jacobs, Jason, and Steven Peacock, eds. *Television Aesthetics and Style.* New York: Bloomsbury, 2013.

Jaramillo, Deborah. "Rescuing Television from 'The Cinematic': The Perils of Dismissing Television Style." Jacobs and Peacock 67–75.

Johnson, Russell, with Steve Cox. *Here on Gilligan's Isle.* New York: HarperCollins, 1993.

Johnston, Claire. "Women's Cinema as Counter-Cinema." *Movies and Methods, An Anthology:* Vol. 1, ed. Bill Nichols. U of California P, 1976. 208–223.

Kalish, Irma. *Quora.* Newsweek.com. 14 July 2014. https://www.quora.com/How-has-the-television-industry-changed-since-the-1950s-and-1960s?ref=newsweek&rel_pos=1. Accessed 1 Mar. 2015.

Kaplan, E. Ann. "Mothering, Feminism, and Representation: The Maternal in Melodrama and the Woman's Film 1910–40." Gledhill, *Home* 113–37.

———, ed. *Women in Film Noir.* London: BFI, 1980.

Kawin, Bruce. "Authorship, Design, and Execution." Grant 190–99.

Kearney, Mary Celeste, and James M. Moran. "Television Programmes and Series Episodes Directed by Ida Lupino." Kuhn 159–86.

Kemp, Philip. "From the Nightmare Factory: HUAC and the Politics of Noir." *The Big Book of Noir.* Ed. Edward Gorman, Lee Server, and Martin H. Greenberg. New York: Carol and Graf, 1998. 77–86.

Keogh, Peter. "One Tough Mother: Ida Lupino." *Film Ireland* 88 (Sept./Oct. 2002): 2–23. London: British Film Institute, Reuben Library.

Khoshbakht, Ehsan. "Femininity and Language in Ida Lupino's 'Checked Out.'" *La Furia Umana* 14 (Autumn 2012). http://www.lafuriaumana.it/index.php?option=com_content&view=article&id=614:-1 -r-femininity-and-language-in-ida-lupinos-no-5-checked-out&catid=66:la-furia-umana-nd14-autumn-2012&Itemid=61. Accessed 15 July 2013.

King, Susan. "A Very Independent Streak." *Los Angeles Times,* 15 Oct. 2002. Margaret Herrick Library, Academy of Motion Picture Arts and Sciences, Beverly Hills, CA.

Klein, Amanda Ann, and R. Barton Palmer. *Cycles, Sequels, Spin-offs, Remakes, and Reboots: Multiplicities in Film and Television.* Austin: U of Texas P, 2016.

Koszarski, Richard. *Hollywood Directors: 1941–1976*. Oxford: Oxford UP, 1977.

Kozloff, Sarah. "Empathy and the Cinema of Engagement: Reevaluating the Politics of Film." *Projections* 7.2 (Winter 2013): 1–40.

——. *The Life of the Author*. Montreal: Caboose Press, 2014.

——. "Melodrama." Friedman et al. 80–119.

——. "On Dangerous Ground: Directors in the 1950s." *Directing*. Ed. Virginia Wright Wexman. Behind the Silver Screen. New Brunswick, NJ: Rutgers UP, 2018.

——. "The Social-Problem Film." Friedman et al. 446–83.

Kuhn, Annette, ed. *Queen of the 'B's: Ida Lupino Behind the Camera*. Westport, CT: Praeger, 1995.

Landy, Marcia. "Movies and the Fate of Genre." *American Cinema of the 1940s*. Ed. Wheeler Winston Dixon. New Brunswick, NJ: Rutgers UP, 2006. 222–44.

Lane, Christina. "Stepping Out from Behind the Grand Silhouette: Joan Harrison's Films of the 1940s." *Authorship and Film*. Ed. David A. Gerstner and Janet Staiger. New York: Routledge, 2003. 97–118.

Lee, Edith C. "Horner, Harry." *Film Reference*. http://www.filmreference.com/Writers-and-Production-Artists-Ha-Ja/Horner-Harry.html#b#ixzz3xZ1DNUfM. Accessed 9 Jan. 2016.

Lev, Peter. *The Fifties: Transforming the Screen*. Berkeley: U of California P, 2003.

Levine, Elana. "Charlie's Angels." *The Television History Book*. Ed. Michele Hilmes. London: British Film Institute, 2003. 92–93.

Levy, Ariel. "Dolls and Feelings: Jill Soloway's Post-Patriarchal Television." *New Yorker*, 14 Dec. 2015. http://www.newyorker.com/magazine/2015/12/14/dolls-and-feelings. Web.

Loynd, Ray. "Autumn Years of Ida Lupino." *Los Angeles Herald Examiner*, 6 Mar. 1975. Margaret Herrick Library, Academy of Motion Picture Arts and Sciences, Beverly Hills, CA.

Ludlow, Carter. "Sunset Strip Row at Dawn Features Ida Lupino's Mate." *Los Angeles Examiner*, 1 Mar. 1953. Margaret Herrick Library, Academy of Motion Picture Arts and Sciences, Beverly Hills, CA.

Lupino, Ida. "Me, Mother Directress." *Action!* (May-June 1967). Reprinted in Koszarski 372–77.

——. "New Faces in New Places: They Are Needed Behind the Camera, Too." *Films in Review* 1.9 (Dec. 1950): 17–19. London: British Film Institute, Reuben Library.

——. "Walk Back Rocky Road with Ida." Guest Contributor for Hedda Hopper. *Los Angeles Times*, 29 June 1965. Margaret Herrick Library, Academy of Motion Picture Arts and Sciences, Beverly Hills, CA.

——. Western Union Telegram, to Joseph Breen, 9 Feb. 1949. Production Code Association File on *Not Wanted* (1949). Margaret Herrick Library, Academy of Motion Picture Arts and Sciences, Beverly Hills, CA.

——. "Why I Made *Never Fear*." Advertisement. *Citizen News*, 17 Feb. 1950. Margaret Herrick Library, Academy of Motion Picture Arts and Sciences, Beverly Hills, CA.

Lupino, Ida, and Collier Young. Letter to James V. Bennett, 10 Apr. 1952. Production Code Association File on *The Hitch-Hiker* (1953). Margaret Herrick Library, Academy of Motion Picture Arts and Sciences, Beverly Hills, CA.

"Lupino Legend." *News Review*, 1 Dec. 1949. Margaret Herrick Library, Academy of Motion Picture Arts and Sciences, Beverly Hills, CA.

Mahar, Karen Ward. *Women Filmmakers in Early Hollywood*. Baltimore: Johns Hopkins UP, 2008.

Making Waves: The 50 Greatest Women in Radio and Television. Kansas City, MO: American Women in Radio and Television, 2001.

Malcom, Don. "Sinister Shrinks: A Quick Taxonomy of the 'Couch Trip.'" *Noir City Sentinel*, Aug./Sept. 2007. http://www.transatlantichabit.com/noir/Max-Ophuls.pdf.

Martin, Angela. "Refocusing Authorship in Women's Filmmaking." Grant 127–34.

May, Elaine Tyler. *Homeward Bound: American Families in the Cold War Era*. New York: Basic Books. Ebook. 2007.

Mayne, Judith. *Directed by Dorothy Arzner*. Bloomington: Indiana UP, 1994.

McGilligan, Patrick, and Debra Weiner. "Interview with Ida Lupino." Patrick McGilligan, *Film Crazy: Interviews with Hollywood Legends*. New York: St. Martin's Press, 2000.

McHugh, Kathleen Anne. *American Domesticity: From How-to Manual to Hollywood Melodrama*. New York: Oxford UP, 1999.

Melbourne International Film Festival Program Guide. "*The Trouble with Angels*." http://miff.com.au/festival-archive/film/21532. Accessed 1 Dec. 2015.

Mendelson, Scott. "'Wonder Woman' Shocker: Director Michelle MacLaren Drops Out." *Forbes*, 13 Apr. 2015. http://www.forbes.com/sites/scottmendelson/2015/04/13/michelle-maclaren-leaves-wonder-woman/#4a913006fcf7. Accessed 5 Dec. 2015.

Merck, Mandy. "*Hard, Fast and Beautiful* (1951)." Kuhn 73–89.

Meskin, Aaron. "Authorship." *The Routledge Companion to Philosophy and Film*. Ed. Paisley Livingston and Carl Plantinga. Oxen: Routledge, 2009. 12–28.

Metz, Walter. *Bewitched*. TV Milestone Series. Detroit: Wayne State UP, 2007.

——. *Gilligan's Island*. TV Milestone Series. Detroit: Wayne State UP, 2012.

A Mighty Girl. Carolyn Danckaert and Aaron Smith. http://www.amightygirl.com. Accessed 10 Nov. 2015.

Mills, C. Wright. *The Power Elite*. Oxford: Oxford UP, 1956.

Minoff, Philip. "TV Personalities" (on *Mr. Adams and Eve*). *Family Circle*, Mar. 1958. Margaret Herrick Library, Academy of Motion Picture Arts and Sciences, Beverly Hills, CA.

Mittell, Jason. "The Quality of Complexity: Vast Versus Dense Seriality in Contemporary Television." Jacobs and Peacock 45–56.

Morreale, Joanne. *The Donna Reed Show*. TV Milestone Series. Detroit: Wayne State UP, 2012.

Moss, Morton, "In Spite of Herself." *Los Angeles Herald Examiner*, 9 Nov. 1972. Margaret Herrick Library, Academy of Motion Picture Arts and Sciences, Beverly Hills, CA.

Mulvey, Laura. "Visual Pleasure and Narrative Cinema." *Screen* 16.3 (Autumn 1975): 6–18.

"*Never Fear.*" Review. *Variety*, 4 Jan. 1950. MPAA Collection, Margaret Herrick Library, Academy of Motion Picture Arts and Sciences, Beverly Hills, CA.

Newcomb, Horace. *TV: The Most Popular Art.* Garden City, NY: Anchor Books, 1974.

Nolan, Jack Edmund. "Ida Lupino." *Films in Review* 16 (1965): 61–62.

O'Brian, Hugh. Interview. *Archive of American Television.* http://www.emmytvlegends .org/interviews/people/hugh-obrian. Accessed 15 June 2015.

O'Dell, Cary. *Women Pioneers in Television: Biographies of Fifteen Industry Leaders.* Jefferson, NC: McFarland, 1997.

O'Reilly, Julie D. *Bewitched Again: Supernaturally Powerful Women on Television, 1996–2011.* Jefferson, NC: McFarland, 2013.

Orgeron, Marsha. *Hollywood Ambitions: Celebrity in the Movie Age.* Middletown, CT: Wesleyan UP, 2008.

Osteen, Mark. *Nightmare Alley: Film Noir and the American Dream.* Baltimore: Johns Hopkins UP, 2013.

Palmer, R. Barton. *Shot on Location: Postwar American Cinema and the Exploration of Real Place.* New Brunswick, NJ: Rutgers UP, 2016.

Parker, Francine. "Discovering Ida Lupino." *Action* 2.3 (May–June 1967): 19–23.

Parsons, Louella O. "Ida's Is a Working Marriage." *Los Angeles Examiner*, 3 Aug. 1957. Margaret Herrick Library, Academy of Motion Picture Arts and Sciences, Beverly Hills, CA.

Pilato, Herbie J. *Twitch Upon a Star.* Lanham, MD: Rowman and Littlefield, 2012.

Place, Janey. "No Place for a Woman: The Family in Film Noir." http://www .filmnoirstudies.com/essays/no_place.asp. Accessed 1 June 2015.

Pomerance, Murray. *Moment of Action: Riddles of Cinematic Performance.* New Brunswick, NJ: Rutgers UP, 2016.

"The Producer." *Gilligan's Island.* First draft by Gerald Gardner and Dee Caruso. 26 May 1966. Arts Library, archive of Fuller French, Fort Worth, TX. Accessed 13 May 2016.

Quart, Barbara Koenig. *Women Directors: The Emergence of a New Cinema.* New York: Praeger, 1988.

Rabinovitz, Lauren. "*The Hitch-Hiker* (1953)." Kuhn 90–102.

Rickey, Carrie. "Lupino Noir." *Village Voice*, 29 Oct. 1980, 43–45.

"RKO Refuses to Blunt Its 'Hitch-Hiker' Blurbs Tho Ride-Thumbers Beef." *Variety*, 17 April 1953. Margaret Herrick Library, Academy of Motion Picture Arts and Sciences, Beverly Hills, CA.

Royle, Nicholas. *The Uncanny: An Introduction.* Manchester: Manchester UP, 2003.

Sarris, Andrew. *The American Cinema: Directors and Directions 1929–1968.* New York: Dutton, 1968.

Schatz, Thomas. *Boom and Bust: American Cinema in the 1940s.* Berkeley: U of California P, 1997.

———. "Desilu, *I Love Lucy*, and the Rise of Network TV." *Making Television.* Ed. Robert J. Thompson and Gary Burns. New York: Praeger, 1990. 117–36.

Scheib, Ronnie. "Ida Lupino." Curatorial Essay for MoMA Retrospective on Lupino, 1 Feb.–9 Mar. 1991.

——. "Ida Lupino, Auteuress." *Film Comment* (Jan./Feb. 1980): 54–64.

——. "*Never Fear* (1950)" [*sic*]. Kuhn 40–56.

Schleier, Merrill. *Skyscraper Cinema: Architecture and Gender in American Film*. Minneapolis: U of Minnesota P, 2009.

Scorsese, Martin. "The Lives They Lived: Ida Lupino; Behind the Camera, a Feminist." *New York Times Magazine*, 31 Dec. 1995. 43.

Seger, Linda. *When Women Call the Shots*. New York: Henry Holt, 1996.

Sélavy, Virginie. "Bloody-Minded Women." *Sight and Sound* (Oct. 2015). Web.

Shorris, Sylvia. Interview with Harry Horner, Sept. 1985. Transcript. Special Collections, Margaret Herrick Library, Academy of Motion Picture Arts and Sciences, Beverly Hills, CA.

Silver, Alain, and James Ursini, eds. *Film Noir: The Directors*. Milwaukee: Limelight, 2012.

——. *Film Noir Reader*. Pompton Plains, NJ: Limelight, 1996.

Silver, Charles. "Ida Lupino's *Never Fear (The Young Lovers)*." MoMA Blog *Inside Out*, 6 Nov. 2012. http://www.moma.org/explore/inside_out/2012/11/06/ida-lupinos-never-fear-the-young-lovers.

Sklar, Robert. "James Agee and the U.S. Response to Neorealism." *Global Neorealism: The Transnational History of a Film Style*. Ed. Saverio Giovacchini and Robert Sklar. Jackson: UP of Mississippi, 2012. 71–72.

Smith, Jeff. "Movie Music as Moving Music: Emotion, Cognition, and the Film Score." *Passionate Views: Film, Cognition, and Emotion*. Ed. Carl Plantinga and Greg M. Smith. Baltimore: Johns Hopkins UP, 1999. 146–67.

Snelson, Tim. *Phantom Ladies: Hollywood Horror and the Homefront*. New Brunswick, NJ: Rutgers UP, 2014.

Sobchack, Vivian. "'Lounge Time': Post-War Crises and the Chronotope of Film Noir." *Refiguring American Film Genres: History and Theory*. Ed. Nick Brown. Berkeley: U of California P, 1998. 129–70.

Spencer, Kathleen. *Art and Politics in Have Gun Will Travel: The 1950s Television Western as Ethical Drama*. Jefferson, NC: McFarland, 2014. Ebook.

Spigel, Lynn. *Make Room for TV: Television and the Family Ideal in Postwar America*. Chicago: U of Chicago P, 1992.

Staggs, Sam. *Born to Be Hurt: The Untold Story of Imitation of Life*. New York: St. Martin's, 2009.

Stamp, Shelley. "Lois Weber." *Women's Film Pioneers Project*. https://wfpp.cdrs .columbia.edu/pioneer/ccp-lois-weber/. Accessed 12 Aug. 2015.

——. *Lois Weber in Early Hollywood*. Berkeley: U of California P, 2015.

Stanfield, Peter. "'Got-to-See': Teenpix and the Social Problem Picture—Trends and Cycles." *The Wiley-Blackwell History of American Film*: Vol. 3, *1946–1975*. Ed. Cynthia Lucia, Roy Grundmann, and Art Simon. Chichester: Wiley-Blackwell, 2012.

Stewart, Lucy. *Ida Lupino as Film Director, 1949–1953: An 'Auteur' Approach*. New York: Arno Press, 1980.

Stone, Judy. "The Life of a Glamour Queen?" *New York Times*, 24 Aug. 1969. Margaret Herrick Library, Academy of Motion Picture Arts and Sciences, Beverly Hills, CA.

Strauss, Theodore. "A Most Retiring Lady." *New York Times*, 21 Sept. 1941. Margaret Herrick Library, Academy of Motion Picture Arts and Sciences, Beverly Hills, CA.

Studlar, Gaylyn. *Have Gun—Will Travel*. TV Milestone Series. Detroit: Wayne State UP, 2015.

"Suspension." *Mr Adams and Eve*. Script by Sol Saks and Louella McFarlane. Four Star Films. Airdate 25 Oct. 1957. Archived at the Harry Ransom Center, University of Texas, Austin. Accessed 12 May 2016.

Swartz, Tracy. "Female Directors, Writers from Chicago Area Weigh in on Sexism in Hollywood." *Chicago Tribune*, 23 Nov. 2015. http://www.chicagotribune.com/entertainment/ct-hollywood-directors-writers-chicago-area-20151123-story.html.

Thomas, Bob. "Lupino Trying Low Budget 'Unwed Mother' Drama Film." *San Diego Tribune-Sun*, 9 Feb. 1949. Production Code Association File on *Not Wanted* (1949). Margaret Herrick Library, Academy of Motion Picture Arts and Sciences, Beverly Hills, CA.

Tischler, Stanford. Interview. *Archive of American Television*. http://www.emmytvlegends.org/interviews/people/stanford-tischler. Accessed 15 June 2015.

"The Torpedo." *The Untouchables*. First draft by Ed Adamson. 4 Mar. 1963. Desilu Productions. Arts Library, archive of Fuller French, Fort Worth, TX. Accessed 13 May 2016.

Tresniowski, Alex. "The Miracle Girl." *People*, 31 Mar. 2003. http://www.people.com/people/archive/article/0,,20139640,00.html.

Tunis, John. "Mother of a Champion." *Harper's Monthly Magazine*, Feb. 1929, 275–89.

Ursini, James. "Angst at Sixty Fields per Second." Silver and Ursini, *Film Noir Reader*, 275–88.

Varney, Ginger. "Ida Lupino, Director." *L.A. Weekly*, 12 Nov. 1982. Margaret Herrick Library, Academy of Motion Picture Arts and Sciences, Beverly Hills, CA.

Wager, Jans. *Dames in the Driver's Seat: Rereading Film Noir*. Austin: U of Texas P, 2005.

———. "Ida Lupino." Silver and Ursini, *Film Noir: The Directors*, 224–41.

Waldman, Diane. "*Not Wanted* (1949)." Kuhn 13–39.

Williams, Linda. "'Something Else Besides a Mother': *Stella Dallas* and the Maternal Melodrama." Gledhill, *Home* 299–325.

Wiseman, Rosalind (with Elizabeth Rapoport). *Queen Bee Moms and Kingpin Dads*. New York: Random House, 2006.

Wlodarczyk, Holley. "The Cultural Meanings of the *Leave It to Beaver* House." *Archi. Pop: Mediating Architecture in Popular Culture*. Ed. D. Medina Lasansky. New York: Bloomsbury, 2014. Ebook.

Wocjik, Pamela Robertson. *The Apartment Plot: Urban Living in American Film and Popular Culture, 1945 to 1975*. Durham, NC: Duke UP, 2010.

Zavattini, Cesare. "A Thesis on Neo-Realism." *Springtime in Italy: A Reader on Neo-Realism*. Ed. and trans. David Overbey. Hamden CT: Archon Books, 1978.

INDEX

ABC (TV network), 126, 171

Academy (of Motion Picture Arts and Sciences) Awards, 9, 53, 102, 121, 155, 206n4. *See also* Oscars

"Academy Award" (TV pilot), 155–57, 217n14, 217n16

action (genre), 134–35, 162, 165, 167, 174, 189, 196, 198, 218n18

Action (magazine), 32

"Active Duty" (TV episode), 217n14

Adams, Dorothy, 72

Adams, James Truslow, 90

Affair, The (TV series, 2014–), 201

Agee, James, 63–64, 66

Agee on Film (Agee), 64

"A Is for Aardvark" (TV episode), 171–74

Alabama Hills (CA), 17

Aladdin Suite (musical composition), viii

Aldrich, Robert, 11, 144

Alfred Hitchcock Presents (TV series, 1955–1962), 121, 135, 162, 180–82, 185

Alice in Wonderland (Norman Z. McLeod, 1933), 5

All About Eve (Joseph L. Mankiewicz, 1950), 142

Allen, Debbie, 201

Alley, Robert S., 134

Althusser, Louis, 216n8

Ambler (PA), 113

American Cinema, The (Sarris), 35

American Domesticity: From How-to Manual to Hollywood Melodrama (McHugh), 87

American Don Juan in Rome (Murgi), 173

American Dream, 2, 8, 15–17, 27, 40, 65, 68, 71, 75, 80, 87–91, 93–95, 98, 143–44, 151, 197

American Film Institute (AFI), 12, 65, 150

American Home Life, 1880–1930 (Foy and Schlereth), 214n13

American modernism, 17

American realism, 1, 49–51, 66, 122, 211n30, 211–12n32

Amos 'n' Andy (TV series, 1951–1953), 123

Anderson, Ken, 215n16

Anderson, Mary Ann, 24–25, 135, 154–55, 169–71, 180, 198, 206n14, 209n25, 215n5, 216–17n13, 217n14, 217–18n17, 219n22

Andress, Ursula, 179

Andrews, Julie, 111

Andrews, Tod, 42

Annenberg School for Communication and Journalism (USC), 205n3

Antonelli, Louis, 209–10n25

Apartment Plot: Urban Living in American Film and Popular Culture, The (Wocjik), 214n12

Arden, Eve, 159

Arlen, Harold, vii

Armstrong, Charlotte, 182

Arnaz, Desi, 93, 138, 216–17n13
Artists and Models (Raoul Walsh, 1937), 4
Arts Library (Fort Worth, TX), 217n14
Arzner, Dorothy, 3, 24, 29, 32, 67, 213n5
Asher, William, 172, 219n26
Ashland Daily Press, 20
"Assault, The" (TV episode), 194
Astaire, Fred, vii
Austrian Expressionism, 55
Austro-Hungarian Empire, 55
auteur critics, 29
auteurism, 28–29, 35–36, 58, 61–62, 136

Babelsberg, 56
"Bachelor, The" (TV episode), 149, 217n14
Baker, Joby, 165
Baldwin, Alec, 209n21
Balio, Tino, 64
Ball, Lucille, 93, 138, 153–54, 216–17n13
Balsam, Martin, 144
Barbarella (Roger Vadim, 1968), 111
Barbaro, Umberto, 212n32
Barrette, Pierre, 215n7
Bart, Peter, viii, 188
Barthes, Roland, 215n7
Basinger, Jeanine, 31, 213n3
Batman (TV series, 1966–1968), 147, 164
Baxter, Anne, 142
Bazin, André, 28, 136, 216n8
Beatles, The, 111
Beats, The (poets), 41–42
Becker, Christine, 122, 149, 153–54, 157, 159, 215n1
Bel Geddes, Barbara, 182, 184–86
Belton, John, 40, 111–12, 119
Bendek, Therese, 41
Bennett, James, 25
Benshoff, Harry, 40
Berle, Milton, 120
Berlin, 56, 58, 200
Bernstein, Maurice, 51
Best Years of Our Lives, The (William Wyler, 1946), 64–65, 210n26

Betz, Carl, 168
Beware My Lovely (Harry Horner, 1952), 53
Bewitched (TV series, 1964–1972), 149, 167–68, 171–74, 219n26
Bianco e nero (film journal), 212n32
Bicycle Thieves (Vittorio De Sica, 1948), 52, 212n33
Biesen, Sheri Chinen, vii–viii
Bigamist, The (Ida Lupino, 1953), 12, 16–17, 41–42, 62–63, 65, 69, 72–75, 87, 89, 96–100, 122, 128, 161, 164, 189, 206n13, 207–8n19, 208n20, 209n24, 214n14
Bigelow, Kathryn, 28, 58–59
Big Heat, The (Fritz Lang, 1953), 182, 186
Big Knife, The (Robert Aldrich, 1955), 11, 144
Big Lift, The (George Seaton, 1950), 49
Bill Cosby Show, The (TV series, 1984–1992), 219n22
Blackman, Honor, 112
Blot, The (Lois Weber, 1921), 67
Blue Steel (Kathryn Bigelow, 1990), 59
Bob & Carol & Ted & Alice (Paul Mazursky, 1969), 112
Body and Soul (Robert Rossen, 1948), 9
Bond, Anson, 21–22, 205n1, 210n26
Bond, Raymond, 102
Bondanella, Peter, 211–12n32
"Bonny Bonny Banks of Loch Lomond, The" (song), 198
Boone, Richard, 124, 191, 193
Bordwell, David, 211n28
Borgnine, Ernest, 121
Borzage, Frank, 123
Box Office (film journal), 136
Boyer, Charles, 122
Brakhage, Stan, 50
Brando, Marlon, 143
Brasselle, Keefe, 13–14, 70, 217n15
Breaking Bad (TV series, 2008–2013), 199, 215n7
Brecht, Bertolt, 52

Breen, Joseph, 18–23, 25–26
Brenez, Nicole, 212–13n34
Bridgeport (CA), 82–84
Bridget Productions, 149
Bright Lights Film Journal, 206n7
Bronfen, Elisabeth, 214n11
Bronson, Lillian, 193
Bronx, 121
Brownlow, Kevin, 67
Brownworth, Victoria A., 207n19
Bubbeo, Daniel, 5, 23
Bureau of Prisons (U.S. Department of
    Justice), 25
Burke, Jim, 23
Butler, Jeremy, 134, 136, 142, 215–16nn6–8,
    219n27
Byars, Jackie, 64

Caan, James, 187
Cabbage Fairy, The (Alice Guy, 1896), 66
Cactus Flower (Gene Saks, 1969), 189
Cahiers du cinéma (film journal), 28
Calder, King, 194
Caldwell, John Thornton, 215n7
California, 17, 23–24, 44, 50, 57, 77, 84, 87,
    97–98, 109, 128
California modern (style), 97–98
Camel News Caravan (TV series, 1948), 120
"Canary Kid, The" (TV episode), 125
Cannes Film Festival, 122
Capitol City, 42–43, 46, 58, 70–71, 87, 102,
    106, 109
Captain Marvel (forthcoming film), 201
Cardwell, Sarah, 135, 215n7
Carman, Emily, 3
Carmichael, Hoagy, viii
Carné, Marcel, 212n32
Carol (Todd Haynes, 2015), 199
Carroll, Lewis, 5
"Case of Emily Cameron, The" (TV
    episode), 136
Cash, Johnny, 147
Caspary, Vera, 84

CBS (TV network), 20, 120–21, 136, 149,
    155
Centro Sperimentale di Cinematografia
    (film school), 212n32
Chamberlain, Richard, 163
Chambers, Wheaton, 72
Chandler, Raymond, 68
Change of Habit (William Graham, 1969),
    111
Charlie's Angels (TV series, 1976–1981),
    136, 146–48
Chatsworth (CA), 91, 93–94
Chayefsky, Paddy, 121, 212n33
Cheyenne (TV series, 1955–1963), 122, 126
Child, Ben, 201
Chinatown (Roman Polanski, 1974), 69,
    174, 185–86
Cinecittà Studio, 212n32
Cinema (film journal), 212n32
"cinema of empathy," 47, 114, 133, 189
CinemaScope, 120
Cinerama, 120
Clarke, Robert, 42, 45, 79
Cleopatra (Cecil B. DeMille, 1934), 6, 8
Cleopatra (Joseph L. Mankiewicz, 1963),
    111
Clifton, Elmer, 11–12
"Closed Cabinet, The" (TV episode),
    177–78
Coates, Phyllis, 187
Coates, Tyler, 114
Cohn, Harry, 126
Colbert, Claudette, 6, 8
Cold War, 83
Collins, Jo, 214n11
Collins, Roy, 27, 163, 188
Colonial Revival (style), 103–4
Colt .45 (TV series, 1957–1960), 126
Colton, Helen, 23
Columbia Pictures, 110–12, 126
Columbo (TV series, 1971–2003), 147
comedy (genre), 149–50, 154, 161–62,
    167–74

"Come on to Mars' House" (TV episode), 217n14

coming-of-age story, 111

Connors, Chuck, 194

Conried, Hans, 219n25

Cook, Pam, 51, 58, 80, 108–9

Cook, William "Billy," 17, 23–26

Cook Story, The (unproduced film), 24, 26

Coontz, Stephanie, 104

Cotten, Joseph, 162–63

Cowie, Elizabeth, 68, 213n6

Craig, Yvonne, 164–65

Cranston, Bryan, 199

"Crime for Mothers, A" (TV episode), 180–82

Crossfire (Edward Dmytryk, 1947), 64

Crowley, Patricia, 166

Curtiz, Michael, 11, 101

Cyrano de Bergerac (Michael Gordon, 1950), 12

Dallas, Stella (fict. character), 188

Dames in the Driver's Seat (Wager), 213n6

Damron, Forrest, 23, 206n12

Danckaert, Carolyn, 214n15

Dargis, Manohla, 205n3

Davis, Bette, 142, 156, 158, 218n18

"Day in the Year, A" (TV episode), 166

"Deadeye Dick" (TV episode), 195–97

Dean, James, 143

"Dear Variety" (TV episode), 151–52, 217n14

"Declaration of Independents" (Lupino and Young), 9, 37, 39, 49

De Cordova, Fred, 150

DeKova, Frank, 186

DeMille, Cecil B., 67, 142, 144–45

Denver, Bob, 169

de Rochemont, Louis, 9, 49

"Designing The Heiress" (Horner), 53

Desilu (home), 93

Desjardins, Mary, 145–46, 153–54, 216n11, 218n19

Desmond, John, 125

Detecting Women (Gates), 213n6

Detour (Edgar G. Ulmer, 1945), 109

Dexter, Joy, 163

Dickinson, Emily, viii

"Difference of Opinion, A" (TV episode), 168–69

Dimendberg, Edward, 214n12

Director's Guild, 31

Directors Guild of America Quarterly (film journal), 213n3

Diskant, George, 122

Disney, 201

Dixon, Wheeler Winston, 34, 110, 167, 174

Dmytryk, Edward, 64

Doane, Mary Ann, 192

documentary style, 8, 10, 13, 24–25, 35, 47, 51

domestic melodrama, 86, 216n11

"Dominique" (song), 111

Donati, William, 11–12, 36, 51–52, 63, 135

"Donna Reed Show, The" (TV series, 1958–1966), 167–69

Doty, Alexander, 218n19

Double Indemnity (Billy Wilder, 1944), 82, 84, 129

Dowd, Maureen, 145, 200–201, 206n3, 207n16, 209n21, 219n21

Dozoretz, Wendy, 81, 209n20

Dragnet (Jack Webb, 1954), 121

Dr. Kildare (TV series, 1961–1966), 163

Drury, James, 196

Duff, Bridget, 7, 27, 149

Duff, Howard, 121, 136, 138, 147, 149, 153–55, 157–58, 167, 216–17n13

Duncan, Isadora, 115

Dundee and the Culhane (TV series, 1967), 198

Dunst, Kirsten, 199

Dwan, Allan, 5

Dyer, Richard, 61, 213n1

Edwards, Douglas, 120

Ehrenreich, Barbara, 41–42, 211n29

Ehrlich, Jake, 164
Eisenhower, Dwight D., 27
Elliot, Biff, 181
Elsaesser, Thomas, 62
Emerald, Connie, 205n1
Emerald Productions, 18, 39, 205n1, 210n26
Emerson, Faye, 159
Emmy Awards, 206n5
England, 5
Epic of America, The (Adams), 90
epic theater, 52
Erikson, Erik, 41
European-influenced documentary realism, 8, 13, 47
Evans, Dale, 93
Everitt, David, 209–10n25
"Everybody's Playing Solo" (TV episode), 164–65
Expressionism: Austrian, 55; German, 2, 53, 55, 187, 212–13n34

Fabares, Shelley, 168
Family Circle (magazine), 157
Fargo (TV series, 2014–), 199
Farmer, Frances, viii
"Fatso" (TV episode), 189–91, 219n27
Fawcett, Farrah, 146
Federal (house style), 104
Federal Trade Commission, 210–11n27
Feeder, William, 25–26
Feminine Mystique, The (Friedan), 173
feminist auteurism, 29, 58. *See also* auterism
Ferrer, Jose, 12
Fidelman, Geoffrey Mark, 216–17n13
Field, Sally, 111
"Fighter, The" (TV episode), 217n14
Filmakers, The (production company), 1–4, 9–10, 12–18, 21, 24–26, 32, 37–39, 47, 49, 51–53, 55, 63–65, 68, 112, 114–15, 120, 125, 139, 151, 153, 161, 163, 169, 195, 206nn11–12, 210n26, 218n17, 219n23
Film Fatales: Independent Women Direc-

tors (Redding and Brownworth), 207n19
Film Forum, 176
film noir, 2, 17, 29, 33–34, 40, 47, 53, 55, 58, 63–65, 67–71, 73–90, 92, 96, 98–102, 106–9, 123, 127–34, 143–44, 162, 167–68, 174, 178, 180–82, 184, 187, 189–92, 194–95, 197, 206n13, 208–9n20, 214nn11–12, 219n27
Film Noir and the Spaces of Modernity (Dimendberg), 214n12
Film Reference (journal), 55
Films in Review (journal), 37
Firestone, Shulamith, 113
Fisher, George, 19–20
Fiske, John, 134
"Fist of Five, A" (TV episode), 186–87, 192
"Flack, The" (TV episode), 217n14
Fleming, Victor, 11
Florey, Meb, 194
Flying Nun, The (TV series, 1967–1970), 111
Flynn, Errol, 94
Fonda, Jane, 111
Fontaine, Joan, 17, 72, 149, 160–61
Ford, John, 11, 123, 196, 206n4
Forrest, Sally, 11, 13–14, 16, 22–23, 32, 65, 70, 76, 164, 217n15
Fort Apache (John Ford, 1948), 206n4
Foster, Gwendolyn Audrey, 26–27, 32, 206nn6–7
Foster, Jodie, 2
400 Blows, The (Francois Truffaut, 1959), 212n33
"Four Star" (acting group), 121–22
Four Star Films, 149
Four Star Playhouse (TV series, 1952–1956), 123, 136, 139, 141, 215n1
Foy, Jessica H., 214n13
France, 28, 209n25, 213n3
Francis, Anne, 135
Franciscus, James, 165
Franco, John, 52

Frank, Nino, 67
Frank, Robert, 50
Frankenstein (Shelley), 144
French, Fuller, 217n14
French cinema, 212n32
Freud, Sigmund, 115
Freund, Karl, 216n13
Friedan, Betty, 41, 113, 173–74
Friedman, Kim, 64, 66, 201
Frost, Jennifer, 205n2
Frye, William, 110
Fryman, Pamela, 201
Fugitive, The (TV series, 1963–1967), 189–91, 219n27
Fuller, Graham, 170, 215n2
Fuller, Samuel, 34, 194
"fun-nun" movies, 111, 215n16

Gable, Clark, 75, 151
Gaines, Jane, 61–62, 213n1
Galligan, David, 5
Game of Thrones (TV series, 2011–), 199
Garfield, John, 9, 121
Garrison, Sean, 198
Gates, Philippa, 68, 213n6
Geller, Theresa L., 213n5
Gender Meets Genre in Postwar Cinema (Gledhill), 213n1
General Electric Theater (TV series, 1953–1962), 135
Gene Siskel Film Center (Art Institute of Chicago), 209n25
"Genius of Genre and the Ingenuity of Women, The" (Gaines), 61
Gentleman's Agreement (Elia Kazan, 1947), 64, 210n26
Georgakas, Dan, 15, 17, 34
George Burns and Gracie Allen Show, The (TV series, 1950–1958), 152
Georgian (house style), 104
Geraghty, Christine, 215n7
German Expressionism, 2, 53, 55, 187, 212–13n34

Ghost and Mrs. Muir, The (TV series, 1968–1970), 167–68, 171
G.I. Bill (1944), 90
Gilligan's Island (TV series, 1964–1967), 136, 167–70, 216n9
Glatter, Lesli Linka, 200
Gledhill, Christine, 213n1
Godard, Jean-Luc, 29
Godfather, The (Francis Ford Coppola, 1972), 187
Goldbergs, The (TV series, 1949–1956), 123
Goldfinger (Guy Hamilton, 1964), 112
Goldsmith, Jerry, 174
Gordon, Michael, 12
gothic (style), 26, 53, 88, 144, 146, 177, 216n11
Graham, Sheilah, 156
Granet, Bert, 216–17n13
Grant, Catherine, 29
Grapes of Wrath, The (John Ford, 1940), 64, 152
Great Depression, 39, 87, 152
Great Expectations (David Lean, 1946), 177
Gregg, Virginia, 162–63
Greven, David, 17, 27, 76, 206n7
Grey's Anatomy (TV series, 2005–), 201
Griffin, Sean, 40
Griffith, D. W., 67
Griffith, Edward H., viii
Grossman, Julie, 68, 143, 213n6, 216n10
Guinle, Pierre, 124
Gunsmoke (TV series, 1955–1975), 135
Guy-Blaché, Alice, 66, 213n3
Gwenn, Edmund, 73, 75
Gypsy (Mervyn LeRoy, 1962), 215n17

Halper, Donna, 24, 28
Hal Roach Studios, 123
Hamilton, Lillian, 54, 102
Hammett, Dashiell, 68
Hanalis, Blanche, 110

Hanson, Helen, 68, 213n6

Happy Homes Real Estate agency, 15–16

Haralovich, Mary Beth, 113

Hard, Fast and Beautiful (Ida Lupino, 1951), 11, 16, 30, 32, 42, 63, 65, 70, 76–81, 89–92, 94–96, 105–6, 112, 140, 164, 180, 207–9nn19–20, 214n14

Harding, June, 110

Hard Way, The (Vincent Sherman, 1943), viii, 4

Harper's Monthly Magazine, 76

Harrington, Alan, 41

Harrison, Joan, 180

Harrison, Rex, 171

Harry Ransom Center (University of Texas), 217n14

Hartley, John, 134

Haskell, Molly, 30, 34

Hastie, Amelie, 38, 209n24, 214n14, 219n22

Have Gun—Will Travel (TV series, 1957–1963), 124, 184, 191, 193, 195

Havinhurst, R. J., 41

Hawaiian Eye (TV series, 1959–1963), 126

Haynes, Todd, 199

Hayward, Louis, 218n17

HBO (TV network), 202

Headland, Leslye, 201

Heartland (TV series, 2011–), 200

Hearts of Men, The (Ehrenreich), 41

Heck-Rabi, Louise, 36–37

Hedda Hopper's Hollywood: Celebrity Gossip and American Conservatism (Frost), 205n2

Hefner, Hugh, 41

Heiress, The (William Wyler, 1949), 53–54, 102, 104

Her First Affaire (Allan Dwan, 1932), 5

Herman, Judith, 65

Heston, Charlton, 121

High Sierra (Raoul Walsh, 1941), 17

Highsmith, Patricia, 199

Hinkson, Jake, viii

Hitchcock, Alfred, 8, 10, 70, 82, 84–85, 114, 121, 134–35, 162, 175, 177, 180–83, 185–86, 215n5

Hitch-Hiker, The (Ida Lupino, 1953), 16–18, 23–24, 26–27, 41–42, 59, 69, 75, 108, 123, 133, 144, 160, 164, 186, 188, 206n6, 206nn13–15, 209n25, 218n18

Hoch, Winton, 206n4

Holliday, Kate, vii

Hollywood Heroines: Women in Film Noir and the Female Gothic Film (Hanson), 213n6

Hollywood Reporter (magazine), 135, 170

Home in Hollywood: The Imaginary Geography of Cinema (Bronfen), 214n11

"home noir," 63, 78, 82–83, 85–86, 88, 90, 92, 96, 99–102, 106–7, 123, 129–31, 167–68, 181, 195, 214nn11–12

Home of the Brave (Mark Robson, 1949), 9

Homeward Bound: American Families in the Cold War Era (May), 43

Honey West (TV series, 1965–1966), 135

Hopper, Hedda, 4, 23, 205n2, 206n12

Horner, Harry, 37, 53–55, 57, 102, 104, 212–13n34

Houseman, John, 213n2

House Un-American Activities Committee (HUAC), 9–10, 38, 64, 121, 149

"Howard and Eve and Ida" (TV episode) 158–60, 171, 217n14

"Howard Goes to Jail" (TV episode), 217n14

Howdy Doody (TV series, 1947–1960), 120

Huber, Christopher, 218n18

Hughes, Howard, 16, 169, 210n26, 213n2

Hunt, Martita, 176–77

Hurd, Mary, 10

Hustler, The (Robert Rossen, 1961), 9, 53

Hutchins, Will, 125

"Ida Lupino" (Wager), 34, 68

"Ida Lupino, Auteuress" (Scheib), 110

Ida Lupino: Beyond the Camera (Anderson and Lupino), 135, 171, 198, 209n25, 217–18n17
Ida Lupino: Noir Queen Crosses Taboos in Hollywood (program book), 210n25
I Love Lucy (TV series, 1951–1957), 138, 154, 159, 216–17n13
Inside/Out (MoMA blog), 210n25
Introduction to Film Genres, An (Friedman, et al.), 207n18
Irma la Douce (Billy Wilder, 1963), 111
Italian neorealism, 2, 49–53, 55, 211–12n32
Italy, 38, 211–12n32
It's the Pictures That Got Small (Becker), 149
"I Will Be Remembered" (TV episode), 146–47

Jack Benny Show, The (TV series, 1950–1965), 123
Jackson, Kate, 146
Jacobs, Jason, 136–37, 215n7
Jakobsen, Janet, 113
Janssen, David, 189, 191
Jaramillo, Deborah, 215nn6–7
Jarrico, Paul, 19
Jenkins, Patty, 201
Jervis, John, 214n11
"Joan Fontaine Story, The" (TV episode), 160
Johnny Belinda (Jean Negulesco, 1948), 102
Johnny Staccato (TV series, 1959), 219n27
"Johnny's Too Long at the Fair" (song), 49
Johnson, Russell, 216n9
Johnson, Samuel, 201
Johnston, Claire, 29, 67
Johnston, Eric, 19, 64, 213n5, 213n7
Jolie, Angelina, 2, 201
July, Miranda, 145

Kabat-Kaiser Institute, 14–15
Kalish, Irma, 125
Kaplan, E. Ann, 76, 213n6

Karloff, Boris, 174, 176, 179
Kawin, Bruce, 29
Kazan, Elia, 52, 64, 159, 213n2
Kearney, Mary Celeste, 134, 191
Kearns, Joseph, 156
Keenan, Vince, viii
Keith, Robert, 175
Kemp, Philip, 70
Keogh, Peter, 32, 219n22
Khoshbakht, Ehsan, 215n3
King, Susan, 11–12, 32
Kino International, 209n23
Kinon, Richard, 219n22
Kipling, Rudyard, 6
Kobe, Gail, 188
Kohut, Heinz, 116
Koszarski, Richard, 32, 206n13
Kozloff, Sarah, 47–48, 52, 62, 64, 66, 206n8, 207nn17–18, 210n26, 213n2
Kramer, Stanley, 9, 49
Kuhn, Annette, 14, 35, 43, 51, 80, 109, 178, 206n7, 208n19, 209n20, 209n24

La Centra, Peg, vii
"Lady on the Wall" (TV episode), 191–93, 195–96
Landay, Lori, 218n19
Landy, Marcia, 63
Lane, Christina, 180
Lang, Fritz, 8, 51, 55–56, 89, 182, 186
Lange, Hope, 168, 171
"Last of the Sommervilles, The" (TV episode), 175–77
Laura (Otto Preminger, 1944), 77, 82, 84, 184, 192
L.A. Weekly (magazine), 36
Lawson, Linda, 194
Lean, David, 177
Leave Her to Heaven (John M. Stahl, 1945), 63
Leave It to Beaver (TV series, 1957–1963), 103–4
Lee, Edith C., 55

Lee, Gypsy Rose, 110, 115, 215n17
LeFauve, Meg, 201
"Lethal Ladies, The" (TV episode), 176, 179
Lev, Peter, 64
Levine, Elana, 216n12
Levy, Ariel, 200
Life in the Crystal Palace (Harrington), 41
Life of the Author (Kozloff), 62, 207n17
Life with Mother Superior (Strahey), 110
Light That Failed, The (William A. Wellman, 1939), 6
Lincoln, Abraham, 162–63
Literature, Film, and Their Hideous Progeny (Grossman), 216n10
Little Foxes, The (William Wyler, 1941), 54–55
Litvak, Anatole, 101
Lloyd, Norman, 121
Lockhart, Gene, 9
Lois Weber in Early Hollywood (Stamp), 66–67
Lolita (Stanley Kubrick, 1962), 111
Lonely Crowd, The (Riesman), 41
Longstreet (TV series, 1971–1972), 165
Lorre, Peter, 57, 123, 127, 130–31
Los Angeles, 17, 42–43, 51, 55, 69, 74–75, 93, 97–98, 106, 108–9, 165, 217n14
Los Angeles Herald Examiner, 5, 217n16
Los Angeles Philharmonic, viii
Los Angeles Times, 206n12
Lost Boundaries (Alfred L. Werker, 1949), 9
Lost Weekend, The (Billy Wilder, 1945), 64
"Love in the Wrong Season" (TV episode), 166
Lovejoy, Frank, 75
Loynd, Ray, 218n17
Luc-Gabrielle, Sister, 111
Lucy Book, The (Fidelman), 216–17n13
Lucy/Desi Comedy Hour, The (TV series, 1957–1960), 153–54, 216–17n13
"Lucy's Summer Vacation" (TV episode), 153, 216–17n13
Ludlow, Carter, 217n16

Lumière Festival (Lyon, France), 209n25
Lupino, Rita, 5
Lupino, Stanley, 5
"Lupino noir" (Rickey), 33–34, 63
Lynch, David, 128

M (Peter Lorre, 1931), 51, 53, 55–58, 127, 212–13n34
MacDonnell, Norman, 135, 171
"Madeira, My Dear" (TV episode), 171
Mad Men (TV series, 2007–2015), 215n7
"Magazine Story" (TV episode), 217n14
Mahar, Karen, 23, 66, 213n4, 218n20
Making of The Hitch-Hiker, The (Anderson), 24–25, 59, 206n14, 209n25
Making Waves: The 50 Greatest Women in Radio and Television (American Women in Radio and Television), 161
Maltese Falcon, The (John Huston, 1941), 68, 127
Mancuso, Gail, 201
Man I Love, The (Raoul Walsh, 1947), vii
"Man I Love, The" (song), vii
"Man in the Cooler, The" (TV episode), 187–88
Mann, Delbert, 52, 121–22, 212n33
Manners, Margaret, 182
Mantee, Paul, 194
Man Who Shot Liberty Valance, The (John Ford, 1962), 196–97
March, Hal, 107
Marchand, Nancy, 121
March of Time, The (newsreel), 49
Martin, Angela, 28
Marty (Delbert Mann, 1955), 52, 121–22, 212n33
Marvel, 201
Marvin, Lee, 186
marxist political economy, 50
*M*A*S*H* (TV series, 1972–1983), 206n5
"Masks, The" (TV episode), 175
Maverick (TV series, 1957–1962), 122, 124, 126

May, Elaine Tyler, 43, 45–46
"May Day, May Day" (TV episode), 166
Mayne, Judith, 24, 67, 213n5
McCarey, Leo, 123
McGilligan, Patrick, 10–11, 18, 47, 53, 162, 218n17
McGraw, Charles, 188–89
McHugh, Kathleen Anne, 87
McLaglen, Andrew V., 124–25
McLaran, Michelle, 199, 201
McPherson, Virginia, 20, 23
Melbourne International Film Festival, 114, 209n25, 215n4
Mellen, Albert, 42, 49
Mellencamp, Patricia, 218n19
melodrama (genre), 31, 58, 62–63, 66, 70, 76, 86–87, 94, 97, 125, 132, 143, 148, 163, 188, 194, 207nn18–19, 213n1, 216n11
Men, The (Fred Zinnemann, 1950), 9
Mendelson, Scott, 201
Menzies, William Cameron, 54
Mercer, Johnny, vii
Merchant of Venice, The (Lois Weber, 1914), 67
Merck, Mandy, 81, 209n20, 213n8
Meskin, Aaron, 28
"message pictures," 1, 47, 64, 82, 152
Metz, Walter, 136, 173–74, 219n25
Mexican landscape, 16, 75
Mexico, 17, 23
Mighty Girl, A (website), 214–15n15
Mildred Pierce (Michael Curtiz, 1945), 63, 76, 101, 208n20, 213n9
Miller, Alice, 116
Miller, Ann, 82–84, 101, 128
Millionaire, The (TV series, 1955–1960), 125
Mills, C. Wright, 46
Mills, Hayley, 110, 116
Mills, John, 198
Miracle on 34th Street (George Seaton, 1947), 75
Mittell, Jason, 137, 215n7

Mizrahi, Simon, 124
Modern Women: Women Artists at the Museum of Modern Art (Butler), 210n25
MoMA (Museum of Modern Art), 209n23, 209–10n25
Money for Speed (Bernard Vorhaus, 1933), 5
Monster (Patty Jenkins, 2003), 201
Montgomery, Elizabeth, 168, 219n26
Moody, Ralph, 127
Moore, Mary Tyler, 111
Moorehead, Agnes, 173
Moran, James, 134, 191
Morra, Anne, 209–10n25
Morreale, Joanne, 219n24
Morse, Barry, 189
Moss, Morton, 5, 217–18n17
Mosser Family, 26
"Mother of a Champion" (short story), 76
"Mothers, The" (TV episode), 217n14
Motion Picture Association of America (MPAA), 19, 25, 37, 64, 83, 111
Motion Picture Exhibitor (magazine), 210n26
Motion Picture Magazine, 160
MPAA. See Motion Picture Association of America
Mr. Adams and Eve (TV series, 1957–1958), 136, 138, 149–61, 167, 171, 216–17nn13–14, 217n16, 219n22
Mr. Adams and Eve (Anderson), 209n25
"Mr. George" (TV episode), 174–75
Mr. Novak (TV series, 1963–1965), 162–63, 165–66
"Muffin Man, The" (nursery rhyme), 49
Mulhare, Edward, 171
Mulholland Drive (David Lynch, 2001), 128
Mulvey, Laura, 114–15
Murnau, F. W., 187
Murphy, Rosemary, 179
Murrow, Edward R., 156

musical (genre), viii, 169, 215n17
"musical film noir," vii
Mussolini, Vittorio, 212n32
"My Brother's Keeper" (TV episode), 198
mystery (genre), 174, 182, 184

Naked City, The (Jules Dassin, 1948), 9, 64
Naked Kiss, The (Samuel Fuller, 1964), 194
Nation, The (magazine), 63
National Housing Act of 1934, 90
National Organization for Women
    (NOW), 111
NBC (TV network), 120–21
Negulesco, Jean, vii, 102
Neilson, James, 111
neorealism. *See* Italian neorealism
Neutra, Richard, 93
Never Fear (Ida Lupino, 1949), 9–16, 18,
    31, 55, 65, 70, 112
Newcomb, Horace, 134, 168
"New Faces in New Places: They Are
    Needed Behind the Camera, Too"
    (Lupino), 37
Newman, Paul, 53
new realism, 49. *See also* American real-
    ism
Newsweek (magazine), 30, 66
New Wave, 212n33
New York, 120, 151–52, 176
New York Times, 23, 35, 205–6n3,
    209–10n25, 218n17, 219n22
"Nice Girl" (proposed film title), 46. See
    also *Outrage*
Niven, David, 122
"No. 5 Checked Out" (TV episode),
    123, 126–31, 133, 135, 137, 146, 162–63,
    215nn3–4
"Nobody's Safe" (proposed film title), 46.
    See also *Outrage*
Nocturne (Edwin L. Marin, 1946), 180
"No Fixed Address" (Cook), 59
Nolan, Jack Edmund, 187
Nolan, Jeanette, 179

Notorious (Alfred Hitchcock, 1946), 186
Not Wanted (Elmer Clifton/Ida Lupino,
    1949), 7, 10–14, 18–20, 22–23, 35, 51,
    55, 65, 69–70, 77, 106, 112, 128, 164–65,
    205n1, 206n9, 206n11, 210n26
Novello, Ivor, 5
NOW. *See* National Organization for
    Women

O'Brian, Hugh, 65
O'Brien, Edmond, 17, 72, 75, 164
O'Dell, Cary, 176, 188, 198
Oklahoma, 24, 26
On Dangerous Ground (Nicholas Ray,
    1953), 131, 186
"One for My Baby (and One More for the
    Road)" (song), vii
On the Waterfront (Elia Kazan, 1954), 52,
    159
On Trial (TV series, 1960), 162
Open City (Roberto Rossellini, 1945), 50
Ophuls, Max, 88
Oppenheimer, Jess, 216n13
O'Reilly, Julie, 219n26
Organization Man, The (Whyte), 41
Orgeron, Marsha, 31, 144, 160, 207–
    8nn19–20
Osborne, Robert, 50
Oscars, 50, 122, 155–56. *See also* Academy
    Awards
Osteen, Mark, 37, 68, 76, 206n7, 209n22
Our Town (Sam Wood, 1940), 54
Out of the Past (Jacques Tourneur, 1947),
    69, 82–83, 85, 101, 128
Outrage (Ida Lupino, 1950), 1, 11, 16, 23,
    25, 37, 42–49, 51–57, 59, 63, 65, 87, 89,
    95, 100–3, 105, 107–10, 112, 128, 140,
    165, 194, 209n22, 212–13n34
Ovesey, Lionel, 211n29

Paley, The (museum), 217n14
Paley, Virginia, 155
Paley, William, 155

Palme d'Or, 122

Palmer, R. Barton, 47, 50, 66, 137, 211n30, 212n33

Paramount consent decrees, 38–39, 211n27

Paramount Studios, 4–6, 38–39, 104, 142, 144, 147, 211n27

Paris, Jerry, 43

Parker, Francine, 6, 30

Parsons, Harriet, 180

Parsons, Louella, 219n23

Peacock, Steven, 137, 215n7

Peeping Tom (Michael Powell, 1960), 115

Penn, Leo, 69, 71, 165

People (magazine), 200

Perlman, Nicole, 201

Person to Person (TV series, 1953–1961), 156

Peter Gunn (TV series, 1958–1961), 219n27

Peterson, Paul, 168

Phantom Lady (Robert Siodmak, 1944), 180

Philco-Goodyear Television Playhouse (TV series, 1948–1956), 121, 212n33

Picard, Yves, 215n7

Pickford, Mary, 2

Pilato, Herbie J., 172

Pillow Talk (Michael Gordon, 1959), 12

Pinky (Elia Kazan, 1949), 64

Pittman, Montgomery, 124–25

Place, Janey, 76

Playboy (magazine), 41–42, 111

Polanski, Roman, 69, 122

"politiques des auteurs" (auteur theory), 28–29, 35, 209n24

Pomerance, Murray, 199

Postman Always Rings Twice, The (Tay Garnett, 1946), 77

postwar American realism, 122, 211n30. *See also* American realism

postwar Italian cinema, 212n32

Powell, Dick, 122

Powell, Michael, 115

Powers, Mala, 11, 42, 45, 65, 217n15

Preminger, Otto, 77, 184

Presley, Elvis, 111

Price of Salt, The (Highsmith), 199

Private Hell 36 (Don Siegel, 1954), 12, 219n23

"Producer, The" (TV episode), 169–70

"Producers, The" (TV episode), 217n14

Production Code Administration (PCA), 3, 18–22, 25–26, 37, 56, 94, 111, 206n9

Progressive Era, 88

Psycho (Alfred Hitchcock, 1960), 177

"quality television" (campaign), 202, 215n7

Quart, Barbara Koenig, 31, 33, 208–9n20, 213n9

Queen Kelly (Erich von Stroheim, 1928), 142

Queen of the B's: Ida Lupino Behind the Camera (Kuhn), 209n24

Quiet Man, The (John Ford, 1952), 206n4

Rabinovitz, Lauren, 24, 27, 206n7

Ray, Nicholas, 8, 18, 34

realism: American realism, 1, 49–51, 66, 211n30, 211–12n32; European-influenced documentary realism, 8, 13, 47; new realism, 49; postwar American realism, 122, 211n30

Rebel Without a Cause (Nicholas Ray, 1955), 17

Reckless Moment, The (Max Ophuls, 1949), 63, 88

Redding, Judith M., 207n19

Redmond, Marge, 110

Red Scare, 38

Reed, Alan, 151

Reinhardt, Max, 54

Renoir, Jean, 212n32

Republican Party, 46

Rethinking the Femme Fatale in Film Noir (Grossman), 213n6

"Return of the Canary Kid, The" (TV episode), 125
"Return of Wrongway Feldman, The" (TV episode), 219n25
Rey, Alejandro, 179
Reynolds, Debbie, 111
Rhimes, Shonda, 201
Rickey, Carrie, 17, 33–34, 63, 138, 162, 207–8n19
Ride the Pink Horse (Robert Montgomery, 1947), 180
Riesman, David, 41
Rifleman, The (TV series, 1958–1963), 194
RKO Pictures, 16, 25, 206n15, 209n20, 210n26
Road House (1948, Jean Negulesco), vii–viii
Robinson, Edward G., 9
Rogers, Roy, 93
Roosevelt, Anna, 7
Roosevelt, Eleanor, 7
Roosevelt, Franklin D., 90
Rope (Alfred Hitchcock, 1948), 10
Rorke, Hayden, 151
Rossellini, Roberto, 8, 50, 212n32
Rossen, Robert, 9, 49, 53
Rowlands, Gena, 163–64
Royle, Nicholas, 214n11
Ruitenbeek, Hendrik, 41
Russell, Rosalind, 110, 116, 215n17
Ryan, Robert, 53, 186

Saint Mary's Home for Children, 113
Saint Teresa of Avila, 114
Saks, Sol, 149, 155
Sam Benedict (TV series, 1962–1963), 163–165
Same Time Next Year (Robert Mulligan, 1978), 189
Samson and Delilah (Cecil B. DeMille, 1949), 210n26
San Diego Tribune-Sun, 20
San Fernando Valley, 93

San Francisco, 17, 69, 97–98, 164
San Quentin (prison), 24–25
Santa Paula (CA), 42
Santa Rosalia (Mexico), 23
Sarris, Andrew, 28, 35–36
Schafer, Natalie, 170–71
Scharres, Barbara, 176, 209–10n25
Schatz, Thomas, 64, 122–23
Scheib, Ronnie, 14, 28, 33–34, 110, 178, 209n23
Schleier, Merrill, 214n12
Schlereth, Thomas J., 214n13
Schwartz, Sherwood, 216n9
Scorsese, Martin, 34
Scourby, Alexander, 182, 185
Screen Directors Playhouse (TV series, 1955–1956), 123–24, 127–28, 130, 135, 162
Sea Wolf, The (Michael Curtiz, 1941), 9
Seger, Linda, 66
Sélavy, Virginie, 179
semi-documentary (style), 9, 23, 49–50, 64
Serling, Rod, 143, 179
77 Sunset Strip (TV series, 1958–1964), 122, 126
Shadow of a Doubt (Alfred Hitchcock, 1943), 82, 84–85
Shelley, Mary, 144
Sherman Antitrust Act of 1890, 210–11n27
She Wore a Yellow Ribbon (John Ford, 1949), 206n4
Shoeshine (Vittorio De Sica, 1946), 50
Shore, Dinah, 157
Shorris, Sylvia, 55
Showtime (TV network), 200–201
Shurlock, Geoffrey, 25
Siegel, Don, 12, 218n18, 219n23
Sight and Sound (film journal), 179
silent film, 66, 73, 142, 148, 212–13n34
Silver, Charles, 210n25
Silvers, Phil, 169
Singing Nun, The (Henry Koster, 1966), 111

Siodmak, Robert, 101

"Sixteen-Millimeter Shrine, The" (TV episode), 143–46

Sklar, Robert, 50, 211n31

Skyscraper Cinema: Architecture and Gender in American Film (Schleier), 214n12

Sky's the Limit, The (1943, Edward H. Griffith), viii

Slide, Anthony, 67

Smalley, Phillips, 67

Smart, Elizabeth, 200–201

Smith, Aaron, 214n15

Smith, Jaclyn, 146

Smith, Jeff, 48

Snake Pit, The (Anatole Litvak, 1948), 64

Snelson, Tim, 180

Sobchack, Vivian, 214n12

social problem film, 2, 9, 15–16, 25, 40, 47, 49, 58, 63–82, 97, 120, 152, 162, 210n26

Soloway, Jill, 200, 209n21

Sopranos, The (TV series, 1999–2007), 215n7

Sorry, Wrong Number (Anatole Litvak, 1948), 101

Sothern, Ann, 159

Sound of Music, The (Robert Wise, 1965), 111

South America, 71

Southern California, 16, 51, 87, 102, 108–9

Special Regulations on Crime in Motion Pictures, 26

Spencer, Kathleen, 124

Spigel, Lynn, 154–55, 219n26

Spiral Staircase, The (Robert Siodmak, 1945), 63

S.S. *Minnow* (ship), 216n9

Staaken Studios, 56

Stack, Robert, 187

Staiger, Janet, 211n28

Stamp, Shelley, 66–67

"Stand-In, The" (TV episode), 135–36, 139, 140–42, 145

Stanfield, Peter, 64

Steiger, Rod, 121

Stewart, James, 196

Stewart, Lucy, 23, 209n24

Stone, Judy, 218n17, 219n22

Stout, Archie, 11, 51, 206n4

Strahey, Jane, 110

Strange Affair of Uncle Harry, The (Robert Siodmak, 1944), 63, 101, 180

Stranger on the Third Floor (Boris Ingster, 1940), 127

Strangers on a Train (Alfred Hitchcock, 1951), 70

Strauss, Theodore, viii

"Strega, La" (TV episode), 178–79

Studio One (TV series, 1948–1958), 121

Studlar, Gaylyn, 191, 193

Sturges, Preston, 152

Sugarfoot (TV series, 1957–1961), 124–26

"Sugar, Spice and Everything" (TV episode), 164–65

Sullivan's Travels (Preston Sturges, 1941), 152

Sunset Blvd. (Billy Wilder, 1950), 37, 137–38, 141–45, 147, 152

Surfside 6 (TV series, 1960–1962), 126

Surratt, Mary, 162–63

"Suspension" (TV episode), 154–55, 217n14

Swanson, Gloria, 142, 146–47

"Swan Song" (TV episode), 147

Swartz, Tracy, 201

Swayze, John Cameron, 120

Sweeney, Bob, 194

"Sybilla" (TV episode), 135, 180, 182–86

"Taken for Granted" (TV episode), 150, 217n14

Talman, William, 16, 59, 75, 123, 127–28

Tambor, Jeffrey, 200

"Teen-Age Idol" (TV episode), 167

Television Style (Butler), 134, 136, 215–16nn6–8, 219n27

Texaco Star Theater, The (TV series, 1948), 120

Thaxter, Phyllis, 176

"Thesis on Neo-Realism, A" (Zavattini), 52

They Drive by Night (Raoul Walsh, 1940), 4, 6

They Won't Believe Me (Irving Pichel, 1947), 180

Thinnes, Roy, 187

This Is Your Life (TV series, 1952–1961), 155, 217nn14–15

"This Is Your Past" (fictional TV show), 155, 217n14

Thomas, Betty, 201

Thomas, Bob, 20

3D, 120

Three Musketeers, The (George Sidney, 1948), 210n26

Thriller (TV series, 1960–1962), 135, 138, 162, 174–75, 177–80

thriller (genre), 120, 123, 162, 167, 174–75, 182, 189, 200

Tierney, Gene, 171

Time (magazine), 206n14

Tischler, Stanford, 12, 206n5

Tobacco Roads (John Ford, 1941), 64

Todd-AO, 120

"Torpedo, The" (TV episode), 167, 188–89

Touch of Evil (Orson Welles, 1958), 68, 71

Tourneur, Jacques, 69, 102, 123–24

"To Walk in Grace" (TV episode), 163–64

Towers, Constance, 194

Transparent (TV series, 2014–), 200

Trauma and Recovery: The Aftermath of Violence—From Domestic Abuse to Political Terror (Herman), 65

Treem, Sarah, 201

Trevor, Claire, 76, 180–81

"Trial of Mary Surratt, The" (TV episode), 162

Trouble with Angels, The (Ida Lupino, 1966), 34, 61–62, 110–18, 132, 162, 170, 174, 178, 200, 214–15nn15–16

Truffaut, François, 28, 212n33

Tunis, John, 76–77, 213–14n10

Turner, Sophie, 199

TV Guide (magazine), 198

TV News (TV series, 1948), 120

TV: The Most Popular Art (Newcomb), 168

Twilight Zone, The (TV series, 1959–1964), 124–25, 145–46, 175, 179

"Typical" (TV episode), 153–55, 217n14

UCLA. *See* University of California, Los Angeles

Ulmer, Edgar G., 109

United Press, 20

United States, 5, 24, 28, 39, 51–52, 54, 87, 90, 102–3, 119, 162

Universal Film Manufacturing Company, 67

Universal Studios, 66–67, 104

University of California, Los Angeles (UCLA), 209n25; UCLA Film Archive, 217n14

University of Vienna, 54

Untouchables, The (TV series, 1959–1963), 138, 162, 167, 186–88, 192

Ursini, James, 187, 219n27

U.S. Centennial Exposition (1876), 103

U.S. Department of Justice, 25

U.S. Supreme Court, 38–39, 210–11n27

Van Upp, Virginia, 180

Variety (magazine), 9, 14, 151

Varney, Ginger, 26

Vatican II (Second Vatican Council), 111

"verist materialism" (Palmer), 50

Vertigo (Alfred Hitchcock, 1958), 185–86

"Very Special Girl, A" (TV episode), 135

Victorian period, 5, 44, 46, 53, 65, 82–83, 88, 97, 101–5, 110, 184, 214n13

Victorian Queen Anne (style), 103–4

Vidor, Charles, 11

Village Voice, 33

Virginian, The (TV series, 1962–1971), 195–98
von Sternberg, Josef, 93
von Stroheim, Erich, 142

Wager, Jans, 34, 68, 213n6
Wait until Dark (Terence Young, 1967), 189
Wald, Malvin, 2, 9, 16, 19, 49, 63, 102, 210n26
Waldman, Diane, 23, 206n9
Waldorf Statement, 83
Walsh, Raoul, vii, 6, 11
war (genre), 49
Warner, Jack, 126
Warner Brothers, 3–4, 6, 122, 126, 141, 201
Warner Brothers Presents (TV series, 1955–1956), 122
Washington D.C., 25
Watts, Carol, 29
Waxman, Franz, 144
Wayne, John, 196
Webb, Jack, 121
Weber, Lois, 66–67
Weiner, Debra, 10–11, 18, 30, 33, 47, 53, 123, 162, 218n17
Welles, Orson, 8
Wellman, William, A., 6, 11
West, Mae, 5
western (genre), 126, 135, 162, 167, 191, 193–201
Weston, Jack, 189–91
Whatever Happened to Baby Jane? (Robert Aldrich, 1962), 144
Wheeler, Edward, 196
Where Angels Go, Trouble Follows (James Neilson, 1968), 111
Where Are My Children? (Lois Weber and Phillips Smalley, 1916), 67
White, Susan, 113
Whyte, William F., 41

Wickes, Mary, 110
Wilder, Billy, 122, 138–39, 144, 147, 152
Wilder, Thornton, 54
Will There Really Be a Morning (unproduced film), viii
Winchell, Walter, 186
Wire, The (TV series, 2002–2008), 215n7
Wiseman, Rosalind, 77
Wlodarczyk, Holley, 103
Wocjik, Pamela Robertson, 214n12
Women in Film Noir (Kaplan), 213n6
Women's Film Pioneers Project (website), 67, 213n5
"women's melodrama," 58, 62–63, 97
Wonder Woman (Patty Jenkins, 2017), 201
Wood, Sam, 54
World War I, 102–3, 213n4
World War II, 7, 40, 42, 65, 87, 103, 211n28, 218n17
Wright, Teresa, 84, 123, 127, 129
Wrong Rut/Birthright, The (alternative titles, *Not Wanted*), 206n11
"Wrongway Feldman" (TV episode), 169, 219n25
Wuornos, Aileen, 201
Wyler, William, 54, 102

York, Dick, 171
Young, Collier, 2, 9 16–18, 24–26, 49, 74, 102, 149, 160–62, 205n1, 210n26, 218n17
Young, Loretta, 159
Young Lovers, The (Ida Lupino, 1949), 10, 14
YouTube, 138, 151, 217n14

Zavattini, Cesare, 51–52
Ziegler, William, 10
Zinnemann, Fred, 123
Zollo, Burt, 41

ABOUT THE AUTHORS

Therese Grisham, Ph.D., is a lecturer in the Film and Media Studies program and in General Humanities, Department of Humanities and Philosophy, at Oakton Community College in Des Plaines, Illinois. She specializes in gender and women in film, American film history, particularly of the World War II and postwar period, and Italian and German cinema. She also teaches special topics in film in the Film School at Facets Multimedia in Chicago. She is currently working on a book project with coauthors Alison McKee and Merrill Schleier, *Home Noir: Gender and Domestic Space in Postwar American Film (1946–1959)*, forthcoming from Rutgers University Press.

Julie Grossman, professor of English and Communication and Film Studies at Le Moyne College, has published numerous essays on film and literature in scholarly journals. She is author of *Rethinking the Femme Fatale in Film Noir* (2009, 2012) and *Literature, Film, and Their Hideous Progeny* (2015). She is coeditor (with R. Barton Palmer) of the book series Adaptation and Visual Culture and the forthcoming collection *Adaptation in Visual Culture: Images, Texts, and Their Multiple Worlds*.